Upside Down

Upside Down

Seasons among the Nunamiut

MARGARET B. BLACKMAN

UNIVERSITY OF NEBRASKA PRESS
LINCOLN ❖ LONDON

"August" first appeared in *In Short: A Collection of Brief Creative Nonfiction*, edited by Judith Kitchen and Mary Paumier Jones (New York: W. W. Norton, 1996). "Remembering Susie Paneak" originally appeared as "One Died Alone, the Other in a Community's Arms" in the *Rochester Democrat and Chronicle*, December 14, 1997. "Fifty Years in One Place" originally appeared in *North American Review*, vol. 286, no. 10.

Library of Congress
Cataloging-in-Publication Data
Blackman, Margaret B.
Upside down: seasons among the
Nunamiut / Margaret B. Blackman.
p.   cm.
ISBN 0-8032-1335-2 (cloth: alk. paper)
1. Nunamiut Eskimos—Alaska—
Anaktuvuk Pass—History.
2. Nunamiut Eskimos—Alaska—
Anaktuvuk Pass—Social life and customs.
3. Ethnology—Alaska—Anaktuvuk Pass.
4. Anaktuvuk Pass (Alaska)—History.
5. Anaktuvuk Pass (Alaska)—Social
life and customs.   I. Title.
E99.E7 B6562   2004
979.8'7—dc21
2003013924

Contents

List of Illustrations   vii

Acknowledgments   ix

Introduction   1

August   5

Tulugak Lake and Beyond   9

Maps   17

Anaktuvuk Pass, You Copy?   21

They Come In; They Go Out   31

Picking   41

The Upside Down Season   47

Fieldnotes   51

Writing History from the Pass   59

The "New" Eskimo   69

Of Meat and Hunger and Everlasting Gob Stoppers   73

Staying Home   85

Masks   89

The Only Road That Goes There
Is the Information Superhighway   97

Remembering Susie Paneak   107

The Exhibition   111

Airplane! Airplaaane!   119

Dispatches from the Field   129

Fifty Years in One Place   143

Weekend Nomads   151

The Things We Carry   161

Town   169

May—North of North   177

Ed's Place   181

Happy July Fourth   191

Faces of the Nunamiut   197

Notes   205

Illustrations

PHOTOGRAPHS

Fireweed by Suaqpak Mountain, Anaktuvuk Pass   5

Susie Paneak at Tulugak Lake   9

CB talk   21

Dancing for tourists   31

Picking berries   41

Meryn and her friends   47

Anaktuvuk Pass   51

Homer Mekiana in his post office   59

Simon Paneak at home   59

Willie Hugo, on his father's lap, 1963   69

Lela Ahgook and her store   73

291 Main Street, Brockport, New York   85

Caribou-skin mask by Rhoda Ahgook   89

Street corner, Anaktuvuk Pass   97

Cemetery, Anaktuvuk Pass   107

Ethel Mekiana, Justus Mekiana, and
Rachel Riley in Brunswick, Maine   111

The Wien plane, 1963   119

Lela Ahgook and Margaret Blackman   129

Walking toward Giant Creek   143

Coming home from camping   151

Returning from caribou hunting, 1959   161

Going to town   169

Anaktuvuk Valley, May   177

Anaktuvuk Pass, 1959   181

Anaktuvuk women on the Fourth of July, 1959   191

Wooden molds for masks   197

MAP

Map of Anaktuvuk Area   16

Acknowledgments

The essays in this collection balance on a pyramid of encouragement, criticism, and financial support from many sources. While no grant specifically funded this project, the National Science Foundation, the North Slope Borough, The Whatcom Museum, The American Philosophical Society, the Alaska Humanities Forum, and SUNY Brockport got me from western New York to northern Alaska many times and funded a long list of oral history interviews and their transcriptions.

There is an equally long list of those who patiently listened, read, and offered suggestions. As the essays accumulated, my enthusiasm for the project grew, as did my desire to share them. I unabashedly gave "readings" over dinner and on the phone; I distributed essays to friends at my gym, mailed and e-mailed them to family, friends, and colleagues. I handed them out at a city council meeting in Anaktuvuk Pass. Writing and disseminating academic prose is a lonely enterprise; the reading is not for everyone. Not so with essays, as I pleasantly discovered. My distributions paid off. Many friends and family served as my reading public over the years, among them Ann Alger, Mark Anderson, Betty Berlin, Ed Berlin, Jim Berlin, Karen Brewster, Ginger Carlson, Marilyn Colby, Ed Hall, Meryn Hall, Pam Hyland, Sue Kenyon, Joel Latner, Molly Lee, Sarah McConnell, Karla Merrifield, Elaine Miller, Charlotte Reid, Pat Sarchet, Carol St. George, Bill Schneider, Pat Soden, Richard Stern, Marilyn Trueblood, and Robin Weintraub. Anaktuvuk Pass readers of some of these essays include Lela Ahgook, Becky Hugo, Freida Rulland, and Vera Weber.

Cristina Klein, Bruce Leslie, Ulpian Toney, and the members of my writers group—Amy Andrews, Gail Bouk, Carol Burelbach, Bill Capossere, Bea Ganley, Jane Guibault, Jeanne Grinnan, Judith Kitchen, Jenny Lloyd, Betsy Nadeau, Gwen Nelson, Gerry Sharp, Larry Sill, Marcia Ullman, Carol Wisner—offered sustained editorial commentary over the lot of this collection, as did Phyllis Morrow and Janet Berlo, who read the manuscript for the University of Nebraska Press. Jack Campbell provided information on the early history of the village. Grant Spearman carefully read and critiqued the essays with a knowledge of the Nunamiut that far surpasses my own. Judith Kitchen, who is such a fluent and lyrical essayist, helped me break out of academic writing and lent her considerable editorial talent to framing the final manuscript. Most of all she believed these essays were publishable and helped me find a home for them.

To the people of Anaktuvuk Pass—especially those mentioned in these essays—who have welcomed me over numerous seasons of fieldwork in their village and put up with my questions, *Quyanaqpak*. In choosing to use peoples' real names in these essays, I do so in expression of friendship and admiration for Iñupiat, "the real people." I hope, in the process, I have not trespassed on anyone's sense of privacy.

Thanks to all who have shaped and shared the seasons of my writing.

Royalties from this book will go to the Simon Paneak Memorial Museum Endowment Fund in Anaktuvuk Pass.

Upside Down

In the Federal Aviation Administration's lexicon of world airports, it's AKP. To the post office it's 99721. To the state of Alaska, it's one of dozens of "second-class cities." To backpackers and hikers from around the world, it's the portal to the Gates of the Arctic National Park. It's a tourist destination as well to day visitors who fly in from Fairbanks to experience a Native village and real bush Alaska. To the Nunamiut Eskimo who live there it is home. Regardless of what it is called, Anaktuvuk Pass is a memorably scenic place, cradled by the gray shale mountains that rise around it, verdant in the moment of summer, pristinely white in the deep freeze of winter.

One hundred miles north of the Arctic Circle, thirty-five miles beyond the treeline, an hour and a half flight in a small airplane from Fairbanks, there is something about this small settlement in the middle of the road-less tundra that draws outsiders like me. My journey to this place began in 1980 at the end of a summer camping trip in Alaska's Brooks Range with my archaeologist husband Ed Hall and his eight-year-old son, Justin. We stopped in Anaktuvuk Pass just long enough to meet a few villagers and visit the village store and new school before flying on to Fairbanks. But it was long enough to know that I wanted to return. Ed and I did return, as working anthropologists. In the summer of 1988 we came with our five-year-old daughter Meryn to begin what we hoped would be a long-term oral history project with village elders. For each of the next several summers we came back with tape recorders and long lists of questions. We accumulated over one hundred hours of interviews, some of it village history, some of it family history, and some of it stories of hunting, camping, and traveling the land. The oral history project became its own journey as we followed villagers' lives from the 1940s and 50s to the present.

Ed had first come to Anaktuvuk nearly thirty years before and had been committed to arctic research ever since. Coming to "his Arctic," I was, in a sense, as I had been twenty years earlier in graduate school, his student. But I was also learning about Anaktuvuk Pass through the eyes of our young daughter and her Nunamiut playmates. I was exploring my own research interests in the village, and I was eager to tell my own stories of discovery.

Other matters derailed our master research plan. By the summer of 1991, Ed had become noticeably ill with multiple sclerosis. He had difficulty walking and talking, but none of this deterred him from making his an-nual summer pilgrimage north. Villagers mistook his slurred speech and his stumbling for drunkenness. He walked with a cane and soldiered through interviews and conversations, repeating himself when people couldn't understand him. He saved his many frustrations for the privacy of our rented quarters.

Ed was determined to return the following summer, though his condition had worsened both physically and mentally. Two years later, in the summer of 1994, I returned to Anaktuvuk Pass with Meryn, but without Ed. It was a shorter than usual trip; I had planned no specific research, just camping, visiting, finding inspiration to write, and enjoying the arctic summer with Meryn. I found most of what I had come for, but I was ill-prepared for Meryn's preadolescent boredom with village life. Her village friends from childhood now had their own teenage concerns, and camping no longer held the excitement for her that it once did. I knew that summer that Ed would never return to Anaktuvuk, but I did not know then that three years hence we would be divorced.

In the summer of 1997, I returned again to Anaktuvuk with a student but without Ed and without Meryn. I carried with me my essays and the desire to write more. I shared some of them with villagers and talked to the village council about the collection I hoped to produce. I told our village friends of Ed's and my divorce, hoping they would understand, and of the progression of his illness. I extended Ed's greetings—a "big hello," as villagers say—and I relayed Meryn's messages to her friends, a few of whom were now young mothers.

Ed and Meryn have been a large part of my seasons among the Nunamiut, but they are not all of it. I returned to Anaktuvuk Pass in 1999 and again in 2001 and 2002 to work on a new research project involving caribou-skin masks. I experienced, in 1999, for the first time in thirty years, the loneliness of solitary fieldwork and then the exhilaration of forgotten freedoms. I visited villagers; I spent a day without talking to anyone. I hiked up the Anaktuvuk valley and sat for a long time on a ridge overlooking the village. I picked blueberries at midnight. I wrote.

Through writing, I had gradually become aware of my changing relationship to my academic discipline. Like others of my scholarly profession, I learned to write with the objective remove and the dispassionate voice of the social scientist. I mastered the passive, impersonal, omniscient voice—"The Nunamiut *are* . . ."—and appropriately absented myself from my writing.

Eventually, though, I tired of academic writing—my own and others'. I disliked its strictures, its repetitiveness, its jargon, its arrogance. In my annual search for reading materials to engage my introductory anthropology students, I became increasingly irritated with the uncanny ability of so many anthropologists to render, in stilted prose, the most interesting cultures hopelessly pedantic and unappealing. I wanted to write differently about Anaktuvuk Pass and its people.

Even had I wanted to write in that impersonal, omniscient voice, I lacked the authority. My field seasons in Anaktuvuk were short summer ones. I didn't have the sustained perspective of someone who had spent a year or more living in the village. My experience and my knowledge, like the essays in this collection, were episodic. And there was one other thing. My personal life *was* part of my fieldwork. I was drawn as much to watching and reflecting on my daughter's adaptation to village life as I was to observing my Nunamiut friend butchering a caribou.

I'm certainly no maverick in anthropology. More than two decades ago, Clifford Geertz was writing the observer back into the cultural scene, arguing for an interpretive anthropology that emphasized the observer's experience. Many anthropologists since, engaging in what they call "reflexive ethnography," have trained their critical eyes on themselves in the field—the observer self-observed. But these essays are less about that than they are about portraying the summer seasons of a place and a people, and about what one discovers in the process of writing. When I began an essay I never knew where it would lead, nor did I know when, or about what, subsequent essays would be written. I wrote them—ten seasons of fieldwork over a period of ten years—as they came to me. Essays are like that, free to follow their own maps.

It is hard to imagine that, while people have occupied the Pass for almost seven thousand years, this so-called city is just fifty-four years old. It is hard to imagine that its residents have been able to send and receive mail for less time than that; that they have had local K-12 schools for not even two generations; that they have enjoyed electricity and television for just a generation and have just recently acquired running water and flush toilets. Still, modern conveniences have come here in rapid-fire order, and they have been enthusiastically embraced. As an anthropologist, I am torn between following the journeys of some villagers down the likes of the Information Superhighway and following the journeys of others back to a time when technology was a rifle, a distant plane in the sky, and a battery-powered radio that tuned in news of World War II in a foreign language—English. I try, in these essays, to follow both.

Yet as much as these essays were intended to focus on the Nunamiut journey from pedestrian nomads to bush airline passengers to travelers on the Information Superhighway, they also record more than a decade of my own personal journey. For the anthropologist, the journey in the field is a special one. Regardless of place, it is travel from the familiar to the strange. It is leaving behind the material comforts and plenitude of home for cramped spaces, few possessions, and a different and not always palatable cuisine. It is travel across vast geography, with space for reflection and adjustment. It is travel over time, as "the field" draws one back season after season.

August

Fireweed by Suaqpak Mountain, Anaktuvuk Pass.

Anaq = *feces*
tua = *having many*
vIk = *place, source*

The barren-ground caribou pass through this mountain valley in the thousands in the fall as they head to the interior from their calving grounds on the Arctic coast. In the spring, they make the return journey. Like other Nunamiut names that dot the landscape— Kanɲuumavik, "gathering place"; Napaaqtualuit, "looks like trees"; Miluk, "breast mountain"—the name is pragmatic, visual, and unadorned. Although a Nunamiut name, the credit for placing it on the USGS map, and thus officially into the lexicon of Alaska place names, goes not to a Native but to W. J. Peters, a geologist who, in 1901, called the pass "Anaktuvuk" after the Native name for the river that runs through it.

Just over fifty years ago three wandering bands of Nunamiut Eskimos came together to settle in the broad Anaktuvuk Valley. Here, at the continental divide, there was an abundance of water and a lush growth of arctic willows. Here was a major thoroughfare for migrating caribou and a small lake where airplanes might land. Here was a place that held the promise of sustaining the Nunamiut in the two worlds in which they were beginning to live.

"Amigiksivik" on the North Slope Borough calendar that hangs in the village store and post office. "Caribou skins are good for making parka," "the month for skinning caribou." Fall arrives, overnight it seems. By early August, green tundra grasses shimmer golden at their tips, as patches of brilliant red dwarf birch and bearberry flash on the flanks of the Brooks Range. Scrubby willows in autumn yellow drop their leaves, smell like October back home.

August is the beginning of sheep season and the ripening of arctic blueberries and cloudberries. Men take leave of work to go into the mountains in search of Dall sheep; women bend low on the tundra, filling plastic bags and buckets with salmon-colored *akpiks*, cloudberries.

More and more the big U.S. flag flying above the tiny post office unfurls toward the south in the cold north wind that blows off the Arctic Ocean. On any August morning the mountains might be dressed in snow down to their feet; wet snow hangs on the willow branches and leaves, then melts under the midday sun. The light of August is softer, less intense than that of a few weeks earlier. The sun is leaving. Night returns to the Pass, seven minutes more of it each day, the sun sliding below the mountains in its ever-dipping circle.

Fog rolls in, not on little cat feet but on a strong north wind, eating up the mountains in its path. The village becomes small, then isolated. We retreat indoors against the cold, closing the two doors of our little house, bumping against each other in its close confines as we negotiate our individual spaces. Kids don't come by "walking around;" we bury ourselves in our books. A weekend day goes by without any contact with villagers. The skies are silent; no planes land.

We leave the Pass the third week in August, watching autumn turn back to summer as we fly south over the Brooks Range to Fairbanks. Up north the caribou cows are starting to get fat. Soon it will be September—Amigaiqsivik, "when the velvet is shed from antlers"—and the caribou will gather in preparation for their southward journey through Anaktuvuk Pass, the "place of many caribou droppings."

Tulugak Lake and Beyond

Susie Paneak at Tulugak Lake.

Anaktuvuk Pass has a population of just over three hundred, more than ninety percent of whom are Nunamiut Eskimo—the mountain people—the only truly inland Eskimo in Alaska. The village occupies less than one hundred acres in the middle of the broadest and longest mountain pass in Alaska's Brooks Range. As a settlement, it's just over a half-century old, but as a place and a name on the landscape of human memory, it's much older and much larger than its small size would suggest. Archaeological remains of human encampments date back seven thousand years, and the historic seminomadic Nunamiut have hunted through this mountain pass for at least the last two hundred years.

It was a long step from seminomadism to a post office. In the winter of 1943, when bush pilot Sig Wien was flying supplies from Fairbanks to Barrow, he landed southwest of Anaktuvuk Pass at Chandler Lake, where one band of Nunamiut had a winter camp. On subsequent occasional visits, Wien transported the furs they had trapped to the Northern Commercial Company in Fairbanks, using store credit to purchase and supply the Nunamiut with store goods and ammunition. As Wien came to know the Nunamiut over the next few years, they told him that they wanted schooling for their children and supplies on a more regular basis. This meant staying in one place for a longer period of time, which, in turn, demanded a substantial and regular supply of firewood. The Anaktuvuk Valley, with its large stands of tall arctic willows and several small lakes on which float and ski planes could land, promised these things.

Though she lives in a Fairbanks subdivision, Mabel Paneak Burris is a Nunamiut—a mountain person, lean and slight and graceful. Her eyes crinkle when she smiles, and she still giggles like the shy young girl Norwegian ethnographer Helge Ingstad met in 1949 and described in his book *Nunamiut*.

Mabel and I are close in age. She was born at Chandler Lake, some thirty miles west of Anaktuvuk Pass, during World War II—before the Nunamiut knew airplanes and before Helge Ingstad became the first white man to spend a winter with her people. Before the Nunamiut became villagers, and before her father's Eskimo name, Paneak, was given to the whole family by the first census taker.

She was called Sigiaruk by her grandmother, May Kakinya, named after May's young son who died at Chandler Lake. Her father, Simon, gave her the English name Mabel. One of two surviving daughters of Susie and Simon Paneak, Mabel moved with her parents and grandparents as they followed the caribou, returning each summer to Tulugak Lake. Those days they lived in a dome-shaped caribou-skin tent, an *itchalik*, built on a frame of bent willow poles, its floor of willow branches overlain with caribou-skin bedrolls. They cooked their meals and brewed their tea on a tiny handmade sheet metal stove inside the tent. They traveled by dog team and wore skin clothing in winter.

The outside world came to Mabel on her father's battery-operated table model Zenith radio, tuned to station KFAR in Fairbanks. She learned her first English words listening to *Tundra Topics* at 9:30 each evening and learning the lyrics of country and western songs. Like her older brothers before her, Mabel found her way out of the Pass through Bureau of Indian Affairs boarding schools, leaving at age nine to go to Wrangel Institute in Southeastern Alaska and coming home to the land each summer. After graduating from high school, she found a job at Bettles Airfield on the Koyukuk River doing everything from kitchen work to relaying weather information to pilots. There she drank her first Coca-Cola and met the white man who would become her husband. She married Bernie Burris at age twenty-three, in Anchorage, with her father's scientist friend Laurence Irving standing in his place to give his daughter in marriage. The Burrises raised a family of three sons and a daughter, living first in Minnesota, then Montana, then Washington, before returning to Alaska to settle in Fairbanks.

Anaktuvuk draws Mabel back often. Her mother is here, as are four brothers and a village full of nieces, nephews, cousins, and in-laws. She comes to visit as well as to hike the land around the Pass, to camp, eat caribou, and pick berries. She spends a lot of her time in the company of her mother, Susie, sitting on the floor of her mother's house, sewing caribou-skin masks with her. When her visits to Anaktuvuk coincide with ours, Ed calls on Mabel to translate for Susie. He's interviewing her about the biography he is writing of Simon.

On the first weekend in August 1990, Ed, Meryn, and I are out on the land, at Tulugak Lake, where Simon Paneak's band of Nunamiut have camped in summers beginning in 1947 and where Simon and his father-in-law, Elijah Kakinya, continued to live with their families for several winters after the others settled at Anaktuvuk Pass. It was a favorable place to live, for even when there were no caribou, there was always fresh fish from the lake. We've brought our fishing poles in anticipation.

We traveled, not as they did so many summers ago on foot with their pack dogs, but by summoning a floatplane from Bettles Airfield to transport us and our camping gear the sixteen miles from Anaktuvuk to Tulugak Lake. Susie and Mabel came with us, along with Susie's little terrier dog, Aluk, jokingly referred to as her "lead [sled] dog." We will spend the weekend camping, fishing for grayling and lake trout, sifting through the ruins of

Simon and Susie's old sod house, and interviewing Susie and Mabel about their lives here in the late 1940s and 1950s.

Mabel and I fall easily into each other's company. We both like to hike and talk, so we set off in the early evening of the first day to climb a mountain about a mile to the east of the lake. The evening is sunny and warm, and we quickly shed our jackets, hanging them on the bushy willows in the flats. I push myself to match Mabel's long, comfortable strides. She is surefooted over tussocks, and she easily clambers up the steep talus slopes in a pair of flimsy gum boots while I labor to keep from twisting an ankle in my steel shank Eddie Bauer shoe pacs. Mabel walks the land with the agility and assurance of one who took her first steps on the uneven tundra.

Mabel first climbed this mountain as a girl in 1956 with Ethel Ross Oliver, an Anchorage schoolteacher who came to the Nunamiut that summer to teach school in a Quonset-hut tent pitched near Tulugak Lake. We find the stone cairn they built at the very top and look inside it for the paper written with their names and encased in aluminum foil, but it is gone.

It is hot on top of the mountain in the lee of the wind, and we sit down to cool off and enjoy the view. Under a clear arctic summer sky, the mountain-top rewards us with vistas of enormous expanse. Beyond the valley to the north, the low mountains flatten into the Arctic coastal plain. South around a gentle bend lies Anaktuvuk, its orange-roofed health center on the village's highest point just visible through binoculars. To the west, the tiny domes of our nylon tents are bright against the shimmering oval of Tulugak Lake, and Nahauraq, a long-ridged mountain, beyond it. A bull moose browsing in the willows near the lake is the only moving object in the panorama.

Only when our stomachs remind us of dinner do we reluctantly head back, pausing first to take pictures of each other with the camera Mabel has brought. We stop halfway down the mountain as Mabel spots a bird among the rocks. Raising the binoculars, she confirms its identity, naming it both in English and Iñupiaq. Her knowledge of birds is a legacy from her father. For many years, Simon assisted Arctic biologist Laurence Irving in a study of the bird life of northern interior Alaska, and Mabel in turn assisted her father, noting the arrival of nesting birds, collecting eggs, and preparing specimens.

I imagine the memories that walking this land must stir. Trekking from here to Anaktuvuk and back in the 1950s when the mail plane came in, re-turning in the company of Anaktuvuk girlfriends with supplies and a bagful of mail for Simon. Trying to curl straight black hair around bleached, weath-ered caribou ribs and becoming frustrated when the bones fell out. Flying out of the Brooks Range once, dangerously sick with pneumonia, lucky that the twice-monthly mail plane had come when it did. Remembering Nick Gubser, just a few years older than she, who came here as a young anthropol-ogy student from Yale in 1959 to spend the year with her family. His undergraduate thesis, rewritten for publication, became the major ethnographic work on the Nunamiut. "Sometimes I have dreams about living here," Mabel offers. "Not too often, though." Wistfully she adds, "I wonder sometimes what it'd be like if we lived here today."

This morning, we are all going hunting for the past. When they began spending winters at Tulugak, in the mid-1950s, Simon and Susie built a sod house, its skeleton made of spruce hauled by sled from the timbered mountains to the south. They flattened tin Blazo gasoline cans for shingles and siding to cover the sod blocks, and they put a window in each of the south and west walls of the house. As they settled into these more permanent quarters, their possessions grew. "Many, many more things are kept indoors: books, pictures, mirror . . . guitar. I could not take in everything this first visit," commented Ethel Ross Oliver, the summer-school teacher. Susie liked living here. "Sod house warm, alright," she remembers, smiling.

The walls and roof have long since eroded in the quarter-century the house has stood abandoned, but we easily find its square depression. We build a fire in the willows just to the north of the house, where Simon used to stake his dog team, make hot tea, and eat strips of smoked salmon and pilot bread, before moving down to the site of the house. I set up the tape recorder on the remains of an old wooden box shelf and point the microphone toward Susie and Mabel. "About what year was this house built?" I begin.

Suddenly Mabel remembers the ten marbles she once hid here to dig up at a later date. She doesn't find them but does retrieve a rusted can of her father's Prince Albert tobacco, the frontispiece to the old Zenith radio, and an aluminum teapot in which a vole has begun to construct its winter nest. A tiny rubberized mitten falls out with the nest, and we speculate which of her younger brothers the mitten had belonged to. By the end of the interview, Mabel has added to her bounty a broken boat paddle and two rusted sheet metal stoves. Her brother Roosevelt will be amused at her trove of artifacts. "Mabel's been collecting her childhood," Ed chuckles.

The weekend passes in a blur of fishing, eating, napping, hiking, and avoiding the cold wind that blows out of the north. The lake yields a respectable harvest of grayling during our stay, mostly to Mabel, who catches nine of them. We roast the fish in the fire, with potatoes, and eat the leftovers our last day as fish chowder. Inside Susie's tent, the Coleman stove warms us. Eight-year-old Meryn, splayed out on the rumple of sleeping bags, reads Judy Blume's *Otherwise Known as Sheila the Great* for the fifth time. "You making a story?" Susie asks as I open my bound book to write. "Journal," I smile. "Like Simon, I write every day."

Mabel disappears outside the tent while the rest of us continue to bask in the warmth of the stove. She likes being outside. She paces slowly back and forth in front of the tent, hands drawn up in the sleeves of her coat against the cold, looking, as she has since a young girl, for game, for birds, for airplanes. All the while she carries on a conversation in Iñupiaq with Susie, who is still inside. They are enviably companionable, perhaps increasingly so as Susie has grown older and more frail. "I wonder how many more times my mom will go camping," Mabel confesses to me during one of our hikes.

Their talk goes on long into the night. After we have turned in to our own tent, they are still talking. As far apart culturally as they might seem, this Fairbanks suburbanite and her bush village mother, they move today in each other's worlds, Susie journeying to Fairbanks about as often as Mabel comes home to Anaktuvuk. Either way, it's just an hour and a half flight. Yet, from Tulugak Lake, they have traveled farther than most of us.

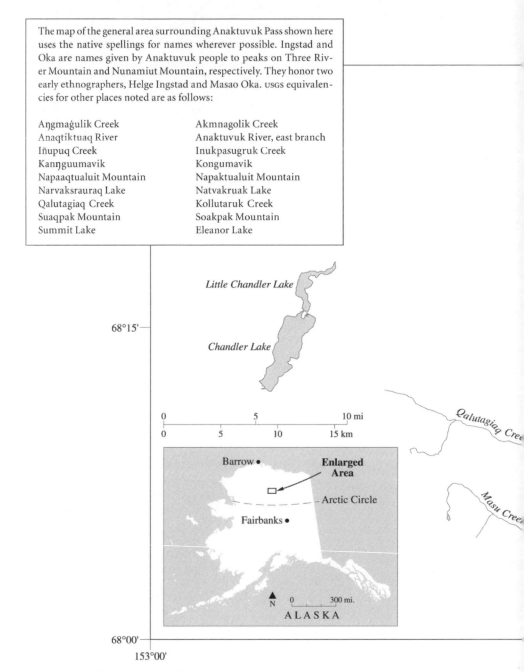

The map of the general area surrounding Anaktuvuk Pass shown here uses the native spellings for names wherever possible. Ingstad and Oka are names given by Anaktuvuk people to peaks on Three River Mountain and Nunamiut Mountain, respectively. They honor two early ethnographers, Helge Ingstad and Masao Oka. USGS equivalencies for other places noted are as follows:

Aŋmaġulik Creek	Akmnagolik Creek
Anaqtiktuaq River	Anaktuvuk River, east branch
Iñupuq Creek	Inukpasugruk Creek
Kanŋguumavik	Kongumavik
Napaaqtualuit Mountain	Napaktualuit Mountain
Narvaksrauraq Lake	Natvakruak Lake
Qalutagiaq Creek	Kollutaruk Creek
Suaqpak Mountain	Soakpak Mountain
Summit Lake	Eleanor Lake

Little Chandler Lake

68°15'—

Chandler Lake

| 0 | | 5 | | 10 mi |
| 0 | 5 | | 10 | 15 km |

Qalutagiaq Cree

Barrow •

Enlarged Area

Arctic Circle

Masu Cree

Fairbanks •

N 0   300 mi.

ALASKA

68°00'—

153°00'

Map of Anaktuvuk area.

Maps

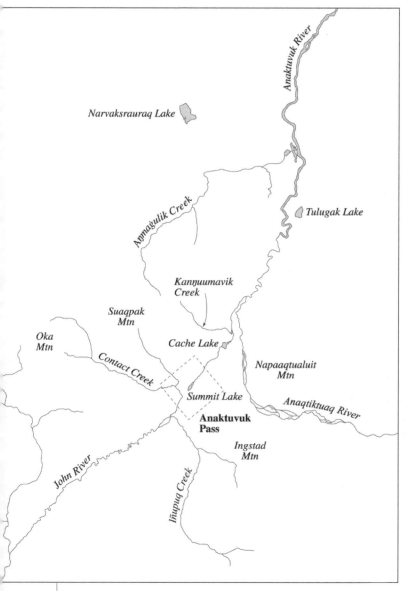

Some early explorers took Eskimos and their knowledge of the land seriously and asked them to draw maps of the surrounding country. The Eskimos obliged. These maps were a great boon to arctic travel and exploration; today they offer an insight into the way Eskimos perceived the space around them. . . . Eskimos, both men and women, produced highly accurate maps of the coastal and interior regions of their homeland. . . . [They] were making and using maps long before they met Europeans, both as mnemonic devices for ordering extensive systems of place names and as navigational aids.

Barry Lopez, Arctic Dreams

We unroll the USGS maps and tack them up, edge to edge, papering an expanse of wall in our little village house. They remain there as a reference while we're in the village. From time to time I look at them, committing names of rivers and creeks to memory, locating lakes and valleys relative to the village so I have some geographical sense of what people are talking about when they mention places they have traveled and hunted. But I'm like the house cat who sees the outdoors only from the windowsill or occasionally from the confines of the fenced backyard under the watchful eye of its owner. I haven't been to many places outside the village; I can't visualize the details of the terrain or gauge the time it takes to get from here to there. My mental map of this country contains the dot of a village surrounded by mountain peaks, many of them nameless to me. The thin blue squiggle of the Anaktuvuk River flows north from the continental divide here, the John River is a blue line wiggling south. The imaginary arc of the Arctic Circle, one hundred miles south of Anaktuvuk, locates this place for me in the north country, and the dots representing Fairbanks and Barrow anchor it on a SE–NW trending line.

The maps mean more to Ed. He's seen almost all of northern Alaska from the air as a USGS archaeologist, and quite a bit of it from the ground in earlier archaeological surveys. As a college student he was a gofer on a geological survey party in the Anaktuvuk region. He's been to the Killik River valley where Justus Mekiana and his sisters Doris Hugo and Rachel Riley spent their early childhood, before they settled in Anaktuvuk Pass. And he knows Chandler Lake, where Simon Paneak's little band wintered in the 1940s. Simon, the one whom Laurence Irving eulogized as "the man with a map in his mind," often drew maps from memory. In one he made for archaeologist Jack Campbell, he drew the fishing locations in ten north-flowing streams, several of which were unnamed on the published maps. "His cartography is remarkably accurate," Campbell wrote.

Simon wasn't the only Nunamiut with a map in his mind. Justus Mekiana has been coming to our place at one o'clock every day to talk about where he traveled and hunted in his younger days. The tape recorder sits on the kitchen table, and Ed unrolls a second set of maps for the interview. Ed and I sit side by side on big plastic storage coolers pulled up to the table. Justus takes his seat at the end of the table on the only chair, canting it at a forty-five-degree angle so that he's facing us. The northern sun streams in the window over the kitchen table, falling on the maps and darkening Justus's photosensitive glasses. I can't tell whom he's looking at when he talks, but it's probably Ed, who asks most of the questions. I'm mostly listening and watching as Justus describes his travels and Ed marks on the maps the camping places and hunting spots he mentions. Later, I will interview Justus about making masks, kin relations, and oral history, but these interviews are about travel and maps. Ed is prepared with a map for everywhere Justus has traveled in his sixty-one years. They pore over them. Every place Justus camped or killed an animal, Ed puts a number. Today they're following the Killik River.

"Uqpigruaq, One time we stay in the fall time right there."

"Oh, way down the Killik?"

"Yeah, way down there."

Ed writes "21" just above where the Uqpigruaq flows into the Killik River. "Lots of marshy ground around there?" Ed asks. He knows the territory. "Yeah, we stay down there for all the way to Christmas, in the fall time, after we go hunting good skin, you know, down there. There is a lot of caribou."

Justus lifts an imaginary rifle, bracing it against his shoulder to aim at a fat bull caribou. Holding a knife, he makes a cut into the belly of his freshly killed caribou, then, placing his foot on the carcass, tugs at the hide, demonstrating how to skin a caribou in the traditional manner. When they talk about hunting wolves and their pups in the spring for the bounty, Justus looks up from the map and squints into his imaginary scope to focus on a full-bellied wolf, taking food to her pups in the den. When he thinks about his travels, he smiles. Suddenly he moves his bunched fingers emphatically across the map to remind us, "We don't stay in one place, just move around all the time. Move around all of the time where there is a lot of caribou."

But now that Anaktuvuk people are in one place and surrounded on three sides by the Gates of the Arctic National Park, Justus gives us a lesson in *tannik* geography. The Park Service looks only at the land on the map, he says. "Here's mine, here's mine, they say. Here's mine. They don't know anything about if there's siksrikpak [marmot] in there. They don't know if they have fish over there in the creek. There is a lot of sheep, but they don't know anything. We know everything in this land. Siksikpuk, or where there is a lot of sheep, or fish. Everything we know. But Park Service says, that's mine. That's mine."

Ed and Justus return to discussing the old days. Pretty soon they have mapped out an entire year, the numbered places on the map keyed to kills, campsites, a lost pack dog, a wolf den. Is it possible to map a man's life so literally?

"Maybe this is a good place to stop," Ed says after nearly two hours. Justus puts his cap on and stands to go. Ed rolls up the map, satisfied. "We covered a lot of country."

Anaktuvuk Pass, You Copy?

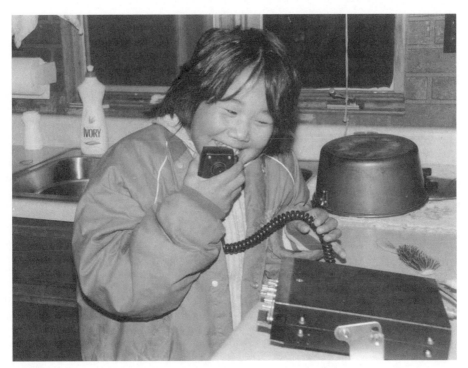

CB talk.

In Anaktuvuk Pass there are fewer than one hundred houses, a small community hall, and just one school building for the entire population of village kids. The little village store is the only obvious commercial establishment, the post office the only obvious government presence. Beyond the village airstrip, the pristine wilderness stretches for miles in every direction. This is a village settled so recently that the older people still speak longingly of themselves as nomads. A village so closely knit that only seven surnames— Paneak, Mekiana, Hugo, Morry, Ahgook, Kakinya, Rulland—occur among its original founders and most of today's residents. A village where everyone knows everyone else, not just by face, but, just as importantly, by voice on the CB *radio. And everyone knows just about everyone's business, too.*

Midsummer 1991, late one Sunday morning. Sundays are quiet here. Only the occasional crunching of tires on gravel breaks through the incessant buzzing of the cluster flies that have come to life in the warm air. It's the crackling of the CB radio that reveals people stirring on this lazy morning.

"Hello, Anaktuvuk Pass, you copy?" The caller is James Luke, a bachelor in his sixties who lives alone in a tiny house with a giant spike of a radio antenna stuck into the ground beside it. Luke spends many hours a day seated before his CB radio talking to other villagers, and his is often the predominant voice on the airwaves. He begins the round of wake-up greetings that are a weekend ritual here:

"Good morning, good morning, Riley."

"Good morning, Luke."

"Not too hot and no mosquitoes, looks like a nice day maybe."

"Yup. Everybody just waking up slowly."

They talk for a few moments, then Luke's voice moves on:

"Joby Ahgook, Joby Ahgook, Good morning."

"Good morning."

"Nice day alright."

"Yup. Gonna go toward Masu today, after I fix my muffler."

"Lotsa blueberries down there maybe."

"Yeah. Alice and the girls want to go picking."

"Good day for it."

"Yup. Well, finally going to get up, maybe."

The "good morning" rounds continue into the noon hour, but like every summer weekend, many of the villagers are away, having traveled in their Argos [1]—the all-terrain summer vehicle of choice—north or south of the village, where there is likely to be game and berries. From June to October every Friday evening a convoy of Argos, laden with tents and tarps and tent poles, cookstove, fishing poles, rifle and binoculars, kids and clothes and disposable diapers, and followed by the family dog, makes its way out from the village and onto the tundra. Late Sunday night or in the early hours of Monday morning they return. Slowly wakening villagers this Sunday morning inquire on their CBs about those out camping for the weekend, or they attempt to rouse the campers themselves, who stay in touch with the village on the mobile CB units mounted in their Argos.

Bonnie, a little girl out camping with her parents toward Chandler Lake, comes on the CB, her words choked out between sobs. She has just awakened from a nap and can't locate her mother or father. Minnie Mekiana, at her home base CB, tries first to reach Bonnie's father: "Gilbert Lincoln, Gilbert Lincoln." When he doesn't answer, she tries to calm the little girl: "Maybe they've gone to the bathroom or are picking berries. Is your dad's rifle there? Stay in the Argo or the tent," she advises. "They won't leave you." Her words must have helped, for Bonnie doesn't call back. About fifteen minutes later a male voice from the village asks Bonnie if her parents are back yet. "Not yet," she answers. "Call again if you get lonely," he urges.

At 12:30 the CB goes silent for awhile. Then Raymond Paneak calls for Jimmy Jack to consult about a problem Ray is having with his Argo. The malfunctioning vehicle has kept him confined to the village this weekend. Ray describes in some detail what he's already done to the machine, and Jimmy offers a possible solution to his problem. They sign off after commenting on the weather: "August, fall time weather almost; time for sheep and bull moose."

As the afternoon wears on, the talk is between the village and people out on the land, most of it initiated by those sitting at their home base CBs. Caribou dominates the conversation—who got what, whether bulls or cows, and how many. Late in the afternoon an invitation to share the bounty of the hunt is announced on the CB: "Anybody who wants to eat meat, come to Noah Ahgook's."

The village social calendar for the day unfolds on the CB as well: "Early birthday party for Justus, Brian, and Robert. Everybody's invited." "Snerts [a lightning-fast double-solitaire game] at Olive Morry's at 10:30." Villagers welcome home Rhoda Ahgook, who has returned from the hospital in Fairbanks, where she has undergone tests for the last two weeks. In the early evening, Riley Morry wonders if anyone is going "up the hill" to the poker tent for what will surely turn into an all-night high-stakes game. Almost every summer evening there is a poker game in session in the white canvas tent on "Poker Hill." "Nobody there yet," he laments.

The CB crackles on, with requests for Argo parts and a woman wanting to "borrow" a Pamper. Another woman advertises her Argo for sale—a thousand dollars. She's trying to raise the airfare to fly to Fairbanks to see her boyfriend. A grandmother gives advice to a granddaughter while the entire village listens in. Riley Morry reports the halftime score of the Seattle Seahawks–Phoenix Cardinals football game to those out camping. Village children pick up the microphone seeking playmates.

"Meryn Hall, Meryn Hall." "Go ahead," my CB-shy daughter responds. "What you doing?" "Nothing." "Who all's over there right now?" "Nobody, just my mom and dad." "Can I come over?" "Sure." A few other calls for Meryn follow, and within ten minutes our little house has filled with girls.

The CB sits in a prominent place in every village home—on an end table beside the sofa in the living room or on the kitchen table or the kitchen counter. Everyone is tuned to channel 14, the primary talk channel, but when it is actively being used or when folks want to converse without interruption, they direct the person they call to another channel, usually 5, 9, 21, or 40. I soon mastered the quick flip of the dial, springing from the chair at my computer and shamelessly turning the knob on our borrowed CB to the designated talk channel. Today I listen in on Mabel Burris talking to her sister-in-law, Marie Paneak. "Okay, everybody," Mabel announces when finished, "back to channel 14." I smile, relieved to learn that I am not the only eavesdropper in the village.

Sunday evening often brings music across the CB airwaves. Johnny Rulland, another sixtyish village bachelor, belts out a country and western ballad about never marrying, Zacharias Hugo sings in Iñupiaq, accompanying himself on his drum, and an unidentified person plays "singspiration" hymns sung in Iñupiaq and recorded at a village gathering months before. For a moment I consider adding to the musical repertoire of the community by playing the *Brandenberg Concertos*. But the whole village would know who did it, I remind myself. I go back to my computer.

Late evening. As darkness begins to press down on the land in August, parents are calling for young children to come home. No parent hollers from the back door as they did in the Indianapolis suburb of my childhood. In fact, a visitor walking the evening streets of Anaktuvuk Pass would never know parents might be looking for their children. At 10:30 Maggie Morry calls her granddaughter on the CB: "Hattie Morry, Hattie Morry, you read anywhere?" "Hattie M-o-r-r-y, Hattie M-o-r-r-y," her voice rises and falls, "Time to go home." A mother looks for her young son: "Anthony Ahgook, Anthony Ahgook. Anybody see Anthony, send him home." Children frequently don't heed these calls, especially the first one. An hour later, at 11:30, Hattie's grandmother has begun to get impatient: "Hattie Morry, Hattie Morry, come home right now!"

Just before I turn off the CB for the evening, a man, obviously angry, complains about his CB not fine tracking, then abruptly lashes out: "I'm tired of this fucking community, anybody want some trouble, come over!" No takers answer. The caller makes vague complaints about people giving out things—drugs and alcohol—that they shouldn't, then disappears from the airwaves. Drunks get on the CB and say "anything," villagers complain, noting that sometimes the only solution is to go to the caller's house and take away his mike until he sobers up. One villager offers another solution. "Mostly we just turn off our CB when people are drinking."

Midnight. Parents have located their wandering children, and weekend campers, including little Bonnie and her family, have returned to the village. Most villagers, mindful of work on Monday, turn in earlier than on the weekend. Night owls who leave their CBs on will catch the occasional conversation and perhaps loud rock music played by teenagers. Invisible by day and less inclined to speak on the CB than younger children, teens come into their own late at night on the airwaves.

I flick the radio's off switch, cutting my link to every other household here. An anthropologist's dream, I tell myself, this "fly-on-the-wall" ethnography. I've seen no one today, talked to no one, intruded in no villager's life, not even left the house. Yet my fieldnotes brim with more than twelve hours of CB conversation. I smile. I could get used to such armchair anthropology.

Citizens band radios came to Anaktuvuk Pass sometime in the late 1970s, just as their popularity on the nation's highways was peaking.[2] The village was electrified in 1976, and by early 1978 television, one phone, and a few CBs were present. The Nunamiut have always been quick to adopt new technology, and it seems that they acquired CBs as soon as they were readily available and affordable.

CB radios became a village fixture unencumbered by most of the CB culture that had evolved in the lower forty-eight. Aside from "you copy," "roger," "you read," and "say again," CB jargon is not used in the village. Nor do people have any need of colorful "handles" that mask one's real identity and make it easier to talk to strangers. There are no strangers in this village of Ahgooks, Hugos, Mekianas, Paneaks, Kakinyas, Morrys, and Rullands. No CB operator calling another person identifies himself or herself, except the visiting anthropologists who have the occasional need to pick up the CB to order water, locate their child, or arrange for an interview. But our self-identification is probably unwarranted because, after a few days in the village, our voices are known as well. Even young children know most villagers' voices. "Who's that?" I would repeatedly ask, and five-year-old Emily Hugo, or six-year-old Bernice Rulland, would instantly tell me.

Virtually every house in this village has a CB radio that is on during the waking hours of its members, and families who own Argos equip their vehicles with a mobile CB unit. All the public buildings, like the post office, the school, and the washeteria, have CBs. So do the assortment of public vehicles that spend their days driving the five miles of gravel streets each day. "Water truck, water truck," brings the tanker that pumps drinking and washing water for each household. "USDS, need a new pallet," gets rid of the ballooned garbage bags of human waste in the cardboard honeybucket containers that sit before each home. Calls for "Fuel truck, fuel truck," become more frequent as summer comes to an end and heating oil tanks need filling.

The rhythm of CB talk is different during the week than on the weekends. People are up and at their mikes earlier; there are calls for water delivery and for honeybucket pickup. People call into the health clinic with questions: "Can my nine-month-old baby drink orange juice?" And the health clinic calls out to the community: "Tell Valerie she's got to come for her shot." Changes are broadcast in the daily schedule of village life: "The washeteria won't open until three P.M. today," and special events are announced: "School board meeting tonight at seven o'clock. Anybody who's interested come to the school." Villagers talk back and forth from work, check on an elderly shut-in and kids at home. The kids talk back to their working parents, often to complain about a sibling: "Bernice poked me with a needle;" "Mom-mm, Raymond spit on Carol."

Most CB talk in Anaktuvuk Pass is in English, yet older people do occasionally speak at length in Iñupiaq. As I listened with frustration to long lapses in a language where I understood only the occasional word, I couldn't help wondering if people ever spoke in Iñupiaq to keep information from the handful of *tannik*, or white, residents who have CBs. "No," villagers assured me, no one would do that. I soon learned otherwise. Last summer Ed was experiencing, for the first time, visible symptoms of multiple sclerosis, particularly difficulties in walking and slurred speech. It wasn't long before one man reported to the entire village in Iñupiaq, "Looks like Ed Hall is drunk!"

Listening to the CB over just a few summers, voices become familiar and patterns emerge. Certain people dominate the airwaves, and there seems to be a CB pecking order, especially among the men. James Luke, who is somewhat of an outsider, counting only three cousins as close relatives in the village, talks a great deal on the CB, but he defers to other men if they wish to speak. Men talk more often and at greater length than women, though women are as much a part of the "good morning" circuit as men, and women initiate conversations with both sexes. The handful of non-Natives in the village speak only in some official capacity—as nurse, accountant for the village corporation, school principal, or the like; *tanniks* are not part of the network of people who regularly call and are called, though some, like me, may be routine listeners.

Kids' conversations are short and instrumental, but they are habitual CB users, switching on the mike to talk, mastering turn-taking in speaking, and turning from channel 14 to another talk channel by the time they are four or five years old. Their introduction to the CB starts early. A mother broadcasts her baby to the community; the baby babbles and chortles on the air for about forty-five seconds. Another mother tells a friend, "Junior's sending you a kiss through the CB." One little girl asks another, "Can your little sister turn the CB to channel 5? 'OK, Molly, channel 5.'" Molly makes it to channel 5, but she sounds very young indeed.

It's easy to dismiss the CB as simply a substitute for the telephone in Anaktuvuk Pass. There are only twenty-two resident phones in the village, while nearly everyone has a CB. But the telephone has its own uses. People resort to their telephones when the CB is "too full of talk." And, if a private conversation is your intent, the phone is the instrument of choice. But people are so accustomed to contacting villagers on their CBs that, rather than ringing up someone on the phone, the caller will rouse her on the CB only to instruct, "Call me on the phone."

Most of the time, people would rather talk on the CB. "With a telephone you have to press so many numbers; with CB, it's just easier," explained one villager. And, for anyone who just wants to talk, the CB offers an entire village of potential conversationalists. Almost like a chain reaction, people are pulled onto the airwaves:

At 11 P.M. Riley Morry is calling around the village on the mike. He reaches John Octuck, who has just awakened from a nap; they talk for a few minutes, and then Riley calls Willie Hugo, getting instead his wife, Becky, who reports that Willie is sleeping. Becky's voice brings on Lela Ahgook, who inquires how Becky's father, who has been hospitalized in Barrow, is doing. Riley, hearing his sister, Lela, intervenes as soon as Lela and Becky have finished their conversation: "Your CB sounds like shit," he accuses her. Lela retorts: "That's how my voice is." "Well, you better stay hidden then till you get better." Lela laughs and Riley continues his late-evening rounds on the radio.

"You can visit through the CB," remarked one woman. "It's good to talk on the CB," a man confessed, "It's too lonely and quiet without it." Especially, I imagine, in the dark of winter. And what a forum for self-expression! All those ears out there to receive your speech, song, tirade. One August night Zach Hugo spoke at length in Iñupiaq about the potential impact of hunting guides and sports hunters on the fall caribou migration, and I am told that men often tell stories on the CB in the wintertime. Several times a week Rhoda Ahgook, Johnny Rulland, and Zach Hugo sing Iñupiaq songs on the air, sometimes accompanying themselves on taut skin drums. Candidates for political office find the CB irresistible.

As attractive as the CB is to its community of local users, it can be intimidating to the outsider, especially in a village where even the youngest kids are experts. Accustomed to a cordless phone, which accompanies me to any room of my home for private phone conversations, I find the CB unsettling.

When I pick up the mike, I am conscious of the more than two hundred pairs of ears trained on CB sets. Everyone will hear me. What if someone answers and I don't recognize the voice, or what if I have to request "say again" because I don't understand the transmission? I will make a fool of myself doing something as simple as ordering water delivery, and they will talk—in Iñupiaq—about the foibles of the foolish *tannik* anthropologist. So, I avoid the CB if at all possible. I would rather flag down the water truck on the street.

In a 1991 article in *Phi Kappa Phi Journal* entitled "The Reservation Conditions," Native author Vine Deloria Jr. offers a cautionary tale about modern electronic communication and entertainment appliances in Native American communities. TVs, VCRs, and the like are isolating, he argues. They promote individual, not group, values; they encourage observation but not interaction among the observers. Similarly, the CB radio has added to the growing isolation of the Nunamiut. One can talk to the health clinic, check the mail at the post office, learn the whereabouts of the village transit bus, get a diagnosis on an ailing Argo, call one's children at home, and visit with other villagers without venturing beyond the CB microphone. Not to mention doing armchair anthropology.

But, while the CB promotes a certain physical isolation, it also connects people separated by place, and it furthers, rather than undermines, a sense of community in this small mountain village. Anaktuvuk Pass has a reputation both among locals and outsiders as a friendly place. People see each other several times a day on the village streets, and each time they do, they wave and greet one another. The CB reinforces this, extending the opportunities for personal contact and conversation. In the old days, Eskimo men would gather in the *qarigi*, a community hall of sorts, where they would build and repair sleds and hunting equipment, plan and discuss a hunt, and tell stories and sing songs. Women and children would sometimes join them there. Today the people come together through the CB in an electronic *qarigi*.

Up until the 1950s, the Nunamiut moved across the land in small groups, each unaware of the exact whereabouts of any other at a given time. Not until they all came together could their separate experiences be told. Today, journeys on the land are shared instantly through the CB radio. The story of the hunt need not wait until the hunters return, but can be relayed in bits and pieces as it unfolds. During the fall caribou migration through the pass, the CB radio is used to coordinate the hunt itself.

The CB offers villagers a vicarious nomadism. Those at home follow the journeys of other villagers to favorite camping, hunting, and berry-picking places. If the stay-at-homes can make their way out on the land this weekend, they will know the best direction to head for game, the places the berries are the thickest, and where to find the company of others. If not, then the CB radio has provided them a weekend of mental journeys to Qalutagiaq, Masu Creek, and Narvaksrauraq through other villagers' shared experiences.

The CB radio marks both ends of our summer sojourn here. We plug in the radio, adjust the antenna, and tune in to channel 14 as soon as the electricity in our rental house is turned on. And on our last night in the village, as we are packing gear for the return trip home, Ed picks up the mike: "Hello, Anaktuvuk Pass . . ." He spins out a message of heartfelt thanks and goodbyes, speaking for all three of us. Villagers' voices reply: "Nice to have you here," "Have a safe trip home," "Come back next summer," "Don't forget Anaktuvuk Pass . . ."

They Come In; They Go Out

Dancing for tourists. Photo by James H. Barker.

By the early 1950s, a scatter of ivruliks, *low, semisubterranean sod houses built over a frame of spruce logs, sprang up in the pass, making a village. Wrapped in the tundra grasses that grew on them, these low mounds of houses seemed much more a part of the arctic terrain than the palette of angular modern houses that gradually replaced them. Once a month the mail, addressed to Anaktuvuk Pass 8, Alaska, came in, and the entire village turned out to watch the mail plane land. Younger villagers carried the freight and mail the quarter-mile from the lake to the post office, located in Homer Mekiana's sod house—or tent, depending on the season. Everyone—mothers packing babies on their backs, small children, old men—stood by as Homer sorted and handed out the mail. In the summertime, residents moved out of the cool sod houses and into white canvas tents. And many residents packed up their tents and took off for summer camping and hunting places, leaving the postmaster's lone tent with the American flag flying beside it.*

The only sod house still occupied belongs to the local museum curator, a white anthropologist who has lived in the village for more than twenty years. Today, arctic ground squirrels make the ivruliks *their homes, peer out from between the chinks in the walls, stand on sod roofs to survey the village. Curious kids tag along after summertime visitors, plying them with questions.*

It's on time today. I hear a distant hum in the sky directly to the south, then see the flash of white against Mount Ingstad. "Airpla-a-ane," I yell to Ed on my way out the door. I stride across the street toward the post office and airstrip. The heavy steel door to the tiny post office opens and Mary Mekiana, the postmaster, appears on the steps lugging two canvas bags of outgoing mail. She looks up to see the plane circle above the village, then disappear in a cloud of dust as it touches down at the south end of the runway. A couple of German hikers in polarfleece, climbing pants, and waterproof gaiters sit at the picnic table by the steps, their bulging backpacks propped against the post office stairs. They're a bit grimy now, after two weeks on the land, and are looking forward to returning to Fairbanks on this morning's flight.

Within minutes, the water truck, the village "transit bus," and the sewer truck have all converged on the scene. Their engines idle; their drivers, and the two bus passengers, wonder what this morning's flight will bring. The school truck is here, too, in anticipation of a shipment of school supplies. The public safety officer brakes his four-wheeler to a halt on the gravel runway by the post office, dismounts, and waves to Mary. He trains his eyes on the small, two-engine Beechcraft that has just pulled into the staging area in front of the post office, hoping this will be a routine turnaround, no liquor—illegal here—or drugs coming into town.

But even before that telltale skyward hum is heard—in fact, a sign that it is imminent—a battered red pickup truck pulls up to the fence by the post office. Its one gray door and the assorted children in back identify it as belonging to Steve Wells, agent for the three airlines that serve the village. He is also the tour guide for those who have purchased a package tour to Anaktuvuk from the airlines.

A curly-haired, wooly hulk of a man with a voice to match his size, Steve seems custom-designed for bush Alaska—faded denim overalls, work boots, and rumpled wool shirt. His charges for this morning are equally distinct in appearance. They take uncertain steps down the four tiny, narrow plane stairs, gazing at the collection of vehicles and people gathered about. They zip their fleece-lined windbreakers against the wind, straighten cameras around their necks, put on hats to ward off the cold. Day-trippers. They arrive on the 10:30 A.M. flight from Fairbanks and head back to "civilization" on the flight at 2:30 P.M..

Steve's booming voice and hale-fellow-well-met demeanor put them at ease: "Hey, whadda think of this arctic sunshine? Another heat wave . . . Just have a seat over there at the picnic table while I finish unloading the plane and then we'll take you to the bathrooms and the coffee." "Hey, Ray, had enough of the big lights and the city?" He greets Raymond Paneak, home from "town"—Fairbanks. Steve's nonstop repartee with the pilot and returning villagers engages the new arrivals, who wait, surveying the scene and raising their cameras to photograph the unloading of the plane, the knot of surrounding villagers, and me, the lone anthropologist. "This plane's full of Arctic Samsonite," grumbles Wells, tossing another plastic garbage bag of "luggage" on the airstrip. He loads the outgoing freight, baggage, and mail, assists those who need help up the narrow steps to the plane, shoos small children away from the propellers, and then returns to his charges, directing them toward his truck.

Picking up the styrofoam take-out box containing the soggy remains of last night's hamburger from the truck bed, he kicks aside a rack of caribou antlers to make room for the long planks he places across the bed of his truck. Tourist statistics in Anaktuvuk Pass are measured not only by the number of signatures in the museum guest book but by the number of planks fitted each morning across the back of Steve Wells's truck. Three planks and fourteen tourists today, a record for the summer.

Tourism is big business in Alaska, and has been, in some form, for over a century. Cruise ships and the Alaska state ferries ply the Inside Passage, and caravans of motor homes and four-wheel-drive vehicles venture the Alaska

Highway each summer. By marketing the Aurora borealis, winter visitors, especially the Japanese, are enticed. But more and more people want an Alaskan "experience" that includes a trip to the bush, a visit to a Native village, and some contact with Native Alaskans in their home settings. Native villages and Native corporations in the state are cashing in on the tourist dollars.

It's the rugged beauty of the Brooks Range and the village's location adjacent to Gates of the Arctic National Park, the friendly villagers, and the little log museum that draw the thousand or so visitors to Anaktuvuk Pass each year. Most likely they have seen the advertisements for Anaktuvuk Pass in the *Fairbanks Visitors' Guide* or in *Alaska Magazine,* or they picked up information on the village from the Fairbanks and Anchorage Convention and Visitors Bureaus. The tourists come here from virtually every state, from most of Western Europe, from Australia, China, South Africa, and Japan.

Steve Wells's truck speeds along the road paralleling the airstrip a quarter of a mile south to "camp," a ramble of aging, leaky Atco modular units. They house the village corporation's headquarters, a café, several hotel rooms, and a small store selling engine parts, tires, and other equipment. The day-trippers use the bathroom here and drink a cup of strong, dark coffee. Fifteen or twenty minutes later they're back on the truck, which wends its way over the five miles of graveled village roads. The pickup grinds to a stop before the bridge over Contact Creek. The tourists snap pictures of the village health clinic beside the stream and look for arctic grayling swimming upstream in the rapid waters. A group of young children wade upstream, throwing the glacial river cobbles at the swiftly moving fish. "Rock fishing," they call out to tourist queries.

A hundred yards across the bridge, the truck stops again at the new experimental energy-efficient arctic house, built on a North Slope Borough capital improvement program. It doesn't look that much different from any other village house, but it is crammed with insulation and heat-conserving details. Visitors always wonder how people here deal with the cold, so the new house makes for good conversation. The red pickup continues north, passing little Summit Lake, where planes landed in the days before the runway was built. The road ends at the village cemetery. The tourists gather before a varnished wooden cross with a brass marker inscribed "Masao Oka." A Japanese anthropologist, Wells tells them, who did research here over a period of twenty years. The local people named one of the mountains in the pass after him, and he chose to be buried here beside his Native friends Morry Maptegak and Simon Paneak. The tourists peer down into the old village ice cellar at the margins of the cemetery, where community members once stored meat in the days before salesmen learned to sell freezers to Eskimos. They wonder about the white tent pitched on the ridge just beyond the town boundaries, which fills up with poker players during the long daylit summer nights. They don't know that the Nunamiut were ardent gamblers even in the days before they discovered poker. They settle back into the truck bed for a leisurely drive along the unnamed streets of town. There's much here to explain, and Steve stops the truck several times to poke his head out of the cab and talk to his truck-bed tourists. Predictably, they ask about the lookalike borough housing and honeybucket refuse containers, the silvered wooden meat racks, and those green ATVs—Argos—that look like frogs on eight wheels.

A lone hiker, dwarfed by his large backpack, walks the same village streets, waving at the truckload of tourists as they pass him. Absentmindedly, he tosses a candy bar wrapper into one of the big cardboard honeybucket containers, unaware of their intended purpose. He could be American. Or Canadian, German, Swiss, Dutch, British, Australian, or Japanese. He is one of perhaps four hundred backpackers who will come here in this summer of 1992 to hike the wilderness lands of the Gates of the Arctic National Park. While in Anaktuvuk he'll take advantage of the free showers at the village washeteria, sign his name in the guest book at the museum, and linger awhile in the village store. Come evening his nylon tent will be a bright spot of yellow on the green tundra above the village. And in a day or two he'll be at the picnic table by the post office, waiting for the morning flight to Fairbanks.

I'm always intrigued by the backpackers, and I'm a bit envious of their freedom. They give themselves to the land, crisscross the rugged tundra carrying less on their journeys than the Nunamiut used to in the days before Argos and snowmobiles. I, on the other hand, come to town with an embarrassment of gear for my month's stay. Like that housecat on the window ledge, I remain tied to the village, to my tape recorder and research project.

Stop. Drive twenty-five yards. Stop. One can always tell when the red pickup is on a tourist mission. Crossing back over Contact Creek the truck pauses before one of the remaining sod houses. Cameras focus, shutters hum-snap in succession. Maybe Zacharias Hugo runs out of his prefab house nearby shaking his fist at Steve Wells and demanding payment, and maybe he doesn't. More than once he's hollered, "Twenty dollars a head if anybody want to take pictures." If Zach appears, Steve hustles his flock back onto the truck and they rattle off toward the school and washeteria. Doris Hugo defends her husband: "We don't like tourists to take pictures too much of the sod house without asking. It would be better if at least somebody ask. He would say yes."

Village children playing in the school yard mug for tourist cameras, and the bolder ones descend on the visitors with a lilting litany of questions:

"Who's your name? You come on the plane today?"

"Where you come from?

"How long you stay?"

Familiar words to my ears. Time was when I was trailed by a gaggle of village children posing the very same questions. "How long you stay?" Never long enough, for I disappear well before the first serious snow, but sufficiently long to distinguish me—the anthropologist—from the tourists. And for the kids to know me as the mother of a daughter close in age to them. I quickly became "Hi-Margaret-where's-Meryn?"

The tourists clamber back onto their truck-bed planks, and Wells turns north on the remaining street of town, which ends a block later at a T-corner by the Nunamiut Corporation store. Exploration of the store is saved for the hour between 1:00 and 2:00 when the museum is closed. The truck rambles on, past the new headquarters of the Gates of the Arctic National Park and up the hill to the Simon Paneak Memorial Museum. The small, handsome log museum was completed in 1986, and it honors Anaktuvuk Pass's most famous citizen. The museum curator, Grant Spearman, emerges from the windowless building for his morning stretch in the August sunshine just in time to greet the dismounting tourists. A resident here since 1978, Grant is an anthropologist. Seduced north by archaeology jobs related to the construction of the Alyeska Pipeline and fascination with the traditional Nunamiut life, he stayed.

There's not much pressing business at the museum right now so to-day's guests get the fully narrated tour. Wells departs to grab a quick bite of lunch, promising to collect his charges in forty minutes. He pauses to reassure a woman who worries that she might miss the 2:30 plane: "Do something to get yourself arrested and I'll guarantee you'll be on the afternoon plane!"

In the small space of the museum the story of the Nunamiut is told, from the nomadic hunting days of the old-timers to the settlement of the village. A dog with a caribou-skin pack, a fur-clad hunter with bow, a three-quarter-scale model of an *itchalik*, or caribou-skin tent, and a montage of black-and-white photos. There's much to take in.

The visitors gather round Grant, who leads them, exhibit by exhibit, through the one-room museum. "Do they still hunt here? Do they still make skin clothing?" the tourists wonder, trying to reconcile the modern borough housing and large satellite dish outside the museum with the wood and stone artifacts and the photographs from pre-village days inside. "Did they ever live in snow igloos?" asks the stout woman in red polarfleece and stocking cap, pausing before the exhibit of a Nunamiut skin tent. She's thinking of those picture-book Eskimos from the central Canadian Arctic. "With all these rocks around here, why didn't they make rock houses?" It's the man with the New Orleans drawl. Grant winces.

Even the extended tour takes no more than fifteen minutes. The visitors browse on their own as they wait for Steve's return. They check out the small library adjoining the exhibit space, sign the guest register, and thumb through the publications on Anaktuvuk and North Slope topics for sale at the reception desk. Several caribou-skin masks hang above the reception desk. "Why didn't they wear the skin masks in winter to keep their faces warm?" It's the man from New Orleans again. Ignoring the silliness of his question, Grant patiently points out that the art of mask making is relatively new and that the masks are made as tourist art.

No one buys a mask today, but they're all holding up and inspecting "Simon Paneak Memorial Museum" T-shirts. The day-trippers are not big spenders in the village, dropping on the average only three to four dollars in their four hours here. They carry most of their mementos of this place in their cameras.

The hope of places like Anaktuvuk Pass, now entering the tourism business, is that people coming so far will invest in more than just a memento purchased from the museum or village store. Other Native villages in Alaska are trying to market something of the Native "experience." From the village of Huslia in the subarctic interior, visitors go upriver for four days, where they meet and camp with Native people, eat Native foods, and go on guided wilderness hikes. Grant Spearman finds "ecotourism," targeted at an elite audience, appealing. He spins out an ambitious master plan: A sod house north of the village at Tulugak Lake, and another forty miles south at Pu-vlatuuq in the tree line; *itchalik* tents at key locations where the Native people camped, and, most importantly, knowledgeable, interested Nunamiut men or women willing to escort tourists. "Take people out for three or four days, overnighting at these sites, give them all the place names, the origins of the names, show them all of the hunting and camping localities that people have used and explain their use, take them ice fishing." The problem is finding Nunamiut people willing to execute it. They're too busy out on the land for their own purposes, though there's no lack of talk about the tourist dollars that such efforts might bring in.

Heavy steps on the arctic steel grate announce Steve Wells. "Well, whadda think of the farthest north museum?" he booms. The tourists respond enthusiastically as they file out of the museum and back onto their planks. Last stop, the Nunamiut "Corp" store, where they can buy the only postcard in town, a winter scene at Chandler Lake some thirty-five miles away. Here a virtual village of caribou-skin masks keeps sentinel on store walls; their makers trade them for groceries. There are also T-shirts and sweatshirts and hats inscribed "Anaktuvuk Pass." Most tourists settle on some pop and snacks for the plane ride back to town. While the rest shop, one tourist plants himself at the front of the store and pans his camcorder along the length of the mask-covered wall behind the checkout counter, recording the transaction at the cash register in the process. Dorcas Hugo, the store manager, looks up disapprovingly at him from the sale she's ringing up. Steve takes advantage of the store time to buy a gallon of milk, then hustles his charges back to the truck for the hundred-yard ride to the airstrip.

It's not just the tourists who go out. Every day Anaktuvuk villagers board the plane for Fairbanks. Almost everyone has friends and relatives there. Each July the World Eskimo-Indian Olympics draw an enthusiastic group of villagers to Fairbanks for a week of games and dancing. Attending the August Tanana Valley Fair in Fairbanks is often combined with a shopping trip for school clothing. Health problems that can't be treated at the small village clinic warrant a trip to the city. In Fairbanks you buy a snowmobile or groceries you can't find in Anaktuvuk, and there are always the restaurants and bars. Frontier Flying Service, the main bush airline that serves the village, even has its own frequent flyer program: 3,750 miles logged—about eight round trips—earns the enrollee a free ticket to Fairbanks. Anaktuvuk villagers in the 1990s also wander well beyond Fairbanks.

August 1990. Seven-year-old Meryn pounds up the stairs to our rental house, where I'm typing my fieldnotes on the computer.

"Mom, Mom," she begins, breathless from running. "Guess what, Mom? You'll never guess where Freida and her family stayed that we did too."

"The Fairbanks Westmark," I reply absentmindedly.

"No, guess again, not Fairbanks."

I'm clueless.

"The Travel Lodge in Port Moresby."

I look at her in disbelief. We had gone, that spring, to Australia and Papua New Guinea and indeed stayed in the Travel Lodge in PNG's capital city. Just a few months before, Freida, her parents, and next-youngest sister had been the guests of the Tokyo Broadcasting Company, which arranged and filmed a cultural exchange between a family from Rabaul, PNG, and one from Anaktuvuk Pass.

It all began, Freida's father, Paul Hugo, reflected, "when I just had a long hard day at work and somebody came by and said, 'Are you interested in going on a trip?' 'It all depends on where,' I said." The two families exchanged places for three weeks, meeting at a formal dinner in Tokyo, then continuing on to their respective host communities. A Japanese film crew accompanied each family. "Strange," Paul mused, "I like that place. I enjoyed it. I never got homesick. I don't know, I just wanted to see the world, I think. A little bit anyway." His Air Niu Guinea tickets are still thumbtacked to the paneled living room wall of his Anaktuvuk home.

Paul loans us the two-hour videotape—in Japanese—which, since we have no TV or VCR, we watch with a troop of giggling Anaktuvuk kids at the village fire hall. *The Equator–The Arctic: The Reversal Special Program* was made for Japanese television and aired throughout that nation on New Year's Day 1990. Up on the TV screen the Hugos swelter in the tropical sun and romp in the surf. Caribou hunters look up in casurina trees for fruit bats. The kids laugh, accurately predicting the Hugo family's next moves. They've seen this tape before. Cut to the Papuans, outfitted in down snowmobile suits, riding on snowmobiles, eating caribou meat, and dancing to Eskimo drums in Anaktuvuk Pass. In Anaktuvuk, the excited Japanese narrator holds up a thermometer registering minus thirty-five degrees and with great effort drives a nail into a frozen banana.

A few days later I find Meryn and her friends in their usual play spot on the *qanitchaq*, the entryway to our house. They have gathered rocks and grasses, soil and willow leaves and twigs, and are bent over them, making things and talking. I can't help asking the obvious: "What are you girls playing?" "House," Meryn, Freida, and Frances respond in unison. Then they add, without looking up, "In Papua New Guinea."

Today I'm sitting at the picnic table by the Anaktuvuk Pass post office, read-ing my mail, when the telltale dust cloud at the end of the runway announces the plane. A shivering tourist from New Jersey, eager to return to the warmth of Fairbanks, asks, "What brings you to this godforsaken place?" I explain that I'm an anthropologist from western New York and that I've been doing oral history research here. He shakes his head, "Why would anybody want to live here?"

I watch the sunlight and shadow play on the flanks of Mount Ingstad, now burnished yellow and red in the gathering autumn. I think about how, thirty-some years ago, Anaktuvuk Pass opened to Ed a door to life as an anthropol-ogist, and how it has remained his personal touchstone. I think about Meryn, the five summers of her young life spent here and the remarkable things she will carry of this place and these people into her adulthood. I think of the promise a village friend holds out to me: "Someday, Margaret, I'll tell you my story." I smile at the questioning tourist. "Why," I want to answer, but don't, "would anyone want to live in New Jersey?"

Steve Wells stays with his flock, answering their final questions, spinning yarns about life in the bush. Today the plane is on time, and by 3:30 the woman in the red polarfleece, the shivering New Jerseyite, the New Orleans drawl, and the intrusive camcorder have all flown down the valley of the John River toward Fairbanks. If the warm wind blows from the south tomorrow, it will bring more tourists, but if the weather is foggy and rainy in the Pass, it will be a tourist-less day. I ask Steve about tourists, but he shies from being interviewed. "What can I say," he quips. "They come in; they go out."

Picking

Picking berries.

*From the village of Anaktuvuk Pass a web of trails to camping
and hunting places radiates in all directions. Southwest to Chandler Lake, where Sig Wien first met the Nunamiut in 1943, where
Nunamiut go to fish through the thick lake ice each May, where
they hunt caribou throughout the summer. South to Masu, where
the blueberries grow thick in August. North to Narvaksrauraq, the
best place for* akpiks, *cloudberries. Along the way is Aŋmagulik,
where people stop to rest and smoke and visit before resuming the
long ride to Narvaksrauraq. The names along the way tell a history.
Like the place where Elijah killed his big grizzly bear. Or Kawasaki
Creek, named for the snowmobile that died on its banks.*

Ethel says to pick the large, unripe *akpiks* and put 'em with the ripe
ones and they'll get ripe. When old people talk, I always listen.

LELA AHGOOK

For a short time, in August, berries loom as large in village talk as the game
animals that shape the daily conversations of the Nunamiut. On the CB, in
the washeteria, at the village store, the people talk about which berries—
especially *akpiks* and blueberries—are ripe, and where. Berry pickers travel
out onto the tundra, becoming distant bright spots of color that shift as they
move from patch to patch. Elderly grandmothers, remembering when they
used to walk all day to find berries, ride out of the village onto the saddle
of the nearby mountains in family Argos to spend the day picking. The
destinations of weekend campers depend on where the berries are. Purple
stains ring the mouths of village kids, splotch their palms. It's blueberry time.

It is August 1992, and Meryn and I are camped for the weekend with
Lela and Noah Ahgook. The "Nunamiut Experience," we all jokingly call it.
We're at Narvaksrauraq, twenty miles northwest of Anaktuvuk Pass, where
the *akpiks* are ripe. Lela, Tupperware bowl in hand, opens the flap of the
white canvas tent to go picking the minute breakfast is over. She picks *akpiks*
for two hours in a cold drizzly rain, Noah following her in the Argo, listening
and talking on the CB radio to other campers. From time to time Lela returns
to the Argo to empty her bowlful of salmon-colored berries into a gallon
Ziploc bag. When she's picked one area clean, she straightens up and waves
at Noah, who fetches her and transports her to another patch.

Arctic berries grow small and rather sparsely; they hug the ground and
hide beneath their own leaves. To my untrained eye the tiny fruit are easily
lost among the lichen-covered rocks and grassy tussocks. Picking requires
patience, nimble fingers, and a lot of bending over. But for those who perse-
vere, the tundra yields enough berries to savor in the deep freeze of winter.

Noah pokes his head into the tent, where I'm jotting notes about the camping trip. "You're not camping, you're writing!" Lela, having returned with her berries, chimes in: "Write down that you lay in bed all day." "That's not Nunamiut Experience," Noah teases me, "that's Tannik Experience. Come out and enjoy the weather or I take you home!" I fold up my journal and grab an empty Tupperware bowl. Picking *akpiks* is not one of my favorite activities, and these Nunamiut delicacies are my least favorite berry. The tart, mushy *akpiks* grow in cold, sodden, foot-numbing ground, but picking berries is what this trip is largely about.

Lela has enormous fortitude for berry picking, as do the other women of Anaktuvuk. They pick all day. Younger women, like Minnie Mekiana, who joins us, pick with their babies balanced on their backs, held fast by the mothers' generously cut parkas. Little Rhoda Mekiana is sound asleep, her head poking out from her mother's brightly flowered summer parka. She rolls against her mother's back to the rhythm of Minnie's movements. Nunamiut women are incredibly flexible, bending straight from the hips, rather than squatting, to pick the low-lying berries. Lela and Minnie move slowly across the land, together in my field of vision, alone with their thoughts.

Meryn and I venture off to drier, rockier ground to pick blueberries. The *tannik* way, on our stomachs, arms level with the tiny fruits. Above us the Argos ply the ravines; Lela bends and straightens, bends and straightens. I work slowly, the possibility of an entire day of berry picking stretching before me. The tiny berries accumulate slowly, but they bring fruit from the past with them.

I'm among the ruins of the old Haida Indian village of Kasaan in Southeastern Alaska with my first husband and fellow graduate student, Jim Blackman. It's the summer of 1971, and I am working on my doctoral dissertation project, which includes mapping this village site. Our camping gear has been packed up for some time; we listen, anxiously, for the distant buzz of the plane that was to have picked us up yesterday. To while away the waiting, I pluck the world's largest red huckleberries. They fall with a reassuring plop into the large tin can suspended around my neck by a string. Pick three, eat one. My very favorite berries—filling for a pie if we make it home today; sweet sustenance in case we're stranded here.

We picked a lot of berries that summer in the lushness of the Northwest rainforest—huckleberries, blueberries, thimbleberries, salmonberries, elderberries. We left for home before the salal berries ripened in the autumn, but we took with us a whole case of assorted berry jams that we had put up. I look at the handful of tiny arctic blueberries I have just picked; each is less than half the size of the Northwest Coast blueberries.

By the summer of 1994 several Anaktuvuk women had a blueberry "picker," mail-ordered from Samson's Hardware in Fairbanks. It's a bright red enameled metal contraption, reminiscent of a box-style cheese grater, sporting a handle topside and a comblike appendage on the business end. Grasping the handle, the berry picker can work the blueberry bushes with it like a pair of clippers, shearing off the tiny leaves while raking in the succulent berries. The mechanical "picker" flies in the face of how things used to be done, changing the choreography of berry picking, so that fingers no longer pluck berries from stems. But it is efficient.

I'm not sure, though, that berry picking is about getting more in less time. It has its own purposes and rhythms.

In the summer of 1983 Ed and I, Meryn, and Ed's eleven-year-old son, Justin, are camped with an Eskimo family near Kotzebue at their summer fishing grounds on Alaska's northwest coast. Ed has chartered a small plane and is off flying with Justin, showing him the countryside. I am, of necessity, grounded by my seven-month-old daughter. I go picking blueberries with Eskimo women, Meryn on my back. Marveling at her huge gray-blue eyes, they nickname her "Blueberry Eyes."

Meryn stretches and sighs, breaking my reverie. "I'm hungry," she announces. "Eat berries," I tell her. She frowns, digging into the Ziploc bag. She flattens her berry-filled hand against her face so as not to drop a single precious berry, and a third of our harvest disappears into her mouth. "I like blueberries better than akpiks," she reminds me. "Me too," I agree.

Back in southeast Alaska in 1984, I'm on a sentimental journey to old Haida village sites courtesy of my friend, marine zoologist Bill Lawton, who works at a fishing resort there. I have my field maps from 1971 with me and two-year-old Meryn in the backpack. She learns the names of all the berries. "Huckleberry, thimbleberry, blueberry," she demands, holding out small berry-stained fingers. I pass an uninterrupted supply of berries over my shoulder to her open mouth. "More berries," she laughs when I quit feeding her. We call her "The Berry Kid."

Tired of picking and eating berries, Meryn goes off exploring. Lela and Minnie are still focused on *akpiks*. Noah sits in the Argo, now talking on the CB, now scanning the distant ridges for caribou through his binoculars. I move to another patch of blueberries.

The summer of 1990. I am on the Queen Charlotte Islands, in British Columbia, the site of most of my doctoral dissertation research with the Haida.

I have returned here to work or visit almost every year since 1970. The northern Queen Charlottes, Haida Gwai, has always been "the field" for me. Meryn has joined me to pick wild strawberries with three of the Davidson family women at Rose Spit, a tongue of meadow and beach that juts out into the Pacific Ocean. Each woman selects a promising patch of strawberries and sits or kneels on the wet ground as she picks. All these women have strawberries at home; they are here in the misty rain out of need. "Nice to get away," explains Emily, "No one to tell you what to do, looking over your shoulder like at work." Back home they gather around their mother's old oaken kitchen table, cleaning the berries, talking. It's a woman's thing, berries.

The Argos have moved off in the distance, and I decide to join the others. It's taken me two hours to pick two-thirds of a quart of tiny arctic blueberries. Lela, on the other hand, has picked almost three gallons of *akpiks* in the two days we've been here. Enough to remember this place, this berry season, next winter.

Picking stirs memories for Lela, too. She tells me of the time, in the 1950s, when she and two other Nunamiut women walked the twenty miles from Anaktuvuk to this place, small children in tow, babies on their backs, to pick *akpiks* while their husbands hunted nearby for caribou. "When the akpiks are ripe, we always go north."

Late at night, cocooned in our sleeping bags inside the tent, soporific conversation rises to the peaked tent roof. It winds down, we're almost asleep. Suddenly Lela laughs her hearty, raucous laugh. "Every time I close my eyes, I just see one big akpik!"

The Upside Down Season

Meryn and her friends.

*A ripple of summer grasses and fireweed soften the gravelly vil-
lage yards. Wooden drying racks, silvered smooth from sun and
strong winds, hold drying caribou skins or slabs of red caribou
meat and brightly colored yarn tassels to scare away gluttonous
ravens. Snowmobiles and big wooden sleds for hauling gear and
caribou carcasses, green eight-wheeled Argos, and, increasingly,
newly purchased four-wheelers are parked before the houses, along
with the occasional automobile that is confined in its travel to the
five miles of village streets. Jumbled skeletons of expired snowmobiles and the green carapaces of former Argos lie among the still-
functioning machinery, together with an arctic workshop of miscellaneous Argo and snowmobile parts and a tangle of children's
bicycles. And everywhere there is the scatter of caribou bones—
bleached mandibles, freshly gnawed long bones in the dog yards,
antlers in velvet, and, atop plywood storage sheds, the gray, weath-
ered antlers of seasons past.*

Summer is a brilliant, fleeting moment in the Arctic, announced by softening
snow and the breakup of rivers. Mosquitoes arrive, and waves of migratory
birds. The tundra in full green summer dress is shot with spikes of fuchsia
fireweed, deep-red-leafed sourdock, white puffs of cottongrass, and yellow
arctic daisies. Streams and lakes shimmer in the intense northern sun; the
snow retreats to the mountaintops. Daylight is endless. By June, the sun
scribes a horizontal circle above the crest of the Brooks Range for fifty-six
days, and the caribou travel to the coast to have their calves.

Summer is special. It is the season when people follow the light, staying
up all night, sleeping very late. At every opportunity villagers travel the land,
hunting and camping. To the village children, summer offers a delicious and
heady freedom. The children of Anaktuvuk Pass have considerable latitude
to begin with, for as soon as they are old enough to walk away on their
own they have the run of the village. Small children here don't hold their
mothers' hands, something I quickly discovered the summer of my first field
research as five-year-old Meryn instinctively reached for my hand on our
walks through the village. The village is "safe," everyone echoes, in contrast
to Fairbanks, "town," where children, especially *tannik* children, must live by
rules.

The absence of "rules" is especially notable in Anaktuvuk in the summer,
beginning with the lifting of the 10 P.M. village curfew at the end of the
school year. Well past midnight, children swing toward the sky, run dizzying
circles on the merry-go-round at the village schoolyard, and play pickup
basketball games on the cement court by Contact Creek. Six- and seven-
year-olds walk the village streets and ride their bikes with abandon into the

early-morning hours. They may be expected home for meals but there are no serious repercussions if they don't show up, and as often as not, they don't. Neither do they necessarily come home to sleep, staying first with a friend, then a grandmother, then a cousin before they return home on their own. Older children sometimes stay up two days in a row, and it's a sure bet that a child on the village streets at 8 A.M. in the summer has not arrived there fresh from a night's sleep. Alice Ahgook, uncrowned queen of the village CB radiowaves and mother of five, summed it up when she chatted with another mother on the CB one summer day: "Just like my kids got no stomach summertime," she laughed. "Always out."

For five summers, Meryn luxuriated in the freedom of village life. Now I worry, for as an eleven-year-old, she is pushing for more freedom than I am comfortable with in our small hometown in western New York. This is, after all, a part of the country where the abduction of children is routine headline news. One day she walked off to Wendy's, several blocks away, to meet a friend for lunch, and two and a half hours later they had not returned. Yet two summers ago I didn't even flinch when I spotted her through a pair of binoculars half a mile away from the village with a group of village girls, picnicking on the tundra. Nor did I worry when, as a six-year-old, she played all day without adult supervision, and I didn't even know where she was at 10 P.M.. She had only to get off the small plane when we first arrived in the village to be swept into the company of her village friends; later we would spot her with the other girls, trying to catch grayling in Contact Creek or playing hide-and-go-seek in the scrubby willows. Or she and her friends would descend on us for a few moments to play blind man's bluff in our tiny rental house while we unpacked our gear. By then she would be covered in dust churned up from the gravel streets, her clothing stained from spilled pop and junk food purchased at the village store, her voice already affecting the cadence of the village patois. For all intents and purposes, Meryn became an Anaktuvuk Pass kid each summer, absorbed in village life in ways that her parents could only envy. She ate and slept in villagers' homes, swam in the frigid waters of the small lake by the cemetery, and went camping miles from the village with a Native family. She too stayed up all night and slept long into the day.

Her father and I, on the other hand, always arrived here hewing to the anthropologist's regimen. A project to do, funding for which we must answer, so many blank tapes to fill with oral history interviews in just a month's time. Hours spent tracking down villagers reluctant to commit to an appointed hour when the perpetual light beckoned them out on the land. Worry when a day or two passed without an interview. Renewed efforts to line up interviewees. A field season measured not in the freedoms offered by the welcoming summer light but in hours of tape-recorded interviews and the ethnographic gems they held.

Yet there are freedoms that the interior Arctic summer bestows even on an anthropologist at work. The routines of the workaday world at home fall away—no phones ring, my attendance is not required at any meeting, no television for us—to be replaced by the more elemental routines of securing water, emptying the honeybucket, and making sure the propane tank doesn't run out on the weekend. The immense light expands to hold within the day a long, solitary hike down the valley, watching children at play, reading, reading, reading (I bring a stack of pleasure reading that has begged for my attention all year), and even writing. I fall into bed late, sleep later than is humanly possible at home. I am, finally, by the end of my stay here, "upside down."

"What season do you like best?" I asked Lela and Noah Ahgook one summer evening. Meryn and I had gone with them and two grandchildren a few miles south of the village down the broad valley of the John River to picnic and pick berries. The sun warmed our faces and backs. From our vantage point on the ridge above the river, the village was a mere island of tiny buildings and roads floating on sea of green tundra. "Summer," Noah responded, without hesitation or further explanation. "I don't like it when it's hot," Lela replied, popping a sweet arctic blueberry into her mouth, "but I like summer. Because of the berries."

I have not lived through an arctic winter and I don't really want to, though that admission causes me some professional guilt. It is customary for a cultural anthropologist to spend at least one calendar 'round in the field, experiencing the people, the community, the culture in all seasons. I did that once, as a graduate student, for my doctoral dissertation fieldwork in northern British Columbia and Southeastern Alaska. It is harder now, I tell myself, with a child and pets and a large home, to pack up and go away for a year. Though, if I really wanted to, I know it could be managed. I try to make up for what I am missing by methodically questioning people about the winter: how they spend the dark days, whether talk on the CB radio differs, what the school year is like for children, how it is when first the cold and then the darkness come. I ask about the city basketball tournament held in Anaktuvuk Pass in December and the Christmas games and dances that fill the holiday season. In the long light of the arctic summer, I want to know all about their winter, and whether they, like I, face that season with apprehension and a sense of loss.

In 1984, I spent a week in Anaktuvuk Pass in early November, wintertime—even if just a taste—by any calculations. But I have not lived winter here and cannot write of it. So I write from the green, transitory summer. Here for just a moment before winter descends, making its own rules. That intensity of light, that freedom. The upside down season, like a love affair.

Fieldnotes

Anaktuvuk Pass. Photo by James H. Barker.

The hiker walked over the pass into Anaqtiktuaq Valley and then toward the modern houses and gravel airstrip marking the North Slope home of a few Iñupiat people.

Before he reached the village, he stopped for awhile in the cemetery and read once again the names carved on the grave markers—Jack Ahgook, Elijah Kakinya, Homer Mekiana, Abraham Kakinya, John Hugo, Emily Hugo, David Mekiana. He was flooded with memories—of what might have been; no, what was, what was. Elijah was almost 90 when he died, Emily but 3. The hiker had so much to learn. He stopped last at Simon's grave, then headed toward the village.

As we walk along you may wonder what role I play, who I feel I am: a detached scientific observer, Simon, a passionate participant, the hiker. Travel with me for a while and somewhere along the journey we may both understand.

Ed Hall, unpublished manuscript 1990

Anthropologists are inveterate note takers. We're supposed to "record" everything we do and see in the field. You can't write enough. You should write descriptively, with great detail, and above all else, objectively. You should never be without your notebook. You write longhand, on tablets, on spiral-bound notebooks, later typing up your notes—in the old days on a typewriter, always with a carbon copy that you mailed home as soon as possible; today, on a laptop computer. Anthropologists devise clever techniques to take notes in situations where note-taking is inappropriate: writing with the stub of a pencil on a teeny notebook hidden inside a pants pocket, making frequent trips to "the bathroom" to jot down observations, and, when all else fails, simply committing notes to memory. Fieldnotes are our data, and they become the measure of the anthropologist: a larger stack suggests more thorough fieldwork. But we're secretive and proprietary about our fieldnotes. One anthropologist's informal survey of seventy anthropologists concluded that we are reluctant to share our fieldnotes with anyone. Our attachment to them is so special that, in the words of a respondent, "If the house were burning down, I'd go for the notes first."[1]

The journal is a different critter, but as essential to a field anthropologist's psychological well-being as the fieldnotes are to proper scholarly research. Keep fieldnotes and journal separate, we are advised by the research methods texts, lest emotions, judgments, and other subjective or subversive thoughts belonging to the latter taint our scientific observations in the former. I did that during my early days of fieldwork, even recording the gossip from one community separately from both my fieldnotes and my personal journal. But by the time I began working in Anaktuvuk Pass, my "fieldnotes" included characters and conversations, impressions and reflections, and occasional observations of Meryn and Ed, as well as straight ethnographic data. The personal jostled with the scientific, the boundaries blurred. I came home from the field each summer with a single set of writings—notes-journal-gossip, demarcated only by day.

By the time I went to Anaktuvuk to do fieldwork the journal had also become well entrenched in my personal life. But only in my adult life. I was never much of a diarist as a girl; I found it difficult and embarrassing to write down intimate thoughts and feelings. I made up for that reticence in later life. My longest-running journal revolves around Meryn. I chronicled her journey (and mine with her) from before her birth through middle school. So strongly did I believe in the value of journals that, as soon as she was old enough to write, I gave Meryn a journal with the expectation that she would record her child views of our summer field seasons. I thrilled when, as we sat on the runway in Rochester waiting to take off for Alaska the summer she was seven, she asked for her journal and printed her first entry. Several days, a few thousand miles, and many memorable experiences later, the journal lay forgotten in the pile of her belongings. I begged and cajoled, and finally exercised a mother's prerogative: Write in the journal, *now*, before you go out and play. She stomped off, retrieved her journal and dived beneath the kitchen table, where she opened it to a blank page. How do you spell "journal," she asked. Followed by, How do you spell "making"? In less than a minute she slammed the journal shut, shoved it into my lap and was out the door to play. I turned to her entry: "July 24. My mom is making me write in my journal and I don't want to."

Meryn's required grade-school journals have a similar obligatory quality to them, a definite impatience with this daily imposition: "Really gotta hurry," she exclaimed through nearly 180 school-day pages in the fifth grade.

But the personal diary, that guardian of secrets, is another matter. I know, for in a fit of intellectual curiosity about the epistemological differences between diaries and journals, I committed the transgression of reading my ten-year-old daughter's diary. No, that wasn't the real reason I read it. I read it because, like every other snoopy mother, I was intensely curious about my daughter's inner thoughts. And when I finished, I felt appropriately guilty. But I did satisfy my curiosity about the differences between obligatory journals and personal diaries. She made no excuses here for writing at length; to the contrary: confessed feelings, a shared intimacy between author and audience, so unlike the public journals.

Anthropologists are familiar with Bronislaw Malinowski's *A Diary in the Strict Sense of the Term*, which caused such a ripple in the anthropological community when it was published in 1967. Malinowski, working in New Guinea's Trobriand Islands during World War I, set the standards for rigorous fieldwork and meticulous ethnography. His diary revealed another side of fieldwork. Most shocking was his distaste for the Trobrianders and his blatant reference to them as "niggers," but we could all sympathize with his escape into trashy novels, his malaise, and his longing for home. More surprising than the contents of Malinowski's diary, however, was its dismissal by the anthropologist Ian Hogbin, who reviewed it for the *American Anthropologist* in 1967: "the volume holds no interest for anyone, be he anthropologist, psychologist, student of ethnography, or merely a gossip. Why the journals were translated from the Polish, let alone printed, must remain the publishing mystery of the decade."

Hogbin was clearly uncomfortable being the unintended audience of private mental meanderings, and it's patently obvious that he never experienced the "rush" from reading his own daughter's diary. But how he could conclude, even in 1967 in the days before anthropologists discovered reflexivity, that there was nothing to be learned from such personal narratives is more of a mystery than the publication of Malinowski's diaries.

I can, however, understand Hogbin's discomfort at reading something that was never intended for public consumption, and not just because I read my daughter's diary. A few years before I committed that sin, I was on the other side of the fence—with Malinowski—and Meryn. My fieldnotes were stolen.

In 1988, during our first summer field trip to Anaktuvuk Pass, Ed had talked me into recording my fieldnotes the way he did, using a minicassette recorder. Since that field season predated our purchase of a portable computer, recording notes on tape seemed a worthwhile time-saver during our short field season. As soon as a tape was filled, we copied it and sent the copy home to be typed up by the research assistant Ed had hired. Only after we got home could we review our fieldnotes.

At the end of each day Ed would take the recorder, and, either sitting on the steps of the house or walking about the yard, he would speak the day's activities onto a tape. He'd begin with the date, military style ("6/8/88" for August 6th, 1988), followed by a summary of the day's weather, and then he'd recount what he had observed and what research we had accomplished that day. I found his method of recording fieldnotes less satisfying than writing. While taping had the feel of being conversational because I was talking to *something*, it seemed distanced. I couldn't edit as I went along, and when I had completed a day's entry, I couldn't see at a glance what I had said. When I finally did see the transcribed entries, it was weeks and thousands of miles later. I had only to read the transcripts to realize how differently I spoke than I wrote. Even so, notes, journal, and gossip blended in my tape-recorded entries just as they did in my written notes.

One day, returning home after an interview, we discovered the minicassette recorder and our fieldnote tapes missing! And—Meryn was quick to point out—a bag of frozen blueberries had disappeared as well. It was probably kids, we concluded. We posted notices about town, noting that we only wanted the tapes back, but we never saw them or the recorder again. For the rest of our stay I was haunted by this image: A group of young Nunamiut boys gather behind the school, closing ranks around the one who's taken possession of the recorder, their bikes thrown down in the dirt beside them. He pushes the play button, black heads incline toward the tiny machine. A slightly monotone female *tannik* voice speaks, "August 6, 1988. Cold today, and little sunshine, temperature in the forties." "Play the part about your aka [mother] again," one giggles." The tape rewinds. I returned to writing my notes in a notebook that I kept with me at all times and eyed the village kids nervously. Which one had my fieldnotes?

Just as the personal insinuated itself into my fieldnotes, the anthropologist was firmly entrenched in my personal journals. I was the ethnographer enthusiastically recording my daughter's development, and I was the ethnographer sadly, and often angrily, recounting the progression of Ed's illness.

When Ed was diagnosed with multiple sclerosis in 1980, I was hopeful. "His symptoms are very mild, sensory only, just surface numbness. That's a good sign," his neurologist reassured us. And so it seemed, for ten years. The numbness came and went along with occasional bouts of double vision. Ed carried on, so unfazed that he didn't even bother to tell his parents he had MS, though I suspect that the stigma of the disease had something to do with his secret as well. We continued to teach together as faculty colleagues. We played squash, collected Native American art, and did fieldwork together. We read each other's work, talked and argued anthropology. We had our daughter.

MS receded into the background. But following our vacation to Australia and Papua New Guinea in the spring of 1990, when a bad infection from an insect bite sent him to the hospital for several days, Ed began to experience more serious problems.

July 21, 1990

This will, I think, be a challenging and exhausting field season. Though it has been smooth settling in to Anaktuvuk life, there is a great deal of tension in our working and personal relationships this year. Ed has had a major attack of MS, making him more dependent upon me, shorter tempered, and somewhat physically debilitated. His speech is badly slurred, which he bravely ignores and talks through; I want him to explain it to people lest this village with its share of alcohol problems think him perpetually drunk.

It was a difficult summer. Our small rental house in Anaktuvuk offered little personal space, especially when filled with Meryn and her Nunamiut girlfriends. We were fortunate, in that prelaptop era, to be able to take a portable computer to the field, but we had to share it, and no sooner would I be midway into typing my fieldnotes when my "hour" on the computer was up and Ed was demanding his turn. I was very worried about the course his MS had taken, but I was also angry and indignant that he wouldn't talk about what he was going through, that he alternately lashed out at Meryn and me and was withdrawn. We argued constantly, it seemed, sometimes profitably, more often not.

August 14, 1990

My life is in limbo. Ed and I had a long, sad, rather hopeless discussion last night. How ironic that the field season has gone so well while our marriage is falling apart. Meryn is rereading a book by Judy Blume about divorce. Undoubtedly our arguing is taking a toll on her. I wonder if Margaret Mead ever wrote about her considerable marital troubles in her field journal. She was undoubtedly too professional for such personal indulgences.

The number of "Ed" entries in the index to my fieldnotes continued to grow. I thought about separating my personal entries from my fieldnotes and giving my Ed rantings their own journal, just as I had a separate journal for my much more pleasant ruminations about Meryn. It might have been more professional to do so, but I couldn't compartmentalize. The personal and the professional were impossibly intertwined; my colleague was ailing– my husband was sick. Ed's every action and my reaction affected our research and shaped our days. I escaped in long walks on the tundra and in sweats at the village sauna. When I returned to the house, I sat down for my hour at the computer and continued to pepper my fieldnotes with my frustrations about Ed, taking a perverse delight in writing about him as he fumed at me from across the room. It would be another two years before I launched a journal dedicated to him and his illness, at a time when the professional and the personal no longer wrestled in the field. But for two more years Ed lived on in my fieldnotes. The following summer in Anaktuvuk brought more of the same.

August 2, 1991

Ed's hands are really bothering him. I have to help him put in his contact lenses, serve his plate at dinner, and, though he wants to cook, I suspect it will be virtually impossible for him to do so. He seems tired, withdrawn, almost antisocial, and very frustrated as well as depressed at his condition. He told me that he was going to read the book on MS that I got him next, but he is reading The Blue Nile *instead. He seems swallowed up by his illness, but he's not addressing it.*

That summer my parents had driven up the Alaska Highway to Fairbanks, and they flew up to Anaktuvuk Pass to see the village and visit us for a week.

August 5, 1991

A thoroughly awful day. I really hated to see Mother and Dad go. I enjoyed their visit immensely and they were a breath of fresh air into this troubled household. Even the fieldwork isn't going that well. I am discouraged about the poor planning that went into this field trip, our desultory interviews, our lack of participation in village life, and the sheer amount of effort living here requires which falls almost exclusively on me. To make matters worse, the cold I've had for the last week has invaded my lungs. Who will care for me when I'm sick, I wondered, as I put my mother on the plane. I WANT TO GO HOME.

Writing History from the Pass

Homer Mekiana in his post office.
Photo by Wayne Hanson.

Simon Paneak at home. Photo
by Ward Wells. Courtesy of the
Anchorage Museum of History
and Art.

Following the establishment of the Arctic Research Laboratory in Barrow after World War II, scientists began coming to the Brooks Range to study the flora and fauna as well as the Nunamiuts' adaptation to their arctic environment. To Dr. Kaare Rodahl, head of the Air Force's Arctic Aeromedical Laboratory in Fairbanks in the 1950s, the "rather primitive and isolated Nunamiut village" provided a supply of human research subjects whose lifestyle contrasted markedly to the military control subjects at the Air Force base.

Simon Paneak and Homer Mekiana were, in 1950, the only men in the village of Anaktuvuk Pass, Alaska, who spoke and wrote English. For the nomadic bands of Nunamiut who made up this new village one hundred miles north of the Arctic Circle, they were the translators of the radio news programs that crackled over the three Zenith radios in town. They interacted with the bush pilots who landed on the small lake at the headwaters of the John and Anaktuvuk Rivers, dropping mail and bringing tobacco and coffee, tea and sugar, and ammunition. They welcomed the first census taker in 1950 and the successive waves of geologists, biologists, medical researchers, and other scientists who started coming to this section of northern Alaska in the 1940s. And they wrote—voluminously—corresponding with their new friends, composing letters and mail orders for relatives, writing stories (Simon published at least one in *Alaska Sportsman* magazine in 1960), and chronicling their days on lined paper in bound journals.[1]

Much of their written legacy found its way into the Polar Regions archives at the Elmer Rasmuson Library at the University of Alaska Fairbanks, where I and other anthropologists have pored over it. And some of it has gone the way of all documents whose historical value is recognized too late: to the village dump in the annual village-wide summer trash cleanup. Other missing pieces are rumored to be held fast in the hands of one or another descendant who is not ready to part with them. Whatever the fate of the missing parts, their mere existence heightened the interest with which I read this record.

It was the journals, in particular, that held my attention, though I found the letters, especially Simon's large collection, often more informative and reflective.

A personal narrative of almost any kind, authored by a Native person and allowed to fall into anthropological hands, is nothing short of a gift from the gods. An even more remarkable offering if that narrative spans a great deal of time. Such are the gifts—the journals—left by Homer Mekiana and Simon Paneak.

Homer Mekiana was a Taremiut, a coastal Eskimo, who moved inland after he married a woman from the interior, a Nunamiut. But Barrow, on the Arctic Ocean, was home; he was born there in 1904, and his family was apparently sufficiently sedentary that he managed to complete six grades at the Barrow Bureau of Indian Affairs school. He left Barrow in 1920 and did not return for forty years.

I don't know what turned Homer into a journal writer, but he was writing long before Anaktuvuk Pass became a village. "Even when I was born, at Sheenjik [River]," remembered his son Justus Mekiana, now sixty-five, "he's got a story. He's got a story." "When we used to live at Killik [River]," his fifty-seven-year-old daughter Doris Hugo said, "he got some kind of papers, little book or something; he write 'em down in that book." Unfortunately, when his first wife died in 1947, Homer apparently burned all his early journals.

Homer and his family and several others settled in Anaktuvuk Pass in 1949. Two years later he was appointed the first postmaster of the village, and the mail began to be regularly delivered once a month. For a time the post office moved seasonally up and down the valley, following the still-nomadic villagers, and especially its postmaster, but it was never more than ten or fifteen miles away, and the bush pilots with the mail bags seemed to know where to find it. In the village the canvas post office tent was pitched beside Homer's sod house, its big U.S. flag whipping in the strong winds that sweep north or south through the pass. In this tent, warmed by a wood-burning stove made from a five-gallon Blazo can, Homer bagged and sorted the mail. Villagers had their own descriptions for his activities in this new line of work. "Homer's banging the mail," a villager once told a visiting geologist, referring to the new postmaster's wielding of his cancellation stamp. Here in the post office tent, Homer wrote letters, read the *Life* magazines he now subscribed to, kept his Sears and Roebuck catalog, and took villagers' orders from the "wishbook." Here, too, on a shelf out of reach of his own and other village children, he kept his journal. Faithfully, he wrote in it. "I always see him writing," Doris remembered, "especially at night. Sit down and relax and start writing."

[1950] June 29 Thursday. Cloudy and overcast in the afternoon. Lots of mosquitos are flying in the afternoon when the wind dies down, three boys went over to John River to look for some wolves. We saw 2 caribou but the dogs are hollering and chased them away. War at Korea. Big planes go over us to both ways, north and south.

Over time, Homer's entries became longer, if not more elaborate. His commitment to his journal and the record it represents of village activities is impressive, for its 178 (now typed) pages begin in May 1950 and end in April 1964, three years before he died. More revealing of the journal's importance is the presence of a surrogate author who wrote entries when Homer was off hunting or otherwise absent. That person was his daughter Rachel, who returned to the village in the summer of 1959 from the BIA boarding school in Chemawa, Oregon. Her first entry is in July, and she finishes out the entries for that year. Rachel's voice is more personal than her father's:

> [1959] August 14. Today the weather is clear and warm, wind from north. . . . Time 12:00 P.M. My dad and Frank are playing cards now. They started around 9:35 and they are still playing. The name of the game is 15–2 [cribbage]. I don't know the game. I mean, I just can't understand it. They always get real excited alright but I don't know what for. Me and my girl friend, Ada Rulland, are watching them and listening to the radio. Some of the records make us lonesome, especially the ones we used to hear in school. Today Alice and I went up to pick berries and we picked about 10 lbs each. There sure are lots of berries.

After Homer Mekiana died in 1967, his journal passed to the keeping of his son Cyrus, who was persuaded by a scientist who had read the journal to deposit it with the Naval Arctic Research Laboratory in Barrow. John Schindler, the laboratory's director, who published the journal in 1972 as a special report, praised its contents for their historical importance, notwithstanding the fact that several years' entries are missing. The journal is filled, he said, "with the everyday items of natural history that were important to the people of the village."

Indeed. The book brims with the minutia that fuel ethnohistorians. There, for the taking, are several years of:

WEATHER REPORTS
> Foggy and frost on the willows. [10/28/50]
> Cloudy and ice fog today and breeze from south [12/10/50]
> Little snow is getting soft [4/15/51]

SUBSISTENCE ACTIVITIES, COMPLETE WITH NUMBERS
> Billy and I shot 12 caribou and Ahugak shot 2 and Zacharias shot 2 caribou too [5/23/51]
> Justus, Jonas and Bob came home and caught 6 wolfs and 2 of them were eaten by Jonas's pups [6/29/51]
> The girls and women went to pick some berries [8/20/51]

BENCHMARKS IN THE HISTORY OF THE VILLAGE, MOST OF THEM TIED TO AIRPLANES
> First time we saw the helicopter in here [6/6/50]

Plane came from Bettles and brought school teachers, James
Hayden and wife [7/4/50]

First time I ride on airplane [4/5/51]

This is the first time the box car plane land here [8/15/62]

VILLAGE DEMOGRAPHY

Susie Paneak had a baby boy but did not live long [June 28,
1960]

This month there was a baby born to Amos Morry's wife, but
it did not live long, only lived about 5 or 6 days [January 1961]

Reading on, we learn about some of the programs and news items Homer
picked up on his Zenith radio, and that, after 1960, he made and listened to
taped letters on his reel-to-reel recorder. We see the comings and goings of
people in this small place—be they Natives out on the land or outsiders flying
in from elsewhere. The scientists flow across the pages of Homer Mekiana's
journal in a continual stream: among them, biologists Laurence Irving and
Robert Rausch, geologists Steve Porter and George Gryc, medical researcher
Kaare Rodahl, and anthropologists Bill Irving, Jack Campbell, Nick Gubser,
and Ed Hall.

Homer lets us know that when he isn't out hunting or setting traps,
he's either awaiting the mail plane, sick, or tending to some home task that
couldn't be put off.

[1950] October 22 I did not go today. I made up a cache and fixed my
sled.

"Going" is not only preferable to staying home, but expected. Movement
is, in fact, the overriding theme of Homer's journal. He watches, tracks, and
reports the comings and goings of everyone into and out of Anaktuvuk Pass
in the same way that he watches and reports, as Eskimo people have for
centuries, the peregrinations of the caribou.

It is not surprising that Homer's journal is neither reflective nor expres-
sive in the ways that we writers and readers of journals expect journals to be.
Death and misfortune, in particular, are recounted very matter-of-factly. But
that too is in keeping with his cultural background. There is just one place
where a certain nostalgia creeps in to Homer's matter-of-fact descriptions:

[May 1960] [W]e heard that Barrow people killed 10 whales and we ate
some muktuk when my brother sent me a piece. . . . Oh, what a flavor
for not having or eating it for quite a while. That is my youngster's
meal in my boyhood days at Barrow in early 1910.

I don't know who the intended audience of Homer's journals is, though comments like the above, and the autobiographical sketch he offers on June 10, 1962, suggest that it wasn't just himself or a local audience, especially since the latter wasn't, for the most part, literate. His daughter Doris told me that visitors to Anaktuvuk Pass knew of Homer's journal and often asked to read it. And most of the time he let them. It is possible that Homer kept a journal because some scientist friend had asked him, or as my daughter would put it, because someone "made him," but his long history of committing his words to paper and the enjoyment he derived from writing and reviewing his journals suggest that he wrote for the same reasons all journal keepers write.

Like Homer Mekiana, Simon Paneak apparently kept a journal long before he authored the yearly accounts that biologist Laurence Irving asked him to write beginning in 1950 in order to track the bird life of this corner of northern Alaska. And, like Homer, he enjoyed writing. "Simon always have pencil beside him," exclaimed one villager, and his eldest daughter, Mabel, reminisced, "Seems like almost the whole mail bag is for Simon." In 1957, when he was hospitalized for an extended period of time, he turned to writing an account of Nunamiut culture and a short autobiography. Simon's early pre-1950 journals met a fate similar to Homer's: they were destroyed, inadvertently carted off, some years after his death, to the village dump.

Unlike Homer, Simon had no formal education, though his spoken and written English were good, learned initially from his work with a white trader on the Arctic coast and honed by the *American Standard College Dictionary* that he carried with him everywhere.

Those who knew him agreed that Simon had a remarkable memory and a sharp intellect. Laurence Irving dubbed him a man "with a map in his mind" because of his recall of geographical features and his ability to sketch freehand maps of areas he had not seen since childhood.

Simon was an interior Eskimo, a Nunamiut, though, like the others of his generation, he had spent some fifteen years at the Arctic coast beginning in 1920. Simon, his second wife, Susie, and their large family did not settle in Anaktuvuk Pass year-round until 1962, preferring to spend the summers sixteen miles north of the pass at Tulugak Lake, because, as Simon asserted more than once, "up there where post office is no fish." He was a frequent presence in the new village, however, showing up when the mail plane was due and often wintering there. Simon died in 1975, five years before I saw Anaktuvuk Pass for the first time, but descriptions of him abound in the writings of the many scientists who came to depend upon his hospitality and his extensive knowledge of the natural environment of northern Alaska.

In the spring of 1945, when bush pilot Sig Wien dropped a party of four geologists at Chandler Lake, from where they would make the first stratigraphic maps of this part of the northern interior, the plane was met by Simon Paneak, who was camped with his own and three other families in the vicinity. He ran nearly a mile down the frozen lake on snowshoes to hand the pilot a bundle of fox skins he wished to send to Fairbanks. The scientists learned at this first meeting that Simon had been closely following the course of the war on his mahogany-veneered Zenith all-wave receiving set, listening to *G. I. Jill, The Voice of America*, and *Tokyo Rose*. He asked us, one of the party reported, "What means this thing democracy?"

Simon observed those first scientists carefully, appearing at their tent around dinnertime and reporting back to the rest of the band of Nunamiut camped down the lake, describing their *tannik* food and strange equipment and mimicking their actions.

Sig Wien and the airline his family established became the conduit for most of the other early scientists who came into northern interior Alaska. Wien brought Arctic biologist Laurence Irving to the area in 1947, and Irving, like the others, quickly made the acquaintance of Simon Paneak. Irving was especially interested in the bird life of this region of Alaska, which was not well known at the time, and he enlisted Simon's help in studying it. In August 1950, at Irving's request, Simon began recording data on birds in the journals, which he kept until a few months before his death in 1975.

Though they contain other information, from May until fall the journals focus on the migratory birds that nest in the Arctic. Simon tallies the sightings of different species reported by himself and other family members; he notes when birds are singing and mating; he comments on their nests and eggs, and when the young of various species first take flight. Over the years he collected numerous bird specimens for Irving, recording in his journal the weight, length, and sex of each, along with the contents of their crops.

Beginning in 1960, at Irving's request, Paneak's field observations turned to an intensive study of ptarmigan. He built a large trap for the birds, which still sits behind the home of one of his sons, and he set snares for them as well. He banded and released those that he caught. By 1963 the journal is dominated by ptarmigan.

Feb. 26 1963 Willow ptarmigans are feeding on mostly common willows. Some male ptarmigans are squaking—see them many ptarmigans but hard to figuring out when ptarmigans moving back and forward; very easy for me counted up to 1000 ptarmigans a day. This winter is high population of ptarmigans.

They appear by the hundreds, by the thousands. Simon's activities are focused on tracking every one of theirs, and they loom so large on the landscape that one wonders how anyone could discuss the Arctic without mentioning ptarmigan.

In the flight of arctic birds, we follow the fortunes of the journals' author. On May 21, 1961, one of Simon's children, perhaps his son Ray, has taken over the entry and the bird watching, noting: "Daddy is going to Hosp. So we use Field Guide to . . . see what birds or ducks going north."

In his later years Simon was bothered by allergies and tuberculosis-weakened lungs, which led to several hospitalizations. When he was hospitalized for an extended period in 1958, his bird monitoring continued. From the Alaska Native Service Hospital in Anchorage, he and other patients watched for birds:

April 7 single robin flew over the hospital seen by patient Peter Ashnok

By the late 1950s Simon's health prevented him from hunting caribou like he once did. In his journals he seems content to track birds, but in his letters his frustrations and longing are apparent. Writing in 1964 to Ethel Ross Oliver, the first census taker, a schoolteacher and longtime correspondent and friend: "I cannot hunt any more. I am like a little boy which is more interesting on Ptarmigan life."

Still, the birds held his attention, even when there was nothing else to write about.

[1971, during a very long, cold spell with high winds and ice fog] March 7 No plane, no mail and no nothings. Only ravens.

And it is the birds that configure these records. In May 1954, he is a few days south of the village when he learns that an epidemic of some sort has reached the Anaktuvuk people. When he arrives home Susie is quite sick and has just delivered a stillborn child. She is sorry, she tells him, that she was too sick to document the arrival of the spring birds, and when Simon himself takes sick, he tells his son Ray to take over and record bird sightings.

Laurence Irving's interest and expertise nourished Simon's own knowledge of bird life, and the two enjoyed a collaboration for some twenty-five years. Irving supplied Simon with a Roger Tory Peterson guide to birds, and from it Simon learned the names of birds in English. Their collaboration and their interest in each others' ways of knowing natural phenomena is evident in their coauthorship of three scientific articles. It is evident in Simon's annual trips that Irving sponsored to the Alaskan Arctic Science Conference and in Irving's genuine respect for Native people "wise in knowledge and appreciation of their own country." When Simon died in 1975, it was Laurence Irving who published his obituary in 1976 in *Arctic*, the journal of the Arctic Institute of North America, eulogizing him as "a guide and instructor of scholars in interior Arctic Alaska."

One could easily assume that a commissioned journal on bird life would contain little else, but what Nunamiut Eskimo with a journal could fail to write about caribou?

[1958] Aug 30 Caribou hunter arrive here and said caribou was so skinny, poor even among bulls, and said several caribou been found dead are along in tundra, starve to death.

[1960] May 2 Beginning of old bulls caribous movement

[1961] Oct 2 Around 10,000 caribous arrive here from north, covered whole valley and several bunches came from south met them here. Among the bulls beginning fight.

Not just caribou appear, but other game and fur bearers important to the livelihood of the interior Eskimos. Wolves and their pups taken in the late spring of the year by village men for the bounty, marmot trapping, sheep hunting, and the occasional moose are noted as well in Simon's lined, leather-bound books.

There is an underlying sameness to the endless arctic winter when it is chronicled sparsely in measures of wind strength, degrees of cold, and intensity of snow and ice fog, but the harbingers of the short, intense arctic summer stand out in Simon Paneak's journals just as they do in Homer Mekiana's.

[1956] June 10 We expect mosquitos at any times

[1956] June 13 The ground is beautiful green color. Now many different plant from one another growing rapidly. Many bumble bee busy making honey from willow buds.

The periodicity of village life unfolds with the results of the annual village council elections, the Thanksgiving feast in the community hall, Christmas with Santa Claus, games and dances between the Christmas and New Year's holidays, the Memorial Day picnic at the cemetery, and the Fourth of July rifle target shoot.

[1961] Dec 23 Tomorrow old man Santa will be arrive in sled in 4:P.M..

Epidemics of flu and other communicable disease give cause for concern:

[1961] Nov 25 Most of the peoples are sick. Sickness being here for long times. No one died so far.

But when they do, they find their way into Simon's journal, just as do the newborns.

Focused as Simon's journal is on what he could observe in the expanse of northern Alaska where he lived and traveled, his vision always extended beyond Anaktuvuk Pass and the mountain fastness of the Brooks Range, thanks to his intellectual curiosity, his many Outside friends, and radio station KFAR in Fairbanks.

> November 22, 1963: President John F. Kennedy was shot this morning, Alaska times at 9:00 o'clock and in eastern time 1 P.M. by Oswald with 7 point 5 German military rifle.

It is highly unusual that, in a Native population of fewer than one hundred people, in bush Alaska where hardly anyone spoke English, there would be two men compelled to record, for a period of more than twenty years and in a language not their own, something of the world as they experienced it. The mere existence of two journals covering the same place and time can't help but invite comparison, but that is another essay for another time. Suffice it to say that the world, as Homer Mekiana and Simon Paneak individually and collectively report it, reminds us that, even in the days before electricity, satellite TV, and scheduled passenger airline service, the lives of nomadic Eskimo people in this remote part of Alaska were, in sometimes highly individual ways, powerfully and inextricably linked to the outside world.

For me, the value of these writings lies as much in the qualities they share as journals as in their content. The immediacy of their entries, the feeling that "this really happened," the ordinariness of the days they chronicle, their unmediated words in "village English." Their unorchestrated final entries.

> April 3, 1964. The cat train from Fairbanks reached Anaktuvuk Pass.
>   Homer Mekiana

> [1975] Saturday February 8 Wind N. high snow drift. Ice fogs very poor visible. Temp. 10 below zero. No mail plane for today because of weather is not available for flying.
>   Simon Paneak

The "New" Eskimo

Willie Hugo, on his father's lap, 1963. Photo by Ward Wells.
Courtesy of the Anchorage Museum of History and Art.

The village began to take on a greater sense of permanence when villagers pitched in, with missionaries, to build the Presbyterian church in 1959, followed by a school in 1961. In 1961, Wien Alaska Airlines also built a mile-long gravel airstrip that followed the north-south orientation of the valley.

At the beginning of the oil boom in 1969, a winter ice road from Fairbanks to Prudhoe Bay was pushed through Anaktuvuk Pass. Dubbed the Hickel Highway after then-secretary of the interior and former Alaska governor Wally Hickel, it was a temporary road constructed to haul heavy equipment to the North Slope. Excited villagers watched eighty-seven trucks pass through their village in seventeen days, and they hoped the economic boom would spread to the village, where jobs and cash were scarce. One villager, Jack Morry, already had ideas about what Anaktuvuk Pass should be. He shared them in an article he wrote to the Fairbanks Daily News-Miner.

> Will Anaktuvuk Pass ever grow to be a larger town like other Eskimo villages? Or will it be as it is now ever since the first settlement started? What does the village lack that the other villages have now? It lacks almost everything such as recreation, electricity, or other things. At least we've got Hickel Highway coming through the village. But will it ever solve the countless problems? A little. It helps some men solve the greenback problem.

Thirty-seven-year-old Willie Hugo was not a great talker, but he was friendly, like all the villagers. He had a crooked grin set in an angular face, and the baseball cap he invariably wore seldom contained his unruly straight black hair. Short and strongly built, he strode about town with a purpose. He liked his coffee ready when he came home from work and his dinner on the table.

In many ways Willie Hugo was a "new" Eskimo, [1] walking a path that seemed to successfully bridge the consumerism of American society and the hunting culture to which he was rightful heir. He had a good job as assistant to the manager of the Anaktuvuk Pass power plant. His salary bought a big TV and VCR, two eight-wheeled all-terrain Argos, a snowmobile, a new rifle, and trips to Barrow and Fairbanks for his wife and five children. In his free time, Willie performed as a drummer with the village's traditional dance group.

The name Willie Hugo was synonymous with successful hunting. He was a dedicated and determined subsistence hunter, one of the few young ones who really knew the land and the animals. If Willie went out hunting caribou or sheep, he never seemed to come home empty-handed. He sometimes took his two older girls, Julie and Tina, sheep hunting with him and always timed his annual leave from work to coincide with the opening of sheep season. Evenings after work, he tinkered with his Argo, making sure it was ready for the next hunting trip. Every weekend from May to September he was out on the land with his family, camping and hunting. "You can't depend on store food," he frequently told his children, "You have to learn to hunt."

He and his wife, Becky, almost never left the kids behind when they went camping. They even took extra fishing poles so everyone, from twelve-year-old Julie down to baby Kate, could learn how to fish. And several times during our summer stays in Anaktuvuk Pass, Willie invited Meryn to go camping with them. "How's my little tannik daughter," he would greet Meryn each summer when we returned to the Pass. "You should have gone camping with us to Kanŋuumavik," he teased her one weekend when she'd stayed behind in the village, "Lots of big bulls up Kanŋuumavik Creek, Meryn, lots of big bull caribou."

Willie was out on the land even on workdays, packing up the Argo after work to take his family several miles north to the Anaqtiktuaq Valley, where they would fish and picnic and look for caribou until it was time to go home to bed. The Hugo kids would roast hot dogs and marshmallows over a fire and cast their fishing lines into the river for grayling. On one trip he chased a pack of wolf pups, caught one, and held it in his parka so the kids, my daughter included, could see a wolf puppy up close.

He was ecstatic when Willie Junior, his only son, was born, and he proudly displayed Junior's hospital bracelet safety-pinned to his baseball cap for a full year after Junior's birth. But when his fifth and last child, Kate, was born, he didn't hide his disappointment. "A GIRL, another girl!" he complained to Becky when she told him the news by phone from the Tanana Valley Hospital, but he refused to give her up for adoption as Inuit people often do. Months later, as he carried Kate about in his arms, one would never suspect that he had wished she were a boy. She too, in time, would learn about the importance of subsistence hunting.

When people talked about the future of the village, they looked to the likes of Willie Hugo—"Always hunting for his family," they nodded in approval, "always sharing." "His family means everything to him." They said he seldom drank. "He sobered up after he got a family," explained Becky, who recounted their problems with alcohol as teenagers. But on an early December night in 1993, at a party they hosted, they both got drunk, along with their guests. Sometime, along about 11 P.M., Willie took out his hunting rifle, loaded it, leaned his chin on the barrel and threatened to pull the trigger. For five hours, various people, including his mother, a visiting minister, the village suicide prevention officer, and the public safety officer, came and tried to dissuade him, but in the early morning hours, he made good on his threat.

The news came to Brockport in a terse message left on my phone answering machine. Why did he do it? Where were the kids when he blew his brains out? His kids adored him; I knew that. My daughter, along with the other village kids, liked him too.

There was the time a bunch of kids gathered around Willie as he cut thick slices for each of them from the big watermelon he had just lugged home from the village store. There was that grin he always grinned when he headed out of town on his Argo piled high with camping gear—his girls balanced on the tarp-covered pile, holding fast to the ropes that tied it in place, and Meryn right up there with them, off to Nunamiut country I had never seen. There was the last time we saw Willie: "You coming back next year Meryn? You can learn to climb the mountain with my girls for sheep."

How could he, as sole provider for his family, as a Nunamiut hunter, as a father, leave them? There were vague rumors of marital problems; there was speculation that Willie was depressed because of a bad back he feared would render him unable to hunt, a fate his own father had suffered. "It was that awful alcohol," others insisted, pointing to several alcohol-related suicides in the village in recent years. Maybe it was alcohol that gave him the courage to carry through with a plan. In the days after Christmas, people surmised that his death was premeditated, for a new freezer, big-screen TV, snowmobile, and a Bible, all prepaid, arrived in the village to be delivered to Becky.

Maybe that rifle shot fired on a December night was about satellite TV and VCRs, about the pull of the city and all those amenities a salaried job will buy. Maybe it was about the increasing difficulty of going up in the mountains for sheep, about hunting caribou while working a forty-hour week, about the definition of a man as a hunter. Maybe it was about just how hard it was to be a "new" Eskimo.

Of Meat and Hunger and Everlasting Gob Stoppers

Lela Ahgook and her store.

Villager Justus Mekiana was twenty-two years old in the summer of 1949 when his family came from the Killik River Valley to make their home in Anaktuvuk Pass.

> A long time ago, before 1949, we travel everywhere in Nunamiut country, in Alaska. Moving along. No village. No store; no building. We travel like caribou. Follow the caribou somewhere, wintertime, with the dog team. In the summer time, we travel by dog pack. And in 1949 somehow we stick together. In 1949, 62 people [in Anaktuvuk]. Right now the village is everywhere, I guess, in Alaska. Change everything, even in Anaktuvuk.

Now, once-nomadic caribou hunters return home each day to lookalike brightly painted prefab houses plotted along the grid of straight graveled streets. CB antennas rise skyward from shiny aluminum rooftops like so many needles, pull in signals that link all villagers in one giant party-line conversation. Familiar T-shaped poles carry electric and phone lines, hold the streetlights that begin to come on with the mid-August twilight, channeling the view of mountains through parallel wires. Paths, deliberately trod just beyond the chain lengths of mixed-breed Eskimo dogs tethered outside, crisscross tall grasses behind the houses. The dogs lurch against their chains, bark menacingly at people who take shortcuts through their country. Anaktuvuk dogs spend most of their time tethered nowadays, having long ago relinquished their sled and pack dog status to the more efficient snowmobiles and all-terrain vehicles. Their barking spreads like a wave through the village when the high-pitched whine of kids on four-wheelers breaks the silence of a midsummer's late evening.

It's nearly ten o'clock at night, the second week in August, but the candy clientele at Lela's Masks and Snacks convenience store in Anaktuvuk Pass shows no signs of letting up. The metal door swooshes open and shut for what seems like the fiftieth time. For two hours I've been sitting on an upturned metal pop crate chatting with Lela Ahgook while she dispenses candy and sews fur trim onto a caribou-skin mask she is finishing. The store has no posted hours, but everybody knows that whenever the padlock is off the door, Lela is open for business.

Most come in twos and threes. They're young, some really young, though teenagers and adults contribute candy and pop dollars to Lela's cash box as well. The kids head straight to the back shelves, which are stocked with more than fifty kinds of candy, maybe more than in the convenience store down the street from my home in western New York. Meryn, no stranger to candy herself, ticks off the varieties we don't have at home: single Fruit Rollups, Farley's Fruit Snacks, Spin Pops, Candy Callers, Mouth Splashers bubble gum. Lela's customers choose quickly; they know what they want, and they buy in quantity—five, seven, even eight dollars' worth of candy and pop. They dig in jacket pockets for wadded dollar bills and fives, grab their selections with both hands, slam the door on their way out, pausing just long enough on the metal grate landing to unwrap a candy bar before running down the stairs. An hour later several are back to buy more.

The two new candy items Lela has this summer are not available in the Nunamiut Corp Store where every villager buys groceries. The Candy Caller, a plastic portable phone filled with little candies, plays a tune when its keys are punched. More popular is the Spin Pop, a white plastic battery-powered holder for a large lollipop, reminiscent of an electric toothbrush. On the cutting edge of confectionery technology, it spins the lollipop for easy licking. Eight-year-old Phyllis Morry has one, and she's using it when she comes through the door to buy six more Blue Razzberry Blow Pops. Six-year-old Raymond Ahgook heads directly for the box of Spin Pops, announcing, "This is what I want." He puts it back when he learns that his crinkle of two one-dollar bills is four dollars short of the purchase price. He settles for the blow pops without the spinner.

A knock at the door. "Come in," Lela bellows from behind the counter. Another tentative knock. "Come in," she says more gently, figuring correctly that the caller is a small child. "You don't have to knock, it's a store, not a house." The door opens slowly and four-year-old Robert Williams sticks his head inside. He stops ten feet short of the candy shelves, his big eyes taking in their contents. "What's the matter, you got no money?" Lela probes. He nods, glancing wistfully at the candy shelves, and is out the door.

"Marshmallow Munchies, my best sellers," exclaims Lela, getting up from her stool behind the counter to crush the empty cardboard box and toss it in the wastebasket. She surveys her stock. "Time to reorder soon." She buys her candy wholesale from Sam's Club in Fairbanks, and from the looks of it tonight, she has to reorder frequently.

The daily repetition of this scene exacts its toll on the young consumers. Jessie, Lela's four-year-old grandson, has two fillings in his baby teeth, and his not-yet-two-year-old sister, Josie, is already well acquainted with bubble gum, candy, and pop. In 1948, when scientist Carl Henkelman came to the pass to study the effects of an all-meat diet on Nunamiut dentition, eight-year-old Lela Ahgook hardly knew candy; the peoples' teeth were, Henkelman was pleased to report, excellent.[1] Village elder Justus Mekiana, still a consummate hunter, mused, "We could eat only caribou, no white man's food. Only salt shaker and pepper, that's all we left out when they'd go some-where to hunt and come back. No sugar, no coffee, no milk. We only using the animal food."

Today Frontier Airlines' weekly DC-3 freight plane as well as its twice-daily smaller planes bring in varieties and quantities of foodstuffs undreamed of fifty years ago. Avocados and kiwi fruit, cake mixes, taco shells and bagels; cosmopolitan condiments for the regimen of caribou. Before the late 1940s, before airplanes landed in this valley with their cargoes of Outside goods and food, before a white trader set up a trading post at Anaktuvuk, Nunamiut men made fall and spring trading trips. They went south to Bettles and Shungnak in the interior, and north to trading posts at the mouth of the Colville River on the coast, returning to camp with the white man's foods that lent diversion and variety to their hunter diet.

"They brought back coffee, tea, canned milk, sugar, little bit rice," recalls Doris Hugo of her father's trips to Shungnak when she was a small girl in the early 1940s. We are sitting in the village washeteria, where she works as manager, drinking fresh Hills Bros. coffee from her twelve-cup coffeemaker and munching Oreo cookies, our voices straining to rise above the spin cycles of the ten washing machines. "They used to bring some onions, first onions. Some rolled oats, corn meal, little bit butter, little bit jam, stuff like that. They don't last long. But they always try to save 'em. The tea leaves that are already used, and coffee grounds already used, the older people, like our parents, would save 'em. Even us, we save 'em and froze 'em, outside. And when we're out, we start using 'em, over and over until the color goes away."

"A little bit of candy," Doris smiles. "We used to start eating little bit of candy or little bit of gum but we have to save our gum. All the time after you eat, you put it away someplace, chew it later or next day and next day until the smell is all gone."

The heavy metal door to the washeteria swings open and bangs shut with a vengeance that rattles the recording level needle on my tape recorder. It's kids, with little brown bags of Pixie Stixs and Everlasting Gob Stoppers and suckers, and Meryn with her hand out for her daily ration of candy money. We tried to curtail her intake of candy when we first came, but it was im-possible. If she had no money to buy candy her friends would simply share theirs with her, spreading the word that the *tanniks* were stingy. Reluctantly, I peel off three one-dollar bills to feed her pop and candy habit—and to buy some to share with the others.

It's hard to remember, in these days of wage labor and three-hundred-dollar credit limits at the Nunamiut Corp store, that not long ago the Nun-amiut knew real hunger, even starvation. It's harder to imagine that the hungry times were often in summer, when the land is still green and welcoming and soft and the light long, after the caribou have left the mountains for the Arctic coast and before the autumn migration that funnels them southward by the thousands, through the mountain passes to the forested interior.

In the fall of 1994, the caribou did not come through Anaktuvuk Pass as they usually do but instead turned west, then south through the Chandler Lake area. Without the store, without *tannik* foods to fall back on, it would have been a hungry fall. There have been lots of hungry years recorded in Nunamiut country due to fluctuations in the size of the western arctic caribou herd: five lean years alone between the turn of the twentieth century and World War I, which resulted in such a scarcity of caribou that the people gradually abandoned the interior for the Arctic coast. "I kind of remember when they didn't get very many caribou," said Mabel Paneak Burris, born in 1943. One of the better alternatives was moose. But "I didn't like eating moose," she added. "Caribou I could eat day in, day out." Rachel Mekiana remembered, too. She was nineteen when she penned these words in October 1959 in the daily log her father, Homer, kept:

> Some people have nothing to eat. Not much at all. I really hope our hunter will bring some caribou, sheep or moose home soon and our store doesn't have flour, oatmeal, corn meal. Rather don't have nothing to eat except Crisco and cookies. Poor people, sometime we will starve to death (I joke!). As long as we have caribou we won't starve.

I had just discovered, in an upstairs wastebasket, another discarded school lunch that I packed for my seventh-grade daughter. This was the third one in two weeks. The apple slices turned brown and the sandwich got squished in her backpack, Meryn offered in explanation, hastening to add that she used her own money each of those days to buy lunch. "How dare you waste food when the Nunamiut used to starve?" I wanted to admonish her. Instead, I called the school cafeteria manager to see if her lunch consumption could be monitored, worried that I might be seeing the onset of an eating disorder. In the midst of plenty, children become finicky eaters; young girls train themselves to withstand hunger, flirt with starvation.

Doris Hugo knows about starvation. It makes her mad when her grandchildren open her refrigerator and scan the shelves, complaining, "Nothing to eat." "There's lots to eat in there," she insists. "Nothing to eat," they retort. So she tells them, again, about the wolf. About the hungry time when the men had gone off hunting and the women, children, and old men stayed behind. "Listen," she says:

We have hard times because
they never come home for long time, too,
one month.
No caribou
No sheep
nothing.

Our grandpa, Maptegak,
He catch that wolf in the fall time
and he go
he go after it just when
no animals
We got nothing to eat and then
he sure try
he sure try to let us
eat little piece
little piece every day
but it is finally all gone
finally.

Justus Mekiana, Doris's older brother, also remembers—

Before we hunted,
before I hunted,
sometime the year is hard time
Sometimes really good year
a lot of animals everywhere.

Sometimes really hard to see animals
Even right now.

Sometimes lots of them
all over
Like that, too.

One time
we try
to eat wolf carcasses
A lot of fat alright,
but Maptegak really boil it,
boil it
and
boil it

and boil it.
When you chew it,
somehow make you vomit.
Somehow.

After they boil it, no matter
how much boil it
you can smell it.
When you put it in your mouth
make you vomit.

What else would you eat if you were really hungry and there were no caribou, I ask Dora Hugo, who, along with her niece and nephew had partaken of the wolf they described. Willow leaves when they're green, ground squirrels, ptarmigan and ptarmigan droppings, roots, anything from the ground, she answers through Lela Ahgook, who translates for her.

Even the dogs were trained to expect hunger, fed not every day, but small amounts every other day or every two days. And, cautioned Justus Mekiana, "If you are not eating for I don't know how many days, and you're skinny from hunger when you meet somebody and he's got lot of food, he never give you lots. Just a little bit, he give you, no matter how much food he's got. If you eat lots, you kill yourself. First they boil meat and give you only little bit of the juice and they watch you. And next day, give you more, and if you don't get sick, they give you a lot more; finally, all you want. We never get hungry that much," he mused. "But the story goes like that all the time."

It's summer and Zacharias Hugo is on the CB radio: "There's lots of meat, lots of meat." The Nunamiut ethic bids one share when caribou or mountain sheep have been killed. To the Anaktuvuk people "meat" means caribou, and Zach and Doris Hugo are luxuriating in plenty. Their son Paul killed four caribou over the weekend, and they have invited everyone to their home to enjoy the bounty. Outside their house, the red meat lies in slabs and chunks and jumbles of limbs on a plywood board, later to be parceled into plastic garbage bags and tossed in the Hugos' big freezer. Inside, a huge pot of caribou meat and bones simmers on the stove. People are gathered round the kitchen table reaching for the plate piled high with ribs and leg bones and for the bowl of steaming rumen. "You don't dig around and look for the best piece of meat," Doris once explained to me. "And you don't smell the meat before you eat it," she added. "It's law—for men. They get skinnybones caribou the next time if they do that."

Rose Ann Rulland, a woman Doris's age, sits on the floor using an *ulu* to cut long slices of raw meat off the leg bones, then cracks the bones to extract the marrow, a Nunamiut delicacy. We have just had lunch, but we eat a couple of ribs anyway. For the next hour villagers come through the door, help themselves to meat, talk awhile, then leave. Small children accompany parents and grandparents. For them, too, "meat" is caribou.

"What's your favorite meal?" I ask Meryn's young Nunamiut girlfriends, who, swayed by the promise of candy money and curiosity about the machinations of anthropologists, have gathered round my tape recorder for an interview. "Fried chicken," replies nine-year-old Donna Hugo. "Hamburgers and hot dogs," says Julie Hugo. "Spaghetti, macaroni and cheese," Tina Hugo chimes in. "Meat," asserts Frances Hugo. They all eat a lot of meat, there's no doubt about that, as caribou is still the staple in this meat-eating community's diet. Seventy percent of the diet of the people, estimated the city council in the mid-1980s, comes from the land, and most of that is caribou. But *tannik* foods are readily available—from the frozen boxed chicken parts and hamburger patties in the Nunamiut Corp store to the greasy meals at "camp," the village corporation's diner.

On one of my routine evening trips to relax in the sauna at the village washeteria, I find Rachel Mekiana and her sister Doris Hugo sitting in Doris's little office, snacking on dried meat Rachel has brought. Sheep season has just opened and everyone has been feasting on Dall sheep brought back by hunters. There have been lots of caribou around as well: no one lacks for meat. Both Doris and Rachel complain of stomach problems; they had eaten too much sheep and caribou the day before, they say. So much, reports Rachel, that she had to eat something else for a day. So, off she'd gone to the store to purchase stewing beef. She chews on a piece of dried meat. "When all we had was caribou and sheep, it never bothered my stomach; it's all that other stuff, store stuff, that's done it," she laments.

For several years before there was a village store, Rachel, Doris, and others of their generation ate little else but *tannik* foods from September to May. They were the first group of Nunamiut to be sent out to Wrangel Institute and Mt. Edgecumbe Bureau of Indian Affairs boarding schools in Southeastern Alaska, and there they were introduced to what is surely the worst of *tannik* cuisine—institutional food. "The food, and milk, was really hard to get used to. Way too sweet," Lela Ahgook remembered. "We wondered what we were eating. Hardly eat the first three weeks, I guess." Waiting for these mystery meals made the experience even worse. "Always have to stay in line, keep a real straight line; if you get out of line, you have to go way back at the end. And the line is so long." Sometimes a parent would send a package of dried meat, which the lucky recipient would share with friends. Not till the end of the school year, in May, did the children return to the Pass and to their familiar Nunamiut diet of meat.

To watch Lela Ahgook expertly cut up a caribou, one would never fathom those interrupted seasons of institutional meals and dormitory life. I've come to videotape her as she butchers two caribou that her son Chuck and her daughter's boyfriend, Victor, have brought her. Lela just turned fifty-one a few days ago and has been cutting up caribou for more than thirty-five years. She knows exactly what she's looking at, but I have a difficult time sorting out the various parts of the two bull caribou that lie in low mounds on her *qanitchaq*, or storm porch. Lela sits in the middle of it all, right leg bent at the knee, left leg straight out in front of her. Focused on her work, she holds a chunk of meat in her left hand; her right hand alternately wields a hatchet and every Nunamiut woman's indispensable knife, the semilunar-shaped *ulu*, crafted from a saw blade and set into a well-worn wooden handle. "I'm gonna die if I lose it," she says. "Because it can do everything for me." Her brightly colored polyester blouse is splattered with blood, bits of fat, meat, and the green goo of the intestines, her hands and lower arms are deep red. From time to time she rips a sheet of paper toweling off a roll to wipe her hands.

She looks quizzically at my camcorder. "This part of your story?" I tell her my plans to show the tape to Meryn's classmates and to my college students, explaining that Brockport people know raw meat only in plastic wrapped styrofoam packages. "As long as it's for education I don't care." She twists her *ulu* to help break apart the backbone of one caribou. The meat goes into three piles—bones from which the marrow will be extracted and eaten raw, meat in stewpot-sized chunks for boiling, and scraps for her two dogs. All of it will go in separate plastic garbage bags and be placed in the big freezer on her *qanitchaq*.

I ask the anthropologist's obvious question: "How long will it take you to eat up these caribou?" Nine people sit at Lela's table. "About a week, little bit over a week. We can't afford that store food—steaks and pork chops," she adds. They've already had one meal from this kill—caribou stew last night. "We had caribou stew last night, too," I offer, "but we don't make it like people around here," as if she couldn't have guessed. "Probably add too many stuff to it," she suggests. "Yeah, too many stuff." I rattle off my recipe: tomatoes, onions, fried pieces of caribou meat, lentils, a "bunch of spices." "That's tannik style, alright," Lela concludes.

"Nice fat caribou, really fat," Lela holds up a piece of meat with a thick layer of fat on it. "Did they bring the tongue home?" I ask, knowing that this delicacy is the very favorite part. "Yep, we already ate it, first thing." But they hadn't brought back the livers. "I don't eat liver very much. Too much cholesterol," she explains, alluding to her gallbladder problems. "I'm forced to quit lotta things we like." Lela squeezes out the intestines into a box full of discarded remains. She will boil them later, by themselves. "My kids don't want to take it home with them. They don't know it's the best food."

Lela starts on the shoulder, "The front leg is very good when you dry it," she explains. She cuts the thick meat so that it unfolds, accordionlike, into one long piece that will be hung over the drying rack by the side of her house.

She looks up from her work. "You got me really slow cutting the joints. I can't do it very good sitting in front of a camera, makes me nervous," she complains as she twists and presses her *ulu* on a foreleg joint. Luckily my battery has just run out. I tease her about sending recipes when I get home, but she seems genuinely interested. "Yeah, I want ways to cook the caribou more, so if you got recipes, send 'em."

Every summer, in advance of departing for Anaktuvuk Pass, I make a shopping expedition to our local branch of western New York's finest supermarket. Wegman's superstore in Brockport is probably our most notable cultural attraction and the first stop for all foreign visitors who come to our college town. The Russians seem especially impressed by Wegman's. Visitors ooh and aah at the fresh fruit and vegetable section, the many varieties of store-made pizzas, the deli salads and meats, the live lobsters, the thirty flavors of coffee beans, the fresh flowers. I tell my Anaktuvuk friends about Wegman's too, especially about the prices, which are always about three times lower than those for the same items in the Nunamiut Corp store.

Ed, a born meat eater, thought nothing of a two-week regimen of *maktak*, or whale blubber, and catsup during one summer's archaeological survey on the Arctic coast, but I would buy a month's supply of fresh fruit and vegetables to take north with me. Unfortunately, even fruits and vegetables purchased in Fairbanks can't see me through my stay in Anaktuvuk. I settle for nonperishables unknown to the shelves of the village store: Orange Seville coffee beans, various Knorr packaged sauces that will add zest to lean caribou meat, dried black beans, olive oil, balsamic vinegar, basmati and wild rices, dried fancy soups, Twinings teas . . . I mail them all north well in advance of our departure. Such elaborate preparations for such a short stay.

Anaktuvuk kids come by to see what gourmet items Wegman's has yielded this year, and some invariably stay through the dinner hour. They look disparagingly at the funny colored rice but sample it anyway. Like the rest of the world, they eat tacos, but they push the black beans aside. One of them picks up the package from which the beans have come: "Turtle beans" it reads. "Anak [feces]!" they giggle; "turtle anak!" A pile of the tasty legumes actually does bear a striking resemblance to caribou droppings.

The response to exotic foods has two faces, of course. Anthropologists' testimonies about local foods have traditionally been regarded as a barometer of the privations and the culture shock of fieldwork. One anthropologist friend doing her dissertation research some twenty years ago in Southwestern Alaska wrote me about a dream she had. She stood before a buffet table richly laden with the familiar foods of home, greedily filling the line of platters that she balanced on each arm. And another colleague who spent the past year in the Philippines wrote: "Someone finally noticed that I was subsisting on Sprite, peanuts, and crackers—happily, actually, since Filipino food—pigs' intestines, pigs' tongue, stewed chicken, pickled chicken, pickled pork, ox tongue—give me the runs." There is even the reverse case, the anthropologist so committed to the proven nutritional value of the native diet that he pursues it out of the field to prove a point. That's what Arctic explorer and ethnologist Vilhjalmur Steffanson did when he checked into Bellevue Hospital in New York in 1927 to demonstrate that a diet based exclusively on meat was perfectly healthy. For us anthropologist sojourners to the Arctic in the 1990s, the gastronomic low point, the culinary culture shock, comes not from eating the soured contents of caribou stomachs or gnoshing on warble fly larvae but from being reduced to buying TV dinners at the Nunamiut Corp Store.

I have just learned from the *New York Times* that Canadian Inuit, hoping to create badly needed jobs in their territory, are considering marketing their Native foods in the south. [2] To this end, they've called upon the expertise of several renowned French chefs to render Eskimo delicacies appealing to Montreal society. The chefs have applied their own haute cuisine magic to arctic hare, ptarmigan, seal, and caribou, rather than defer to Native methods of food preparation. "To have cuisine, you must cook," exclaimed one chef, referring to the Native preference for raw food. As the chefs are stuffing caribou roasts with foie gras for Montreal gourmets, I imagine that Canadian Inuit children are lining up at village convenience stores to stock up on candy.

Throughout our stay in Anaktuvuk Pass people kindly offer us meat—a chunk of sheep meat, a hindquarter of a caribou, more meat than I would eat in two or three months. And when we prepare to leave at summer's end and send our goodbyes through the CB radio, the farewell gift that is pressed upon us is, of course, "meat." "We got lots caribou meat here; sure you don't want some to take home?" I don't. I will go to Fairbanks, replenish my depleted body stores with vegetables and fruits, my soul relishing every restorative bite. Like Justus Mekiana, who knows the unsettling hunger that comes from eating another culture's food:

I can't go without the Eskimo food yet myself. I can eat the ham, I can eat the food bought from the store, but next day, I'm tired already. I try to keep caribou or something in my body all the time, right now. The young people right now, some of my kids, they can go without Eskimo food, without much caribou meat. Maybe thirty years from now . . . I don't know.

Staying Home

291 Main Street, Brockport, New York. From a painting by Helen Smagorinsky.

*Just twenty years after the first scientific studies, villager Jack
Morry concluded his 1969 newspaper piece about the state of Anaktuvuk Pass with the plea, "Will this village ever be noticed?" He
didn't have to wait long. A reporter for the* Fairbanks Daily News-
Miner *followed the truckers up the Hickel Highway, writing a series of articles about Anaktuvuk Pass. Every one of them contained
the descriptors "remote" and "isolated," tempered with remarks
about the stunning beauty of the mountains.*

*Fly to Anaktuvuk from Fairbanks with a group of village men.
Once in the mountains they peer out the plane's tiny windows,
pointing to familiar landmarks, naming the rivers and hunting
places and scouting the slopes and valleys for game. The sense of
landscape, the map of the mind, begins miles before the village
comes into view.*

The first day of August, 1995, and I sit in the cloying evening humidity in my
front yard, pulling crabgrass. I have never seen early August from my front
yard though I've lived here eighteen years. With the exception of once, more
than twenty years ago, I have always been "in the field" during the summer.

May graduation at the college signals the beginning of field preparations:
We make plane reservations; write letters, then dial anxious phone calls to
secure housing in the village. Air out musty sleeping bags, find field boots,
down vests, tent and poles, rifle. Load files onto the portable computer. Buy
film, check cameras. Piles of supplies accumulate throughout the house and
grow to alarming size. A fan, in case it gets hot; cassette tapes of music; a stack
of books and magazines to read. Good thing we have a kitchen sink where
we are going . . . A list for the house sitter—so complete that it contains
instructions on how to bury the cats should they die—is fastened to the
refrigerator door with a magnet. The piles of gear are organized into duffel
bags or packed in boxes to be mailed ahead. A neighbor with a van transports
us and our incredible baggage to the airport, and finally we are airborne to
another world.

For many summers I never saw flowers between the May tulips and the
September mums. This summer will be different. I have decided to stay
home. Next year would be soon enough to return to Anaktuvuk Pass, I
convinced myself in the spring. This year, for the first time, I will see the
entirety of a western New York summer: the tulips, then iris, peonies, shasta
daisies, day lilies, sunflowers, zinnias, mums . . . Through the open window
of my bedroom I will hear the "who—who-who-who" of a barred owl late at
night, grumble at the starlings nesting in our gutter, spewing their messiness
on the gray clapboard of our house. In July, blue jays will swoop from hedge
to spruce branch, dive-bombing our cats on the porch deck, wingtips nearly

brushing fur. The pink flowers of the coral bells in my garden will attract a tiny hummingbird; a yellow flash of finches will be startled from country wildflowers by my bicycle. By the end of July, the fragrance of new-mown hay will fill my nostrils as I ride. I will put almost two thousand miles on my bicycle this season, all of it on back roads within a hundred miles of home. I will garden, coaxing flowers to bloom for my stepson Justin's late-August wedding. And I will write, from my air-conditioned attic aerie, of Anaktuvuk Pass, three thousand miles away.

In June I send a letter to my friend Lela to let her know that I will not be coming this year. I remind her of the camping trips I've taken with her and Noah: "We'll save the 'Nunamiut Experience' for next year," I tease. I pull out slides, a videotape. I want to "see" Anaktuvuk Pass again. I reread transcripts from our hours and hours of interviews. I look for a tape of an interview with Lela so I can hear her talking to me. I pull out Ed's handwritten journals from 1959 and 1961 and call up my field journals on my computer.

> August 6, 1994. Caribou on the ridges this morning and even on top of the mountains to our immediate south. They go high when it's hot, and come down at night. A little caribou calf walked along the lower ridge. This is the time of year the Nunamiut used to hunt calves for making skin parkas. "The hair's just right, now," Lela tells me.

Last summer Meryn and I returned to Anaktuvuk, leaving Ed behind at his mother's in Tacoma. When villagers invariably asked about him, I explained that his illness made it just too difficult for him to move around. "Tell Ed Hall a big hello from Anaktuvuk Pass," they all said. Truth is, he would have happily come, but I was not prepared to spend my brief time at the Pass as his caretaker. This was to be a different trip, just Meryn and me. And, for once, no research. We would visit and go camping, and I would write.

We traveled light and mailed only one box from Brockport instead of the usual six or seven. We settled into a Quonset hut tent behind the Gates of the Arctic National Park headquarters in the village. Park rangers kindly supplied us with two cots, a honeybucket, and an extension cord to power Meryn's curling iron and my laptop computer. Meryn spent her days sleeping late, reading the tabloids that now come to the Nunamiut Corp store, and trying to connect with her teenage girlfriends. Each weekday morning, as Meryn slept, I hiked up the hill to the museum with my computer to write. And in the evenings we went visiting. Together we prepared simple one-dish meals in our tent on a borrowed Coleman stove. Late at night Meryn and I lay on our cots and talked. "Mom . . . ," she would begin, posing a question about drugs or how the stock market worked, about tastes in musical bands or favorite actors. Finally, one of us would say, "Let's go to sleep now." This year, on the brink of thirteen, she whines, "Do I have to go back to Anaktuvuk with you next summer?"

Ed is home this summer too, but not by choice. Multiple sclerosis has now confined him to a wheelchair, and he unhappily must defer to my judgment on all sorts of matters. He does not mention going back to Anaktuvuk this summer, but spends his days and evenings at his computer. Although MS has affected his clarity and ability to organize materials, it hasn't dampened his desire to create. He is trying to write Simon Paneak's biography, and he is interweaving his own entire professional career as an Alaskan archaeologist with the fabric of Simon's life. The document makes little sense to me, but he seems satisfied with it, with its purpose. He is holding on to his Alaska.

On warm summer evenings we eat dinner on our deck, listening to the shrieks of blue jays and watching for the hummingbird. Conversation is sparse; Ed fumbles with his fork. Cutting meat is strenuous and requires concentration. Dinners once were animated. Discussion of new research and writing projects filled the time between cooking and setting dinner on the table, and many a paper or article was birthed over a glass of wine and a barbecued fillet of salmon. Now Ed asks about my schedule for the evening, the next morning, and if my writing that day went well. When I have finished an essay he listens to me read it, then wheels himself back to his computer. He doesn't complain about the loneliness, or not being able to go to Alaska. But he does lament the divergence of our lives, the separateness now of our journeys.

In June I go to Columbus, Ohio, on a small commuter plane to visit a friend. Returning home, we fly above the wooded hills and patchwork fields of the Finger Lakes region, across the Genesee River. The runway of the greater Rochester airport lies straight ahead. The pilot noses the plane down. I am overcome with longing. The hills are spruce-timbered, it's the Chena River we cross, and the airport runway in Fairbanks welcomes our plane from the bush.

Already cicadas sing of fall. Soon the mums will bloom, school will begin. And I have not been North.

Masks

Caribou-skin mask by Rhoda Ahgook.

It's not hard to find something—an emblem, a symbol—that stands for Anaktuvuk Pass. One need look no further than the skin masks of Nunamiut faces. Since the mid-1950s, when Justus Mekiana figured out how to make caribou-skin masks on wooden molds, villagers have been making this popular tourist art for sale. The animals of the Brooks Range provide the raw materials— caribou for the faces and hair, arctic fox and wolf and sometimes bear for the parka ruffs that encircle the faces. The masks look Nunamiut, like their makers, with their longer, narrower faces than those of the coastal Eskimo people, and they come in a range of sizes and types. Like any successful invention, Anaktuvuk masks have been copied by Iñupiat people from other villages. But the mask has the mark of the place. Villagers say you can always tell if the mask is from Anaktuvuk.

The front doorbell rings for what seems the twentieth time in as many minutes. I snug the leather ties of my mask, fumbling for the candy bowl on the front hall table. Violent base organ chords of *The Phantom of the Opera* vibrate the floorboards beneath my sock feet. I open the door just as the Phantom sends the chandelier crashing to the stage. Two teenaged scarecrows in red plaid and straw and a tiny blond princess with her two-headed father stand under the porch light. "Oooooh," one of the scarecrows squeals, digging into the candy bowl for a Snickers bar and some M & M's, "it's a werewolf!" The princess whimpers, burying her head under her father's arm. "An Alaskan werewolf," I correct the scarecrow in my gruffest *Canis* voice. I smile behind my mask as I gently drop two candies in the princess's bag.

An Anaktuvuk Pass werewolf. A bulbous-nosed humanoid engulfed in a riot of fur. Dark, tea-stained face of caribou skin topped by two wolf ears. Eyelashes of thick caribou hair and a beard formed by the snout of a wolf. "Real scary," its maker, Lela Ahgook, had nodded approvingly when she handed it to me four years ago, in the summer of 1992.

Anaktuvuk Pass people aren't in the habit of making Halloween masks these days. I was in Anaktuvuk Pass for Halloween the year Ed, another colleague, and I were doing a study of all-terrain vehicle use for the borough government. Lots of village kids, bundled in their parkas in the subzero cold, called at our door. "Trick 'r Treat," they giggled, holding open candy-filled pillowcases for us to toss in more. Only a few wore masks, and they were commercial ones purchased at the village store. Except for the temperature, Halloween in Anaktuvuk seemed very like Halloween in Brockport. No Anaktuvuk kid that year, or probably since, wore a mask like the one Lela made for me.

The Halloween mask of caribou skin is somewhat of an oddity anyway, unlike caribou-skin masks of ordinary faces. They're everywhere in the village. Encircled in fur ruffs, their dark, weathered faces multiply along the white-painted walls of the village store, staring at customers who go about their grocery shopping. They look up from display cases in the village school lobby, greet visitors to the Simon Paneak Museum. At times they seem to number more than the living residents of the community. Half completed, stitched to the wooden frames that impart their human shape, they hang to dry—outdoors, from nails driven into the wooden siding of the houses, indoors from coat hooks or clothesline. They bear an uncanny resemblance to their Nunamiut makers, these masks. And they're a village emblem: every art gallery and craft shop owner in Alaska knows the "Anaktuvuk mask." It's a tourist art form with its own serendipitous origins.

Christmastime, 1951. Villagers Zacharias Hugo and Bob Ahgook were away from the village tending their traplines, hoping to catch some wolves or arctic foxes. At night, in their shared tent, they whiled away the time thinking of the upcoming week of games and nightly entertainment—especially dancing—that would take place in the community hall between Christmas and New Year's. One performance in particular held their attention, the spontaneous dance called *puktuluq*. The dancer wears his parka backward, pulling the hood up over his face as a disguise. It's a clownish act, and a good performer keeps the audience laughing while they try and guess his identity. The Nunamiut had no tradition of masking, though older people had probably seen masked performances in the past in coastal communities. But that wasn't where Zach Hugo got the idea for making a caribou-skin mask to wear at the holiday dances. He had visited Fairbanks in October and seen rubber Halloween masks in a drugstore there. He and Bob would craft something similar from the skin of a caribou they had just killed. So, camped out on their trapline, the men set to work, making two masks. They stitched on a separate piece of caribou skin for a nose and applied caribou hair for mustache, eyebrows, eyelashes, and beard. The results were two strikingly human-looking bearded faces. Like some ancient mountain men who had walked right out of Brooks Range prehistory. Zach and Bob hid their creations when they returned to the village, then brought them out to an enthusiastic crowd at the holiday dances. Their story is still told in Anaktuvuk Pass.

Eventually, one of these two handsewn skin masks found its way to the University of Alaska Museum, where it resides today in the ethnographic collections, but not before it had spawned a cottage industry in mask making. A tourist art that led to the production of several thousand skin masks and an article in the prestigious journal *Science*. [1] A tourist art, which, like all successful art, is now widely imitated.

The Anaktuvuk mask was nudged to tourist art status by Outsiders. When a visiting schoolteacher in 1956 suggested that villagers make crafts that she might take to sell in Anchorage, several people began carving wooden masks of human faces. And a few women even tried their hand at sewing skin masks like those Zach and Bob had made. But it wasn't until Justus Mekiana combined these processes of wood carving and skin sewing that a method for turning out masks in quantity was hit upon. Justus carved a wooden face mold to which he applied a piece of wet caribou skin, stitching it to the mold through preset holes in the eyes, mouth, and nose and pulling it taut against the mold with big stitches crisscrossing the back of the mold. When dry, the mask was freed from its frame, and the eye and mouth openings cut. The mask was completed with the addition of caribou fur hair, eyebrows, eyelashes, a moustache and beard if male, and a fur ruff of wolf or fox. By Mekiana's method it took as little as a day and a half from the application of the wet caribou skin to the mold to the final stitching of the ruff in place. An enterprising artisan could prepare several molds at once.

Justus made his discovery in 1957, and he's still making masks. Within a few years, a dozen Anaktuvuk Pass men and women were making masks following his method. Anaktuvuk skin masks are still made the way Justus first made them, and the old molds, some of which have been used since the beginning, are still turning out the same faces. No art is static, though, and the Nunamiut, true to their nature, have been quick to adapt new technology and materials to their skin masks. The early masks, for example, were sometimes colored by rubbing them with raw caribou liver before applying the skins to the molds. Now, an infusion of coffee or Lipton tea does the job; dental floss, and then artificial sinew, replaced caribou sinew for sewing; and some people even began gluing—instead of sewing—eyebrows and moustaches, beards and hair. Anaktuvuk mask makers also quickly catered to the American fixation with sizing and cost. The single size mask rapidly burgeoned into small, "baby-small," and oversize, the price of each commensurate with its size.

The dark, smooth molds, with their simple lines and boldly carved features, closely resemble the masks once carved and used by the coastal Eskimos. It's these patched and patinated molds, darkened from the application of hundreds of wet caribou skins, that are the precious items in this craft. Even the raw material for the molds is scarce, for the closest source of wood is thirty or forty miles to the south, in the spruce-timbered region of the Brooks Range. The faces are male (long, bigger mouths) and female (rounder cheeks, smaller mouths), and everyone has some of both. The molds, or "frames," are known by their maker's name—Amos's frame, Simon's frame, John's frame—and many still used have survived those who originally carved them.

August, 1991. Susie Paneak still has seventeen molds made for her by her late husband, Simon. We've brought the tape recorder to interview her about mask making and the camera to photograph her molds. We find Susie seated on the floor, legs stretched straight out in front of her, holding a partly completed mask on her lap. The sealskin thimble on her middle finger aids her as she works the needle in and out of the caribou skin. A rope of fur that she is sewing to the mask trails off her lap and onto the floor. Periodically she looks up from her work at her big-screen TV to follow the action on *Wheel of Fortune*. Her sewing materials—a skein of commercial sinew, spare needles, razor blades, small scissors—and the fur scraps from her sewing spew across the coffee table in front of her living-room sofa. Susie's daughter Mabel Burris is visiting from Fairbanks, as she does periodically throughout the year. Mabel works alongside Susie, cutting long half-inch-wide strips of calfskin for eyelashes and appliquéing them and other fur parts onto the blank skin faces. The Nunamiut discovered some years ago that dyed black calfskin makes luxuriant eyelashes. Everybody mail-orders calfskin to sew on their masks.

Susie holds up the mask she's working on. "Old woman mask," she announces. The wrinkled caribou skin around the mouth and eyes confirms. It's one of her opportunistic inventions. A few years back she made masks using an old caribou skin that had lost its elasticity and wouldn't stretch properly over the mold, buckling instead about the mouth and eyes. Susie's been making old people masks ever since. That summer of few good skins, Susie also used one damaged by warble flies. The flies burrow into the skin of the living caribou to lay their eggs, and the hatched larvae burrow out, leaving pinprick discolorations over the surface of the skin. These little round marks spread symmetrically across the cheeks of her woman mask. "I tell tanniks it's pimples," Susie offered mischievously.

The untanned caribou skin and especially the fur trim invite insects even after they they've been made into masks. More than one collector who hasn't applied a prophylactic dosage of RAID to his purchase has been dismayed to later find the beard or fur ruff alive with art-eating bugs. Susie takes more pains than most to protect her masks against insect damage, soaking tissues in bug spray and stuffing them in the hollows in the back of the mask, making sure they don't show behind the eyes. She holds the tissues in place with a piece of cardboard sewn to the back of the mask. The cardboard is the finishing touch, and a sure indication—even if she forgets to sign it—that the mask was made by Susie. Even today not everyone signs their masks, though a mask bought in Fairbanks or Anchorage often carries the silver and black tag authenticating it as Native Alaskan, and identifying the artist. When Susie's completed a few masks, Mabel delivers some of them up the hill to the museum to sell on consignment. Others she takes to sell in Fairbanks when she returns to town.

Lots of villagers take their masks to "town" to sell, boxing up several dozen when they go to the World Eskimo-Indian Olympics in July, the Tanana Valley Fair in August, or to visit relatives at other times of the year. They make the rounds of the art shops in Fairbanks, earning enough to pay their airfare with some left over. The Arctic Traveler Gift Shop, on 2nd Avenue, has been buying Anaktuvuk masks for more than thirty years. The manager there especially likes Justus Mekiana's masks. "A mask by Justus is the best," she insists.

The shops carry the skin masks of the imitators as well. A few years back, someone from Barrow, who must have learned the craft from an Anaktuvuk person, started making mother and baby masks like those of Ethel Mekiana. The tiny baby face, molded on a doll's head, peeks out from its mother's fur-ruffed parka hood. The mother-baby masks are popular and sell for more than the single-face masks. The Caucasian doll's face notwithstanding, they look like the Eskimo people from Barrow with their rounder faces. Anaktuvuk masks—the real ones—are the faces of the Nunamiut, longer and more angular. All kinds of fur shows up on the "not-Anaktuvuk 'Anaktuvuk' masks": sealskin eyebrows, beaver fur hair, Icelandic sheep's wool braids. At Nayuiq Omnik Furs on 6th Avenue in Anchorage, the Eskimo owner carries Anaktuvuk-style masks made from commercially tanned skins. The "caribou" is reindeer from Finland; the skins are smooth and evenly colored, the hair shiny. No bug damage problem with these faces.

Across the street from Nayuiq Omnik Furs at the gift shop in the Anchorage Museum of History and Art, one can find a wealth of finely crafted Alaskan Native art, but not any Anaktuvuk skin masks. When I asked the Native clerk why, she replied, "We don't sell them because they're not Native. They're made by Native people but they were made from Halloween masks in the 1950s." God forbid that the Natives should corrupt their "art" by adopting "foreign" ideas! How odd, though, that at the other end of the continuum are those imitators of imitators of imitators—the commercial silicon mold firm in Fairbanks, Alaska Fossil Products, that manufactures imitation caribou-skin masks complete with tanned fur trim. I guess bugs don't bother these faces either.

In the midst of this minimarket flurry over art and not-art and imitation tourist art, Anaktuvuk mask makers keep applying wet skins to the same old molds. After all, masks pay the bills. They can be traded at the village store for credit on grocery bills, at the village corporation store for equipment and fuel oil, and even with the bush airlines for airline tickets. But sometimes Anaktuvuk people tire of mask making, as Doris Hugo explained to me one day. Doris is the sister of Justus Mekiana, who invented the current molding process, and the wife of Zach Hugo, who made the very first skin mask. Zach never made any more masks, but Doris had been making them for thirty years when Zach suggested that she quit her job as manager of the village washeteria and concentrate on mask making:

> No, I told him, too much masks for years and years. I am tired, I told him. I would rather work at something else than masks. I could make masks, but not every day. Because like when you get older, when you look at too much masks, you start dreaming about your masks or see them when you close your eyes. Masks, masks . . . And I am going to get sick with masks. Justus always say, "Too much masks."

Mask making may disappear before Anaktuvuk people get too sick of it. Among other things, mask making rides on the success of the fall caribou hunt. If there are few caribou, there are few skins. And if there is no hunter in the family, it's difficult to get caribou skins. Fewer younger people know how to properly dry the skins for mask making. Fewer and fewer young people are taking up the craft; there's better and more regular money to be made from jobs with the village corporation, the school, and the North Slope Borough. Maybe, in the end, all that will be left will be the silicon imitations. The real masks will be in the hands of collectors and museums and long-ago tourists to northern Alaska.

But even if this happens there are other ways that the "real" masks will still be "sold." Just last spring, for example, there appeared in my mailbox at the office one of those colorful posters advertisers hope faculty members will tape to the outside of their office doors. This one, with four very different, arresting masks, invited viewers to discover anthropology through a certain introductory textbook. I dutifully taped the poster to my door, counting on the Anaktuvuk mask to bring our department more majors as it hawked anthropology for Allyn and Bacon publishers.

Skin masks were never used again at the holiday celebrations in Anaktuvuk Pass after Bob Ahgook's and Zach Hugo's command performance in 1951, though the masquerade dance itself—*puktuluq*—is still performed at Christmastime. How appropriate, though, given the mask's history, that *puktuluq* also means to go trick or treating at Halloween.

9:30 P.M.. A few Snickers bars, Milk Duds, and a lone lollipop are all that remain in the wooden Eskimo food bowl I've been using to hold the Halloween candy. The music has finished; the Phantom of the Opera's true deformity has now been exposed. The doorbell hasn't rung for at least ten minutes. "Have fun in Halloween scaring people," Lela had instructed me when I bought the mask from her. I have. I snap off the porch light, retrieve Meryn's pumpkin from the pumpkin smashers I imagine might later be lurking in the neighborhood, and lock the door. I untie the leather thongs of my mask and slip off my Alaskan werewolf disguise.

My Alaskan Halloween mask rests on the front hall table beside its "better half," a second mask Lela made for me from the same mold. This one is the normal face of a fur-clad Eskimo, a Nunamiut nomad who hunted caribou in the Anaktuvuk valley before there was ever a village there. The homemade Halloween mask is the ugly deformed twin. Its face is not that of the historic Nunamiut, but of something more ancient. Like the Transylvanian werewolves that straddle the slippery boundary between human and animal; like the animals that the Nunamiut know that can change themselves into humans; like the wolves that follow the caribou.

The Only Road That Goes There Is the Information Superhighway

Street corner, Anaktuvuk Pass.

Three years after the convoys of trucks had passed through the village on the winter haul road, Alaskan journalist Lael Morgan delivered Anaktuvuk Pass to the travel section of the Sunday New York Times. *The local accommodations, a hotel of sorts, was a plywood shipping container with a fifty-five-gallon oil drum stove, rented out by a Nunamiut hunter. There is no word for "hotel" in Iñupiaq, Morgan reported; the hotel's name, Aimagvik, meant simply "home." From the vantage point of the Sunday* Times, *remote winter tourism in the Arctic sounded appealing:*

> When temperatures sink to 50 below and winds funnel through the Pass at 30 miles an hour, there is a surprisingly soft beauty to the land. A thin ice fog drifts through the village, playing games with the timid sun, and the stark contours of mountains dissolve into subtle tiers of blue and gray. The nights are even more impressive, with wild displays of northern lights, of glaring moonlight that seems to bring the mountains closer. How much the summer tourists miss! It is in winter when the northland is at its awesome best, and it is also the time when the traveler has least difficulty in making a reservation at the hotel they call home.

No roads lead to Anaktuvuk Pass today. Just the Information Superhighway.

Hunched over my office computer on a wintry evening in January 1998 at the upstate New York college where I teach anthropology, I tried out my new access to the Web. Like everyone else with a computer and modem, I am easily seduced into Web surfing. First I checked for the specs on a prescription drug, then tried, unsuccessfully, to find a particular New Mexico bed and breakfast cookbook, then meandered up the Sepik River in Papua New Guinea to learn the latest tourist opportunities. From PNG I was off to northern Alaska, my area of research. A double click on Infoseek's Weather Channel. Typed in "Alaska," then "Anaktuvuk Pass."

–31 and clear at 9:16 P.M. EST time on January 22nd.

I decided to visit, via the Web. I selected one of the search engines, typed in "Anaktuvuk Pass" and, in a few seconds, was rewarded with over seven hundred Web sites.

Welcome to Anaktuvuk Pass. Welcome to Anaktuvuk Pass. Gates of the Arctic National Park and Preserve. A Brief History. The

Native residents of Anaktuvuk Pass are the last remaining . . .
http://www.nps.gov/gaar/akp.htm

Arctic Development Council: Anaktuvuk Pass Businesses. Anaktuvuk
Pass Businesses. Bob's—Misc. Retail Stores. Lela's Traditional Mask
and Snacks—Misc. Retail Stores. Nunamiut Construction Co—
General . . . *http://www.northslope.org/akpbus.htm*

Alaska—balancing between two worlds. Modern in their methods, traditional in their hearts, the Iñupiat Eskimo of northern
Alaska inhabit two worlds: one that pre-dates history and . . .
http://www.hpcc920.external.hp.com/aboutp/features/alaska/
index.html

I scanned the entire list, pausing here and there to read ones that piqued
my interest.

Frontier Flying Service, Inc. The home page for one of the "bush," or,
as they prefer to think of themselves today, "commuter" airlines
that serve the Pass and several other northern communities from
Fairbanks. A click to the schedule; another to the fare. I stopped
just short of making a reservation.

DCRA: Community Information Summaries. The Alaska Department
of Community and Regional Affairs has a Web page on Anaktuvuk Pass. Current population 306, eighty-five percent Native.
Unemployment rate, median income, and the seventeen-million-
dollar price tag of the new water and sewer project are all here in
this two-page community profile.

Sourdough Outfitters. A Web site for the adventurous. Sourdough
Outfitters is one of several companies offering tours in and
around Anaktuvuk Pass. It was not too late to sign up for their
Brooks Range Dog Sledding Expedition, but I continued scrolling
down the list of Anaktuvuk Pass Web pages, instead stopping to
read the Gates of the Arctic National Park's home page.

Native American K-12 *Schools on Internet.* Sixth on its list is Alaska:
North Slope Borough School District. The Nunamiut School in
Anaktuvuk has a home page with links to the village's Simon
Paneak Memorial Museum and an electronic tour of its exhibits
and library. There's a collection of student-authored essays from
a 1995 journalism class, the journalism class's home page, and individual student Web pages from the class of 1996. "Technology is
one of the most dramatic changes in our small village," writes one

student. "We have a wide area network in our school district and students all over the North Slope of Alaska correspond through e-mail and by on-line chatting," she continues. I clicked another link, and there appeared, in a photo essay, the class of 1998—all six of them.

Toward the end of the long list the entries seemed less relevant. One last try.

I clicked on the *Alaska Department of Public Safety's Sex Offender Central Registry*. Following the instructions, I typed in the zip code for Anaktuvuk Pass, 99721. My screen returned the name of the only registered sex offender in the village.

What is so remarkable about all of this is that suddenly it is no longer remarkable at all. When mainstream newspaper headlines today boast, "Daughter downloads long-lost father from the Web" and "Woman gives birth on the Internet," when the elementary school set blithely sends and receives letters from Santa on the Internet, and when schoolkids from my area of New York are linking up with classrooms all over the world, that Anaktuvuk Pass—or an Australian aboriginal community or any other remote village—can be found in cyberspace should hardly cause anyone to look up from their computer screen. But as an anthropologist with a memory of fieldwork "BC"—"before computers"—I am unabashedly nostalgic about remote places remaining remote, cyberspace to the contrary.

We anthropologists scoff at the popular caricature of ourselves in the field among the isolated, virtually untouched-by-civilization natives, yet we secretly yearn for just such impossible conditions. The way Ethel Ross Oliver, U.S. census taker in the central Brooks Range of Alaska in 1950, made her way to the then still-nomadic Nunamiut people in the region of Anaktuvuk Pass, is more like I want "my" bush Alaska to be.

In late March of 1950 Oliver flew north into the Brooks Range from Fairbanks, hoping to link up with Simon Paneak's band of Nunamiut so she could count them for the U.S. Census.[1] The plans for connecting had been complicated enough. Simon had sent a letter via bush pilot Sig Wien, who flew over the area fairly regularly, noting:

> We are living yet, but we do not stay together. But dog teams can reach any place of people. If you can stay with us three days, I can guide you with my dog team from here. If you can let me know over KFAR [radio] at 9:30, Tundra Topics, but repeat in two nights, because my radio cannot get in some nights. Please let me know what time you will be here.

Oliver followed Paneak's instructions, sending word via *Tundra Topics* that, weather permitting, she would arrive the following Sunday or Monday at the pass. The message was received and Ross was met, on schedule, by Simon Paneak and Homer Mekiana with waiting dog teams.

By any measure taken outside of cyberspace, Anaktuvuk Pass is still remote, eighty miles from the nearest road, an hour an a half flight from Fairbanks across the vast spruce forest and muskeg, over the southern peaks of the Brooks Range, north of the tree line to the gravel airstrip at the continental divide. The only road that goes here is the Information Superhighway.

It's a well-known fact that the Iñupiat have a history of eagerly embracing new technology, from rifles and commercial whaling gear in the nineteenth century to snowmobiles and all-terrain vehicles in the late twentieth. Most technology has come to Anaktuvuk Pass just about as fast as it is deemed useful and can be practically adopted: electricity for all village homes in 1976, the first telephones, CB radios, and TV in 1978, state-of-the-art audioconferencing telecommunications in the 1980s, and videoconferencing capabilities in the 1990s. The school, positioned within the well-funded (from Prudhoe Bay oil revenues) North Slope Borough School District, has had computers since the present building was constructed in 1979. The Information Superhighway reached the village in 1994. And, just in time for the millennium, everyone in Anaktuvuk Pass will have flush toilets and showers.

In the summer of 1997, after an absence of three years, I returned to Anaktuvuk Pass, curious to learn, among other things, where the Information Superhighway was taking the villagers. I resisted making my airline reservations online and called my travel agent instead to book my flights. En route to Alaska I stopped to visit with my parents in Southern California, arriving just in time to help usher them into the computer age. It was my brother's and my idea to get my mother a computer, especially since, after years of announcing she was too old to learn new technology and that her electric typewriter worked just fine, she had finally expressed an interest in e-mail and thought it might be a good way to keep in touch with family. My eighty-nine-year-old father, however, was not happy when my brother and I brought the new computer and printer into the house. He didn't want it in the first place. We were never sure why. Partly it was because someone else was spending a sizeable sum of money on them: "I always provided well for my family," he kept repeating to us. Despite his aeronautical engineering background and his acknowledgment of the computer's essentialness to the space industry, he remained unconvinced of its personal value. Perhaps his doubt was related to his frustration with the computer circuitry of automobile engines, which had effectively deprived him of the working knowledge he had always had of his cars. Perhaps he ultimately feared losing my mother to cyberspace. He voiced concern about the added phone bills, computer upkeep, and repairs. What if he and my mother needed to go into a nursing home at some point? Could they afford the luxury of a computer? My brother and I tried to reassure him, but mostly we listened. He turned to his familiar metaphors—life in the small farming town of Brook, Indiana, where he grew up, and aeronautical engineering, his professional life for forty years. Brook was a self contained, self-sufficient community, he reminded us. Two drugstores, a doctor, a movie theater, thriving small businesses until—the automobile came. Residents then drove farther afield, to West Lafayette, to shop and do their business, and Brook slowly died. He talked about designing airplanes and lamented that what he did by hand is now all done by computer.

Slowly Dad accepted the presence of the new machine and tolerated our hours huddled over it, surfing the Web, learning e-mail on the local server. Finally, at the end of the second day, he said, "Show me a map of Brook and I'll believe it's worthwhile." Sure enough, we found one. He leaned forward, running his index finger over the map lines on the unfamiliar computer screen. He pointed to the ice pond where his family had cut their ice, the surrounding towns where his father used to deliver fuel oil by mule wagon, the approximate location of the family farm. We might have pulled out a Rand McNally atlas and done the same exercise, but there was something mysterious and magical about calling up this map from some ethereal nowhere and coaxing it onto the computer screen.

Midway through the map exercise, which mightily impressed the rest of us, my father turned to my brother, "Let's see how versatile this thing is. I need to figure out my gas mileage!" He was finally won over when my brother located an image of the Fisher P-75 at the Wright Patterson Air Force Museum of Flight's Web site. My father had been the project engineer on that plane.

No one had to work this hard to sell computers to Eskimos.

Bound for Anaktuvuk Pass, I prepared for the usual housing crunch, more pronounced this summer by the influx of Outside workers for the massive water and sewer line construction project. Unable to secure housing before my departure, I came prepared to camp just outside the village in my new REI tent. I also came prepared to be online. It wasn't my idea, but that of the student who accompanied me. She'd never been to Alaska, never been this far away from home, never been away from her husband for this long. A computer technician at our college, he sent her off to the field with a laptop computer and a subscription to America Online so they could keep in daily touch.

The first few days of our stay we lived in my new tent, and it quickly became apparent that camping leaves very little time for fieldwork. But we were close to the Simon Paneak Memorial Museum, with electricity for our laptop computers and a phone line for Internet access. No sooner had we cleaned up camp every day than we hooked the modem up to the fax line to retrieve and send e-mail. It wasn't so long ago that I was amazed that I could even take a computer to the field. Now we were wired to the world, even if, for the moment, we were living in a tent, hauling water, cooking on a Coleman stove, and using a honeybucket in the old church nearby.

The Native museum curator understood our Internet addiction. As a North Slope Borough employee, she automatically has an e-mail account. "Oh, I got one," she exclaimed one morning, checking her e-mail just as we arrived at the museum. "I don't use Netscape," she added, "just the mail." Like the rest of us, she knows how addictive the Web can be. Even e-mail. "I'd rather talk face to face than spend all my time talking to the machine," she added.

Now I wonder how much talking back and forth on e-mail there is within the village, a question I didn't think to ask. Not much in the summer, I suspect, for the largest concentration of the village's computers is in the school, which is off-limits during the summer months. Besides, villagers have used the CB radio for communication for twenty years now, and virtually everyone has one and talks on it daily. Still, there's a fascination that new technology holds. Not long ago when fax machines were new in the village, someone might, at the drop of a hat, fax a copy of a picture or a joke to a villager in another building barely a stone's throw away.

I asked village kids if they used computers. Yep, said little Mary, six years old, naming a game I wasn't familiar with. "We have one at home, too," her seven-year-old sister chimed in, adding, "my dad has one at work." Olive, age eleven, said she does mostly "Mailman," the local server's mail program, on the computer in her classroom. Twelve-year-old Emily said they have to do A+, a computer homework project, before they can do e-mail. Their e-mail correspondence is mostly with other students on the North Slope, within their school system. But some of the older ones communicate with people farther afield. A young Swiss anthropologist who spent the summer of 1996 in the village has kept in touch with several village teens by e-mail. The Homer Mekiana he knows is not the first village postmaster who met Ethel Ross Oliver in 1950 with his dog team, but *hmekiana@*—Homer's grandson.

One afternoon, on my way to the museum, I stopped by the washeteria to visit with Doris Hugo, the manager. I've interviewed Doris many times over the last decade. She's old enough to remember when she walked, with her parents, from the Killik River valley in 1949 to settle in the Anaktuvuk Pass area. "What's that," she asked, looking at the floppy disk I had in my hand. I told her it was a computer disk and asked if she was familiar with computers. "No," she said, "I don't even know what to do with computers." But Doris knows what wonderful computer equipment they have at the school. "So much new ones. Gee, I wish I was a student today. I would be happy." "My grandchildren, so smart with computers," she smiled. One of her daughters, she added, keeps offering to teach her. I told Doris about my eighty-five-year-old mother, newly online. "Gee, I might learn it yet," she laughed. Doris can't help but be reminded of computers at the washeteria these days. There are as many issues of *Byte* and *PC World* as Avon catalogs lying around for customers to read while they do their laundry.

Up at the museum I plugged in my computer to type up some fieldnotes. Two visiting schoolteachers from Baker Lake, in Canada's Northwest Territories, on a tour of the village, had dropped in. They'd just seen the computer facilities at the school and checked their e-mail from there. From Baker Lake their ISP is expensive, a long-distance call to Ottawa, and their school has nothing like the state-of-the-art equipment that the Nunamiut School has. But that may soon change. Ardicom Digital Communications, a northern-based Native-owned company, is in the process of linking up fifty-eight communities across the Canadian Arctic and subarctic to the Internet.[2] Perhaps by the time Baker Lake becomes part of the new territory of Nunavut, it will have cheap and fast Internet access, videoconferencing, and distance education equal to that in Anaktuvuk.

I decided to check out the school facilities for myself. The chief of maintenance and operations, Dick Clark, has been with the school as long as there have been computers there. He has a generous voice and a laugh so hearty that it makes people in the far corners of the building smile. Marching down the halls to the jangle of his keys, we inventoried the computers in the school classrooms and offices while he reeled off the chronology of computer technology in the school district: First, Apple computers when the school opened in 1979, then Wangs in '87, then Dells with Windows starting in 1990. I later learn, from browsing the Web, that the school's Hewlett Packard netserver and satellite connect to an HP 9000 160 computer in the school district's office in Barrow. This system links all eight communities in the eighty-eight-thousand-square-mile school district. Dick's keys opened classroom doors; we stuck our heads in and counted computers. Sixty-four in all: three in the library, three in the school office, and the rest in the classrooms. And not quite a hundred students in the school to use them all. Every child has their own personal "drive" on the system. They spend up to half of the school day at a computer, Dick related, and often after school as well. A teacher in each community serves as a Web master for the school, helping students design Web pages.

I sat down at a computer, making note of the software programs. They would be the envy of my local school district, of my college, maybe even of well-equipped prep schools. The head of maintenance and operations for the North Slope Borough school district, visiting in Anaktuvuk, told me that the newest technology they were showing at conferences last year was already in place in the borough's schools.

The caribou, oblivious to the information superhighway that surrounds them, continued their primal wanderings, coming close to the village on the first of August. The CB radio buzzed with talk of caribou—where they were, who was out hunting and where. Villagers turned from computer terminals to binoculars, scanning the base of Oka Mountain, a mile west of the village, where a herd of caribou, hardly bigger than a cluster of fruit flies, milled about. At the washeteria, Doris was all smiles. "Going to have caribou meat tonight," she exclaimed. Caribou hunters showed up in the village store, buying cold drinks, telltale bloodstains on shirts and hands and shoes. My student and I hiked out on the tundra to watch the caribou too, then turned back to the computer, spending even more time online, e-mailing friends Outside about the excitement in the village over the caribou.

Never mind, for a moment, how computers are changing the lives of Anak-tuvuk Pass people. I'm not sure how I feel about this instant contact with the outside world that I've taken advantage of from the field. One friend in California sent me e-mail every day I was in Anaktuvuk Pass, and while I looked forward to her letters and those from other friends and family, receiving and sending e-mail became a daily, not-to-be-missed, forty-five-minute ritual. When I'd logged off, I took to wandering down the hill to the post office to see if anyone had sent me what the electronic world now derogatorily calls "snail mail." One day when I returned from the post office to the museum, my student was chatting online with her husband. She looked up from her computer as I teasingly fanned out my four letters from three states and two countries.

Real mail, letters. Hold-in-your-hands mail, with the sender's signature, a cancelled stamp, a postmark, and the bends and scuffs of actual travel from there to here; correspondence removed in time and space from the instant "now" of e-mail and chat rooms. In summertime in the 1950s, Simon Paneak, camped north of the village at Tulugak Lake, used to walk the sixteen miles to the pass when the monthly mail plane came in. He came, not just for supplies, but to retrieve the bag of mail that brought responses to the many letters he wrote. Letters to read and reread; to be answered, sealed in envelopes, and walked back to the pass before the next mail plane came. Were he alive today, would he be doing it all by e-mail?

Obviously, there's more afoot here than e-mail, than schoolkids on the Web, and computer magazines in the village washeteria. Big, important, well-funded projects. Since the early 1980s, the North Slope Borough has maintained a GIS (Geographical Information Service) mapping project known as the Traditional Land Use Inventory, or TLUI, which has committed to the computer the locations of all known places the Iñupiat have camped, hunted, fished, trapped, and lived within the vast North Slope Borough region. This database of TLUIs has many uses, foremost the protection of subsistence areas and cultural heritage sites from industrial development.

The Point Hope virtual museum is a new computer-based project that began with a desire to videotape artifacts from the village of Point Hope located in far-flung museum collections. The project is evolving to include interpretive material on natural history and archaeology as well. Intended eventually for the Web, it's a Point Hope museum, designed by Point Hope Native people. Add another stretch of the Information Superhighway that will bring Outsiders to the North Slope.

Back in Anaktuvuk, they talk lightheartedly about the surfeit of computers in their part of the world. "Pretty soon gonna have to have passwords in Eskimo; too many computers!" joked one villager. I watched a group of boys riding their bikes up a mound of gravel piled in the road from the water and sewer construction project, thoughts of computers probably far from their minds. Three teenaged girls in long skirts sashayed up the gravel street toward the village store to the admiring glances and calls of the construction workers. I turned to face the retinue of small elementary school girls that tagged after us in our village rounds. And I realized: every one of these village kids has an e-mail address. There is a new nomadism in Anaktuvuk Pass, not on terra firma but along the bends and curves of the Information Superhighway, the only road in, the only road out. The road that leads nowhere and everywhere. Marking a journey that has only begun.

This year, my departure from Anaktuvuk Pass was accompanied with an exchange of e-mail addresses. "I just write short thing," one Native friend cautioned. During this past winter she and I have traveled the Information Superhighway from Anaktuvuk to Brockport:

Dear friend. Just want to say Happy thanksgiving to you all from AKP.

And, in mid-January:

. . . right now they are out hunting. They went down south to look for caribou. I hope they will see some caribou and kill some because we are out of meat. We are seeing some sun shine now on top of the mountains.

Remembering Susie Paneak

Cemetery, Anaktuvuk Pass. Photo by James H. Barker.

The waters of Contact Creek gather force in the mountain to the west and cut a purposefully channeled swath through the village, spilling over glacial cobbles and drawing village children, who stun and kill arctic grayling with rocks in an endeavor they call "rock fishing." Rock throwing is learned early here, and learned equally skillfully by both genders. On a dry summer's eve, when the creek waters have receded to a gentle murmur, you may see as many as thirty adults and children, rocks in hand, wading in a line upstream in the icy waters. Rocks fly—ka-thunk! Ka-thunk! Ka-thunk! A hit, raucous cheers, and a stunned grayling joins the growing pile of fish on the bank. If you chance to look up from the fishing activity toward the bridge that spans the creek, you may see a small child walking—one foot carefully placed in front of the other, arms extended like a tightrope artist—along the narrow steel railing. Follow the gravel road north across the bridge a quarter of a mile and you come to the abrupt edge of civilization. The village cemetery, at the end of the road, is the last permanent habitation between here and the Arctic Ocean, two hundred miles north across the tundra. Wooden crosses, festooned in plastic flowers laid there each Memorial Day, turn their faces to the mountains and list in the wind that tunnels down the pass. They number almost as many dead as the living.

On Thanksgiving Day, 1997, Susie Paneak died in a Fairbanks hospital. Through several summers of oral history research Ed and I conducted in Anaktuvuk Pass, we talked with her often, interviewed her several times, and knew her large family. No one is sure when Susie was born, though 1919 is written on her medical card. To the outside world, she was known as Simon Paneak's wife. In addition to being a Nunamiut of enormous intellect and knowledge, Simon was a sure-shot hunter, a natural storyteller, and a leader by any culture's measure. He earned the attention of a steady stream of arctic scientists who beat a path to his caribou-skin tent in their studies of the area's wildlife and geology. It was Susie who cheerfully welcomed and fed these folks, who made her large family's skin clothing, who gathered firewood carrying a baby on her back while trailing a toddler clinging to her parka. She helped Simon, too, with his various scientific projects, counting and recording the birds that visited Alaska's North Slope.

Later, in widowhood, Susie babysat her grandchildren, made fine caribou-skin masks for sale to tourists, picked berries on the tundra, and frequently traveled to Fairbanks to visit her daughter. She loved to work the jigsaw puzzles her children bought her, and she often sat on the floor, her legs stretched straight out, her skin sewing in her lap, watching *Jeopardy* on her big-screen TV. Susie lived alone with her dog, but she was seldom without visitors.

Coincidentally, on Thanksgiving Day, a college colleague in my village was also dead. But no one knew it until almost a week later. The unread newspapers piled up on her porch; the mail overflowed her mailbox. Her cat roamed the neighborhood in search of food. Finally, some neighbors noticed. She lived alone, on medical leave from the college, and had no family in the area with whom to share Thanksgiving. It was no one's fault, really, that she died like this. The college community was busy with the last weeks of classes; she wasn't teaching anymore; her health problems had isolated her from colleagues and neighbors alike. Still, not long ago, she, with her passionate intellect, had been an active member of the college community— accounted for, accountable. She died the death that none of us wants to die, in obscurity, unnoticed on the holiday that draws Americans together for fellowship and food.

The *Fairbanks Daily News-Miner* ran an obituary and, a few days later, a longer reflective piece about Susie Paneak. This was not surprising, for Susie was among a diminishing number of Native elders who speak little English and remember life before airplanes, before money, before electricity and satellite TV, not to mention before computers. Susie was a link to a way of life that is rapidly passing from memory.

"Yes, we will miss Susie," a village friend said in an e-mail message, adding, "but the funeral is Thursday." That was not the non sequitur it seems. A funeral in village Alaska mobilizes the entire community. Susie's Fairbanks children and relatives would accompany the body back to Anaktuvuk, where they would be met by other family members; Susie's Canadian Arctic relatives would fly in. With the arrival of the plane, and its coffin cargo and weeping relatives, life in Susie's village would pause for a day. Several days before, messages broadcast on the CB radio would have marshaled the village men to the cemetery in the subzero cold to prepare the grave; village women would supply the gravediggers with hot coffee. The body would be taken to the Nunamiut School gym, where villagers would gather for the funeral service. A choir would likely be put together for the occasion, and the congregation would escort the body the half mile to the cemetery for burial. A potluck supper in the community hall that night would be followed by a guitar-strumming, foot-stomping singspiration that would go on into the early-morning hours. Susie would be carried to her grave by family and friends, put in the ground that holds her husband, Simon, a son, a daughter-in-law, her parents-in-law. She would be laid to rest, in this mountain pass, among the others, every one of whom she knew in life.

Villagers as well as Outsiders lament the alcohol problems in village

Alaska, the insouciance of the teenagers. The old decry the consumerism of this oil-rich society and the loss of old ways. But in this community that has only seven original surnames, children live near grandparents and aunts and uncles and cousins. They look out for all of their own. What happened in Brockport, New York, could never happen in Anaktuvuk Pass.

The Exhibition

Ethel Mekiana, Justus Mekiana, and Rachel Riley in Brunswick, Maine.

*Anaktuvuk Pass has always been a Nunamiut village, their only
village. The North Slope Borough School District's Web site de-
clares: "Anaktuvuk Pass is home to the last of the Nunamiut." The
Arctic Development Council's home Web page echoes a few others
when it describes the village as "the last remaining settlement of
the Nunamiut." Both of these "vanishing race" declarations are a
bit of a stretch, not to mention anachronistic, since the Nunamiut
are more populous now than they were in the early twentieth century, and Anaktuvuk Pass is not the "last" but the only permanent
settlement the Nunamiut have ever had.*

In 1897, following an unsuccessful attempt to reach the North Pole, Arctic
explorer Robert Peary returned to New York with six Polar Eskimos. His
stories of trains and big buildings and sunlight in the winter, and especially
his promises of guns and ammunition and knives, enticed them to make the
journey. Their destination was the American Museum of Natural History,
where anthropologist-curator Franz Boas intended them to reside over the
winter. That way, Boas reasoned, "Much valuable information of an ethno-
logical character could be obtained from them, and . . . their presence here
would be very instructive to scientists interested in the study of the Northern
races." Within a few months four of the Eskimos contracted TB and died. A
fifth secured passage back to Greenland, leaving the youngest, Minik, just
eight years old, in America.

The orphaned Eskimo boy was raised by an American Museum of Natural
History administrator and his wife.[1] Almost a decade later, Minik came upon
an exhibit in the museum containing his father's skeleton, which he had
been led to believe had been buried at the time of death. The newspapers
picked up the story. "Give Me My Father's Body," blared the headlines in the
World Magazine Supplement of January 6, 1907, but Minik was unsuccessful
in regaining his father's bones. Minik returned to his homeland, where he
served as an interpreter for Donald MacMillan's 1913 Crocker Land expedition to the far north of Greenland. Minik came once more to the United
States, to New Hampshire, where he died in the influenza epidemic of 1918.
His father's bones and those of the other Inuit were not "de-accessioned"
from the museum until the mid-1990s, when they were finally returned to
northern Greenland for burial.

Stories of Native peoples being escorted to other lands are even older than
the journeys of Squanto and Pocahontas. By the close of the last century,
many Natives had been brought to the great museums of natural history
and to Chicago's World Columbian Exposition of 1893 as living exhibits. But
it was the journey of Peary's Polar Eskimos that held particular meaning for
me. A full century after the arrival of Peary's entourage, in October 1998,

I'd been invited to the Peary-MacMillan Arctic Museum at Bowdoin College (both Peary and MacMillan were alumni) to give a lecture on Anaktuvuk Pass caribou-skin masks. Also coming were three Nunamiut mask makers from the village. At the museum's expense, they had flown from Anaktuvuk to Brunswick, Maine, to demonstrate mask making in the museum and at the local schools. Theirs was a much different journey, of course, than that shipboard voyage from Greenland to Brooklyn, and they were not 1890s museum "specimens," but 1990s keepers and teachers of traditional knowledge.

"We didn't even know where Maine was," exclaimed Rachel Riley, that first morning over breakfast in Brunswick. "But the kids knew and the schoolteachers showed us." Rachel is a strong, handsome woman of fifty-seven with a broad face and ready smile. She's the bilingual teacher in the Anaktuvuk Pass village school, responsible for every child's forty-five minutes of daily Iñupiaq language instruction. Every spring Rachel takes the entire school population camping, teaching them how to kill, skin, and butcher caribou, along with other traditional knowledge. She's been making masks, in her spare time, for thirty years.

With Rachel are her older brother, Justus Mekiana, and his wife, Ethel. Justus is seventy, short and slight. He's a man of few words, not very confident in English. Justus's interest in this mask-making project is intense because he is dedicated to documenting Nunamiut activities that are disappearing. He has made more than two thousand masks since he invented the process of applying a piece of wet caribou skin to a carved wooden face mold. One of Justus's masks looks very much like Ethel, with its prominent cheekbones and downturned mouth, but he couldn't have known that when he made the mold for it forty years ago. Ethel is a round little woman of sixty-five. She has a high-pitched laugh and a great sense of humor. Ethel also makes masks. In the mid-1980s she began making a popular form of the skin mask, a mother with a baby peeking out from the mother's parka hood. "Arrigaaa, your daughter's so grown up," Ethel smiles at Meryn who has come with me to have her first look at prospective colleges. They last saw her four years ago, when she was twelve.

We catch up on the year that has elapsed since I was in Anaktuvuk Pass in the summer of 1997. Yes, everyone got lots of caribou this fall. There's a new airline that's cheaper than Frontier. Yes, Dorothy is still mayor. "How's Ed doing?" Ethel asks. I explain what multiple sclerosis is and how it has affected him. "I remember when he was young," she says, recalling Ed's first trip to Anaktuvuk Pass when he was nineteen. "He always wear that red hat. We used to let him baby-sit our kids," she laughed.

Up at the museum the staff is busily putting the finishing touches on an exhibit of Anaktuvuk Pass caribou-skin masks from the 1960s. They were purchased by a nurse who was working in the village at the time, and were recently acquired by the museum. This exhibit is what has brought all of us to the Peary-MacMillan Arctic Museum. The "old" masks are powerful, with their bold facial planes and faces shiny from being rubbed with caribou liver. Later this week, Rachel, Justus, and Ethel will be asked to identify the furs that make up their eyebrows, hair, beards, and parka ruffs. They'll be asked too if they can identify their makers. They nod approvingly at the collection, then turn to oversee the unpacking of the new masks they have each brought to sell in the museum.

Meryn and I leave the hive of activity at the museum to take a scheduled campus tour for prospective students and their parents. From my office window at the State University of New York College at Brockport, I frequently see clusters of parents and their college-bound teens being shepherded about campus by student guides, but they hardly cause me to gaze up from my work. As a faculty member, I am not engaged with that part of campus life. Today I am. I listen attentively to the enthusiastic student who walks backward across campus as she addresses our little group of parents and students. She could sell Bowdoin College to the Eskimos, I conclude. Not only is this my first "college shopping" experience, this is my first introduction to a private college. I gaze longingly at the beautiful classrooms, remembering the sink in the chemistry lab above our anthropology classroom that frequently overflowed, ruining the acoustic tiles on the ceiling, staining the carpet and bringing class to a halt. Adjacent to the Arctic museum is the Bowdoin College Museum of Art, with an entire gallery of portraits by Benjamin West, John Copley, and Gilbert Stuart. Everywhere there are plaques recording the endowment of some campus feature. Overstuffed chairs and couches invite conversations in classroom buildings, the student union, and the library. I have been won over. I am already returning, in the brilliance of fall, for parents' weekend. Meryn is more pragmatic. She wants to know about the food and how quickly she can get from here to Boston.

We spend the remainder of the afternoon exploring the college, then hurry back to get ready for the evening's events. The museum staff treats us all to dinner at a local seafood restaurant, where we share giant plates of lobster paella. The Anaktuvuk people have never had lobster before, or mussels. Yesterday they watched lobsters being taken from lobster traps and put in large pots of boiling water. "Those poor lobsters," Rachel winced at the memory. "Funny, we kill caribou and don't say 'poor caribou.' " "I'll try not to think of those poor boiling lobsters," she said, scanning the menu. She succeeds; the paella is a hit. The mussel shells intrigue the Anaktuvuk villagers. Rachel holds a pair against her chin and Justus puts one over each eye. "For masks," Rachel laughs, as she collects all the mussel shells left over from dinner. Anaktuvuk mask makers have adorned their human face masks with wolf paws and caribou hooves, why not mussel shells? "We'll call it Brunswick-miut," Rachel teases. I tell her I want one.

The Friends of Bowdoin College have begun congregating in the lecture hall where my talk is scheduled to be held. The museum staff is in disguise, for the evening's invitation encouraged "masks and disguises." I have brought my Anaktuvuk Pass Halloween mask to wear following my talk.

Justus, Ethel, and Rachel take their seats in the center section of the hall, and suddenly I am alone on stage, the featured "authority" on their art. I tell them beforehand to let me know if I make mistakes, and before beginning I introduce them as the "real experts." Still, it is mildly disconcerting to be lecturing to the natives about *their* village, *their* art. Afterward they willingly answer questions from the audience. "You did OK," they affirm. The lecture hall empties and we walk, en masse, along a campus path lighted by jack-o'-lanterns to the museum reception. Impressively, the museum director has managed to secure caribou for this event. Hosts and guests mingle in the museum lobby, balancing plates of seafood paté, baked salmon, and skewered slivers of caribou teriyaki.

It is midmorning when I arrive at the museum the following day. The Nunamiut are already hard at work preparing the caribou skins they have brought for mask making. A small crowd of visitors, which by day's end will total four hundred people, encircle them. Rachel and Justus, seated on the floor, scrape the dried flesh from caribou skins while they answer questions. Ethel sits nearby at a table, using her *ulu* to expertly shave the caribou hair from the oval pieces of skin cut for masks. Children run to get bags to collect the long caribou hair. "We used to stuff pillows with it, before we got pillows from the store," Ethel notes. Rachel leans into her long-handled scraper made from a two-and-a-half-foot length of pipe fitted to a wooden handle that has been shaped to fit her hand. Her deft strokes remove the flesh. "Do you hunt caribou yourself?" asks a man in the audience. "I've been hunting for myself since I was thirty-eight," she answers. Rachel's been widowed for almost twenty years. "Have to hunt for yourself if you don't have a man in the house." She grins, running a hand through her short spiky black hair: "Hey, are there any single men in Maine?" "How many caribou do you get in a season," asks another who doesn't know that Anaktuvuk people hunt caribou all year long. "Ten for the year," she answers without hesitation. Rachel is an avid hunter, out on the land in the summertime, so much so that I rarely see her in the village when I go to Anaktuvuk.

Ethel hands the shaved skins to Justus, who takes a piece of sandpaper to the flesh side, smoothing out the marks left by his scraper. On a table nearby water boils in an electric teakettle; a stainless steel pot beside it holds a good measure of loose Lipton tea. The boiling water is poured on the tea and stirred, the caribou skin pieces added and left to soak. All the while I am taking pictures with my camera: Rachel scraping a skin with her long scraper, Justus placing a piece of skin over a mold and cutting it to size, Ethel cutting thick hair from the skin with her ulu, Justus pulling a wet skin from the tea infusion.

I emerge from behind my lens to watch as Justus takes a needle and thread—artificial sinew—from his needle case. He begins stitching the mask to the mold at the eye, nose, and mouth through preformed holes. He flips the mold over, making overcast stitches across the back. He tugs at the thread to pull the skin taut against the mold. He works quickly, doing a second and a third mask.

Though I've published a recent article on Anaktuvuk Pass masks, I've never seen the step-by-step process of their making nor had the good fortune to be able to photograph the entire sequence. When I'm in Anaktuvuk, during the summer, people are more likely to be out on the land hunting and picking berries than making masks. Caribou taken during the fall hunt provide the best skins for mask making. I've interviewed villagers about mask making and taken some photographs of drying masks and of people sewing on trim, but I've had to come to a museum in Brunswick, Maine, more than three thousand miles from Anaktuvuk Pass, to see the process from start to finish.

The mask-making demonstration winds down, and after lunch we head to the beach in my rental car. Although I'd been to Acadia National Park almost thirty years earlier, I've never seen the southern Maine coast, and I am just as eager as these inland villagers this sunny fall afternoon to see the ocean. Splashes of bright yellows and reds draw our eyes to the roadside; the warm sun streams in on us. Fall has been over for two months now in Nunamiut country. "Do you know Indian summer?" I ask Rachel. "No, what is it?" she asks.

Popham Beach State Park, a thirty-minute drive from Brunswick, rewards its visitors with a magnificent sandy beach, which, at low tide, connects to a rocky island. We traipse through the soft sand of the dunes to the water's edge. The women pause to study the vegetation. "These berries?" asks Ethel, bending over a wild rose fruited with rose hips. No, I tell her, but you can make jam out of the rose hips. She seems genuinely disappointed that the plump fruits are not berries. I can understand; she picked gallons of salmon-colored *akpiks* and blueberries this summer on the tundra. "People's feet make the sand look like this?" asks Rachel, commenting on the disturbed sand. I nod, remembering that older Nunamiut have spent their lives looking at animal tracks. When we reach the water, we fan out, each of us walking a slightly different stretch of coastline. Heads down, the Nunamiut scour the beach with the same intensity that they look for caribou. Ethel finds a piece of driftwood that fits her hand perfectly. "Ikun [scraper]," she yelps with delight, pocketing the piece. They spend the next hour filling their jacket pockets with shells and driftwood.

We drive to the very end of the peninsula to see old Fort Popham, a Civil War construction that never saw action. It is an imposing structure, with thick blocks of granite and arched brick ceilings. Justus is out of the car before the rest of us and into the fort. He's impressed with its scale. "Ah, Nipuq' Neeser's house," he smiles in wonder. "Just like in the Bible," he clarifies. I puzzle over his words, trying to render his Iñupiaq pronunciation into something recognizable. Finally, it comes to me: Nebuchadnezzar, the Babylonian king and his wonder of the ancient world, the hanging gardens of Babylon.

We sit at the water's edge for a few minutes watching a lobsterman unloading his catch. A crew member bands the claws. "Too bad we can't take back some of those lobster parts," Ethel laments. "We'd do something with them." I imagine a claw emerging from under a fur ruff, or antennae on the forehead in some monster version of a caribou-skin mask. I'd like one of those masks, too, for my collection. Finally, we head back to town for dinner at the museum director's home. Rachel leans back in the front seat, closing her eyes. "Going to be hard to go back home," she says, "We're getting so spoiled." "Getting spoiled all right," Ethel echoes.

Dinner is a feast of conversation and food, attended by museum staff and the department of anthropology faculty. But by 9:30 we are already plotting our next adventure. Meryn and I are as eager as Rachel, Justus, and Ethel to get to L.L. Bean's home store in Freeport, twenty minutes away. It never closes. The best time to go, say the locals, is around 2 A.M., when there's no waiting in line.

By 10:30 P.M. we're heading down I-95. "L.L. Bean, here we come," Rachel chants. I pick up an unexpected bit of ethnographic information. "Simon Paneak bring that L.L. Bean catalog to Anaktuvuk Pass," Ethel announces. I ask how he got it and Rachel suggests it came from Sig Wien, the Alaskan bush pilot who introduced so many items to the Nunamiut back in the late 1940s and 1950s. "As long as I can remember, there's L.L. Bean catalog. We're still getting it." And then, another gem: "Simon order pocket knife from L.L. Bean and everybody copy him," Ethel offers. Villagers looked up to Simon; he was an *umealiq*, a rich man and a natural leader. No wonder everyone wanted the same pocket knife as Simon.

We park by the huge, brightly lit store. The three pause for a moment to look at the display of wild animals in the store windows. No doubt their hunter eyes see them differently than mine. Once inside, Meryn and I head for the clothing, and the Nunamiut take the stairs down to the camping gear and knives. We agree to meet by the entrance in an hour. One hour and three hundred dollars of clothing purchases later, I find Rachel first, buying several sets of heavy gloves. Justus and Ethel emerge from the camping section, carrying a big bag of purchases. "We see lots of knives, but not that famous pocketknife," Ethel says. "Maybe they change the handle on it," Justus offers. L.L. Bean has whetted their appetites for shopping. On the way home, they announce that they want to be sure to get to Wal-Mart while they are in Brunswick. Luckily, Wal-Mart is closed at midnight, and Rachel says she's even too tired to play snerts. She and Ethel have been playing snerts nightly since their arrival, but tonight everyone is going straight to bed.

Sunday morning, my last hours in Brunswick. Meryn has gone rollerblading with my camera to take some photos on campus and I am drinking a morning cup of tea with Rachel, Ethel, and Justus. I broach a serious topic. I want to do a book on Anaktuvuk masks, interviewing each mask maker about their masks and molds. I explain that this trip has taught me how much I still don't know about the masks. They think it's a good idea, that it will help outsiders to know that Anaktuvuk people created the process and that only they make the "real Anaktuvuk masks."

Talk turns to how they are going to spend their "free" day today. They want to go shopping. Ethel's still thinking about the masks. "Maybe they got fur place here," she jests. Rachel has a serious proposition. "Think you can take us to Wal-Mart?" she asks. She doesn't know how I much detest going to our local Wal-Mart, nor my irrational fear of an enforced retirement as a Wal-Mart greeter. It's just as well that I don't have time to accompany them on their Wal-Mart venture before my plane leaves, but I can drop them there if someone from the museum can pick them up.

Meryn and I are packed to go home, our bags loaded in the car. Before leaving I take some pictures of Rachel, Justus, and Ethel on the wide porch of the Brunswick Bed and Breakfast, where we have been staying. Then everyone piles in the car. The bed and breakfast owner gives me the directions to Wal-Mart. "Go down past the Navy base, it's on the right. You can't miss it." We say our goodbyes in the parking lot there. "See you next summer," I promise. I watch the three figures walk toward the store.

When Minik finally returned to his native Greenland in 1909, he arrived empty-handed. But not the Nunamiut ninety years later. They take a shopping cart from the Wal-Mart greeter and load it with purchases they cannot buy at home. Enough to fill the large suitcase that held their masks and caribou skins on the journey east. The skins have been made into masks. The masks they leave behind, on the walls of the gift shop at the Peary-MacMillan Arctic Museum.

Airplane, Airplaaane!

The Wien plane, 1963. Photo by Ward Wells. Courtesy of the Anchorage
Museum of History and Art.

The actual journey to Anaktuvuk Pass always begins in Fairbanks, on what is still called a "bush" airline, even though its office is computerized, its planes painted with the company logo, and its pilots uniformed. The first half of the flight takes you above undulating spruce forest and muskeg till you reach the foothills of the Brooks Range. In clear weather, the pilot flies above the jagged peaks. But when the weather in the mountains is bad, he follows the sinuous valley of the John River, flying considerably below the mountaintops, which repose in the rain clouds. The turbulence they generate buffets the little plane from side to side. Finally, the ground beneath you rises toward the blue-white ice field at the headwaters of the John River. The shiny aluminum rooftops of the village lie just beyond. The pilot banks sharply, scribing a tight circle above the village, then puts the plane down gently on the gravel airstrip.

It's a familiar ritual. Dump the gear on the scale to be weighed, then report—hopefully truthfully—your body weight. Take the boarding pass and head for the twin-engine Beechcraft parked on the runway apron. It's Fairbanks, July 1999, and I'm in the company of six other passengers. The aircraft, a nine-seater, has logged more miles than I care to know. They're evident in the small dents that pimple the fuselage, the grimy, worn upholstery on the seats, the condensation between the scratched plastic window panes, and the bent metal framing around one of the windows. I reassure myself that the neglected exterior means the mechanics have focused all their attention on the upkeep of the engines and instrumentation.

I know all my fellow travelers, which is comforting. They're returning home to Anaktuvuk Pass. Steve Wells, who sits in the very back, yells to the pilot as he ducks into the plane: "I hope your last name's not Kennedy," referring to John F. Kennedy Jr.'s fatal plane crash of the preceding week. The pilot smiles. He's close to my age, which means he's been flying for a long time. He looks competent; maybe he's flown the route to Anaktuvuk Pass a lot. The airline, Frontier, has been flying there since the 1970s, and for as long as I can remember—and that's back to 1984—their pilots have worn uniforms. So, in appearance anyway, they've made the transition from a bush operation to a commuter airline. Frontier even gives frequent flyer miles, and one can book a flight—the price of which now approaches the coast-to-coast fare in the lower forty-eight—on the Web.

By the summer of 1999, the Anaktuvuk "airport," which is really just a mile-long gravel runway, was on the Web, thanks to a University of Alaska PhD candidate who had installed Web cams at three rural airports to provide automated weather reporting systems. Anaktuvuk was chosen because of its heavy air carrier traffic, dangerous terrain, and poor flying weather. I can only hope, along with the Ph.D. student, that this reporting system improves flying there. And I find it understandable that he publicly thanks God as one of the supporters of his project.

No matter how mainstream and technologically advanced this commuter air service, the hour and a half journey from Fairbanks to Anaktuvuk Pass is, for me, an act of sheer will, of principled dedication to the singular importance of fieldwork in anthropology. And I would be the first to admit that, if there were any other way to get there than by air, I'd do it.

Every anthropologist carries a personal folklore of the field—stories of privations, challenges, dangers, and eventual triumphs. The mishaps of flying there and back are part of that folklore. Some tell the story of flight with bravado; others, regardless of what does or does not actually happen, are enveloped in a discomfort that borders on terror the moment they leave terra firma. I'm in the latter category.

The weather's good this fine July day, here in Fairbanks as well as at the Pass. This could be an uneventful flight. But just as we are airborne and Fairbanks slips into the distance, Steve taps me on the shoulder and asks me to tell Ray Paneak, a few seats ahead of me, to notify the pilot that there's a strange rattling noise that sounds like something hitting the outside of the plane. Perhaps, he suggests, a seatbelt buckle that got trapped in the door. I anxiously pass the word on to Ray, who looks back quizzically at Steve, then relays the message to the pilot. By the time the pilot has removed his headphones and turned around, the sound is gone.

But not my anxiety, which heightens as I add the midair "disassembly" of the plane to my list of flight worries. I hate flying in small planes, despite the nearly thirty field seasons I've logged in them in British Columbia and Alaska. And I don't care much for flying in big ones either. The flight from Fairbanks to Anaktuvuk can be visually spectacular, but it can also be frighteningly rough, and more than one airplane flying in that country has slammed into the rock-laden clouds.

Today, though it's clear. The mountains are beautiful, a deep crinkle of brown dusted with white powder from the snowstorm of two days ago. The two Nunamiut men look out the window when we reach the mountains, pointing out camping and hunting places below. I haven't memorized much of the geography from the air, and I'm convinced this pilot hasn't either. Maybe he's lost. I ask Ray where we are. "South of Anaktuvuk, Allen River." He points to and names a couple of mountains. I relax. We seem to be on course after all. Minutes later, I see in the distance a familiar valley and the silver curls of its river. "Is that the John River?" I ask Ray. "Yeah, John River," he answers. I sigh, relieved. We are almost there, and ahead I see the patch of multicolored squares marking the houses of Anaktuvuk Pass. Today we don't even circle the village. The pilot noses the plane straight down, landing to the north. We taxi up to the fence-rimmed apron at the south end of the village.

Now, the ritual on the ground begins. A handful of people have gathered on the runway apron. A few pickup trucks, the village bus, and a couple of all-terrain Argos ring the parked plane. Villagers wait to greet passengers. Others, with their baggage stacked beside them, wait to board the plane for the return trip to Fairbanks, and still others have come to pick up freight for the school and the village store. I descend the plane with my fellow travelers, collect my gear, and throw it into the back of a waiting pickup truck. From now until I leave, I'll be watching planes from the ground.

Like villagers, I know that the morning plane is due sometime after 10, and the afternoon plane sometime after 2:30. Like them, I may look up when I hear or see an incoming plane circling the village to land, but, given the noise level in the village from the several construction projects underway, some planes will sneak in virtually unnoticed by the majority of villagers. During my short summer stay here, I'll see more aircraft than just the scheduled flights of the three carriers that serve the village. When the sport hunting season opens the first of August, single-engine Cessnas with hunters and guides may land here on their way north or on their return trips south. There's the fuel oil plane, an old DC-6, that will make several late-summer flights to fill the big tanks that lie just off the runway with the village's supply of winter fuel oil. Other planes will bring in gasoline and aviation gas, and Frontier's freight plane, a DC-3, will make at least one run while I'm here with supplies for the village store. If I'm really lucky, I may see a C-130 land with a big load of building materials or heavy machinery. And always there are a few helicopters.

Even thirty years ago, Anaktuvuk Pass was busy with airplanes. Lela Ahgook, a village correspondent for an irregular *Fairbanks Daily News-Miner* column called "Anaktuvuk Passages," wrote in March 1969, "Many plane each day. What a noisy little Village now!" In those days, scheduled air service—"the mail plane"—came in a couple of times a week. The hum of its engines would be noted first by the village dogs, whose chorused howling would alert villagers. "Tiŋŋun, tiŋŋun"—"Airplaane, airplaaane!"—kids and adults alike would shout, dropping whatever they were doing and running to the airstrip to see what the plane had brought. Everyone would pitch in and help unload the freight, exclaiming over the store goods and the size of the mailbag. The whole village turned out, even though, commented one observer, it was "a ten-ton assignment."

Simon Paneak, as village leader and assistant to so many scientists who came to the Pass, kept up with world and regional events by listening to his radio, the first one of which—a big Zenith table model—he acquired in the 1940s. According to one scientist who spent a lot of time with Simon in the early 1960s, Simon "knew all the radio frequencies for the airplanes, and he knew where each one was going. Each one of those planes," the observer reported, "assumed a personality. Villagers just talked about them as if they were people because they were so important to their lives."

Given the importance of airplanes in my own family history, it is perhaps strange that I do not care for flying. I would have learned to love flying if my maternal uncle had had his way. He was a B-17 bomber pilot in World War II, and I, born just before the war ended, the first child in the family. Uncle Tom signed the bombs he dropped with my name on them, and he carried on a one-way wartime correspondence with me. "I hope someday to be able to teach you how to fly," he wrote in one of his letters. I never learned to fly—in more ways than one—but his leather flight jacket from the war now hangs in my closet, a gift from my aunt after his death last year. My father and his two brothers were aeronautical engineers. The oldest, Don, designed the P-40 pursuit plane used in World War II. And my father was the project engineer on the P-75, a pursuit plane designed at the end of the war that never saw service. Come to think of it, it was my father's job of designing airplanes that saw me to college, led me into anthropology—a field that mystified my father—and eventually transported me from Middle America to Anaktuvuk Pass.

My father loved to talk about his work, but what he could say about aeronautical engineering that would hold the attention of a small child was pretty limited. So, when I was little, he took to demonstrating how airplanes fly. Holding in one hand a block of wood with a ruler balanced at right angles across it, he launched his "plane" into the air, all the while gesturing with his other hand to show the flow of air over and under the wings and the principle of lift. When I got a little older, he would draw diagrams of airplane wings with arrows depicting the airflow. The lessons never really sank in. Any airplane I'm on gets into the sky because I will it there. "You're safer traveling in an airplane than in a car," he was fond of telling me when I became a teenager with a driver's license. I'd really like to believe that when I fly to Anaktuvuk Pass.

Writers about Alaskan aviation agree that no place on the globe embraced air travel with the enthusiasm of Alaskans and no other place was so vitally affected by aviation as Alaska. How many Alaskan villages, like Anaktuvuk Pass, were born with the creation of a landing strip? The history of civil aviation in Alaska goes back to the 1920s, but it was World War II and the defense of the Aleutians that spurred the rapid growth of aviation in Alaska. And it was during the war that the Nunamiut saw the first planes come into their country. Sig Wien, the youngest of the famous Wien Alaska Airways brothers, had begun flying between Fairbanks and Barrow in 1938, stopping at either Bettles or Wiseman to refuel.

In 1943, on one of those flights, Wien landed his Bellanca on Chandler Lake in the Brooks Range. While pouring gas from five-gallon cans into his plane's fuel tanks, he spotted a speck in the distance, perhaps a caribou out on the lake ice. Moments later, realizing the running speck was a person, he noted, "I wasn't aware there were any humans in the area, so I was a little concerned at who it might be and what any contact would be like. And when he was pretty close, I could see that it was a Native person, and when he got real close, I could see that he had a big smile on his face." The smiling man was Simon Paneak, whose band of Nunamiut was camped at the north end of the lake. To Wien's surprise, Simon spoke English. The two talked for nearly an hour. Simon explained that they traded at the Northern Commercial Company store in Fairbanks and that they even had a credit account there. They were low on ammunition and supplies, he said, but had furs to trade for those items. With this meeting began a long-term relationship between "Sigwien," as the Nunamiut called him, and the people who were, a few years later, to settle in Anaktuvuk Pass. Wien resupplied the Nunamiut at Chandler many times, taking their furs in his plane back to Fairbanks.

On one of those resupply trips in the 1940s, Wien remembered, Simon Paneak said the Nunamiut would like to locate in a permanent place where their children could get schooling and where they might gather to worship once in awhile. The area around Anaktuvuk Pass would be good, Simon believed, because there were ample willows in the valley for fuel. "So," remarked Wien, "it was decided that we would try to work it out." Wien contacted the Bureau of Indian Affairs in Juneau about providing schoolteachers and offered the services of Wien Alaska Airways to fly the teachers and their supplies in. The first teachers pitched their tents and set up school in the summer of 1947 at Tulugak Lake in the Anaktuvuk Valley, where Simon's band had camped for the summer.

The following summer, 1948, brought several scientists into the Anaktuvuk Valley from Barrow's Arctic Research Laboratory. They were there to study everything from bird and insect life of the Brooks Range to Nunamiut dentition. They came by plane and were supplied by plane. The increased air traffic into the Anaktuvuk area made it possible for the Nunamiut to order supplies, particularly foodstuffs and ammunition, on a more regular basis. Several families would pool their orders so that they might charter a plane. The arrival in 1949 of Pat O'Connell, who set up a small trading post at the pass, contributed to the increased frequency of air service to the area, but it was the application for a post office, which was granted in 1951, that clinched regular air service to Anaktuvuk Pass and resulted in the eventual settlement of the Nunamiut. For a decade the weekly mail plane landed on the open water or the ice of Summit Lake, and then in 1960 Sig Wien staked out a landing field, and a bulldozer, brought in overland from Umiat on the Colville River, carved a strip out of the glacial gravel just north of the headwaters of the John River.

From the beginning, the airplane extended the Nunamiut's grasp of their own country. The first questions an arriving pilot would be asked were, "Did you see any caribou? How many sheep did you see?" The airplane and its supporting technology, in time, also provided new artifacts for the enterprising Nunamiut. The traditional caribou-skin tent might have, instead of bear gut, a plastic window from an airplane sewn into it, and its furnishings would surely include Blazo—airplane fuel—boxes serving as cupboards, shelves, and tabletop supports.

From its first appearance the airplane brought medical assistance, transporting the sick and ailing to Fairbanks. Older villagers remember with sadness parents and other relatives who died in the 1930s and 1940s because "No airplane or anything like that. No medicine." "Today," they counter, "if anybody's sick around here, no matter in the nighttime, an airplane coming in, pick 'em up." A fully medically equipped Beechcraft KingAir, dispatched from Barrow, medivacs patients needing emergency treatment from Anaktuvuk Pass to the hospital in Fairbanks.

Medically speaking, at first the airplane may have been a mixed blessing, for while it brought the sick to medical treatment, it also brought sickness to the Nunamiut. Helge Ingstad, the Norwegian amateur anthropologist who lived with the Nunamiut for several months in 1949, reported that after an airplane landed at Tulugak Lake, where the Nunamiut were camped, the entire population came down with influenza, and four of them died.

Like people everywhere Anaktuvuk villagers remember their first flights. In 1951 four village men were flown to Fairbanks, where they served as test subjects for cold adaptation and endurance studies at the Air Force's Ladd Aeromedical Laboratory. What Justus Mekiana, one of the four, remembers about his first flight was how his fellow passengers leaned with the plane as it turned.

For a number of young villagers, first flights were traumatic as they journeyed to new country and a life away from their families at boarding school. Doris Hugo took her first airplane ride in 1952 with several others from the village to attend Mt. Edgecumbe School in Sitka. "So scary, I get sick, sick all the way through," she remembered. "Eh, sure was hate to fly." Doris's younger sister Rachel Riley remembered her first helicopter ride in 1962. "They let us have a ride for fifteen minutes. Sure scare us around every time we start to go up and start to go down. We always start to scream and holler our heads off."

A few villagers, like Simon Paneak, had a more serious interest in flight. Dave Rose, a pilot from California, first came to Anaktuvuk Pass in his private plane in 1963, and he returned numerous times after that. He became friends with Simon Paneak and carried on a correspondence with him for many years. When he visited Anaktuvuk he took Simon flying with him. Arriving on his second trip to the pass, Rose found a barrel of aviation gas with his name on it waiting on the airstrip. Simon had purchased it for him. "Then I knew we were going to be doing some flying," the pilot said. Rose instructed Simon about the general behavior and the controls of small planes.

And from that moment when I turned the controls over to him, I realized that he had a perfect sense of coordination between aileron control and rudder control. It took no second mentioning, so he must have observed me very closely on previous flights. From then on, I let him fly wherever he wanted to go. He knew how many hours and minutes we had of fuel, and when we had to be back. After a number of flights over several years, I just knew he had the capability of landing. So one day I asked him whether he thought he could land it. We were already on a long final approach to the field, into the wind. Everything was perfect for a landing, and so I sat back and he landed the airplane all by himself.

Simon, Rose added, liked simple aerobatics. "I think he did not like the spins, but he did love to loop the thing and he looped it many times, either right near the village or when we were on the North Slope. Particularly when there were some people on the ground who were camping out there and he knew them, he would loop the plane." "Simon Paneak," mused pilot Rose, "was the perfect student."

Both Simon Paneak and Homer Mekiana, the village postmaster, recorded in their journals the comings and goings of airplanes, their passengers, and cargo of note. Among those passengers, of course, were anthropologists, beginning with Jack Campbell in 1956. Three summers later, Ed Hall, having just completed his freshman year of college, made his first flight to Anaktuvuk Pass in a Cessna 180 on skis, piloted by Andy Anderson of Wien Airlines. The plane landed on the rotting June ice at Summit Lake, and Ed enthused in his journal, "Having never been in a small plane, I was kind of wondering but the first five minutes sold me completely. What a beautiful flight." After that, Ed flew in small planes and helicopters every chance he got.

One summer—we're back to the folklore now—when Ed and I and Meryn were headed to Anaktuvuk for research, we left from Kotzebue, where we had met up after a month of separate travels. We could have taken a scheduled flight from Kotzebue to Fairbanks and another from Fairbanks to Anaktuvuk Pass, but that wasn't Ed's idea of airplane travel. It was the journey that mattered. So he chartered a plane from Kotzebue to Anaktuvuk. It was a single-engine four-seater, probably a Cessna 185, though I didn't note the make and model. I only remember that it was cramped and the flight was interminable. On my lap I held the frozen sheefish we'd purchased in Kotzebue, and the pilot, who'd never been to Anaktuvuk before, held on his lap a set of navigation maps. Ed, the navigator for this adventure, guided the pilot on several detours, including a circuit around Walker Lake. It was a Friday, and hours later, when we finally landed in Anaktuvuk Pass, the village store had closed for the weekend, the sheefish had thawed, and Meryn threw up as we touched down on the runway.

Had we arrived thirty years before, our flight too might have ended up in Homer Mekiana's journal of airplane comings and goings. Homer, in his chronicles, noted not only the mundane arrivals of aircraft, but also the first time something new flew into Anaktuvuk Pass. Like the boxcar plane that brought in a huge fuel oil tank for the school in August 1962, and the first four-engine plane to come to the village, which brought fuel in August 1967. That flight was indeed significant, for up to that time villagers had depended on arctic willows for fuel, which, by 1967, they had exhausted. After much debate, the village council voted to remain in Anaktuvuk Pass rather than relocate to some more accessible site, and the Bureau of Indian Affairs agreed to supply fuel oil for a time. Today fuel oil comes in on the same planes that Homer saw.

One summer when my parents visited us in Anaktuvuk, my father and I hiked down to the airstrip to watch the DC-6 fuel plane, which had just arrived. We stood by the fence, talking, watching the silver behemoth pump its load of petroleum through the big hose that snaked across the runway apron to the tank farm. I was reminded of trips we made to the Indianapolis airport during my childhood to watch the planes take off and land. I had my camcorder with me to record the fuel plane's takeoff and flight. Finally, its four engines revved up; gravel and dust billowed from the wash of its propellers, and slowly the big *tiŋŋun* roared down the airstrip. The DC-6 requires little runway to lift off but it lumbers heavily into the air. We watched it climb ever so slowly, turning and inching up over the mountains, like some winged dinosaur. "It's a great plane," my father said, adding with a chuckle, "there goes my tail." I never knew until that day that he had designed the tail on the DC-6.

Tiŋŋun, airplane—"some thing by which to fly." What did the Nunamiut believe it was that made it fly? Did they know about how air flows over and under the wings? I recall a small wooden figure of a shaman from Point Hope, made to hang suspended in midair from the ceiling of the dance house. His neck cranes upward to the sky, one knee is raised, the other leg arched backward as if he is pushing off to leap into the air. (Actually, according to the story told by the carver, the shaman flew that way, from Siberia, with one leg crooked.) Instead of arms he has outstretched wings. Most noteworthy, though, are his closed eyes and the simple smile that creases his face. In his trance he soars. Is this the carver's dream? Is it the dream of us all? In a culture where humans and animals crossed the line between species, pulling back their animal hoods to reveal their human selves and vice versa, the shaman's trance seems the ultimate transformation—to move effortlessly from the earth to the sky.

I have dreams about flying in big airplanes, and they are always unsettling. We are out of place, taxiing down some city street, landing on an interstate highway, flying too low. I also have dreams about flying under my own power. These are exhilarating and magical. No double plastic window constrains my view. I know where I am, I feel every current of air, and I decide where I go. I soar, bank, hover. I see things that I would never know from the ground, including the edge of the earth. This is the ultimate journey.

"Flight's greatest gift," writes author and pilot William Langewiesche in his collection of essays *Inside the Sky*, "is to let us look around, and when we do we discover that the world is larger than we have been told and that our wings have helped to make it so."

Dispatches from the Field

Lela Ahgook and Margaret Blackman. Photo by Judith Gussler.

It may be home, but no one is born in Anaktuvuk Pass any more, or anywhere nearby if it can be helped. Since the 1960s, the Indian Health Service has sent pregnant village women to Fairbanks three weeks before their due dates to assure that they get to the hospital, and medical care, in time to deliver.

Life's final passage is a different matter. Villagers come back to Anaktuvuk Pass to die. Like the village woman who left many years ago to marry a man from a coastal village and who returned as an old woman when she was diagnosed with terminal cancer. Sick as she was on her homeward journey—she died a few weeks later—she began singing and Eskimo dancing from her airplane seat as soon as the Anaktuvuk Valley came into view.

I'm alone for the first time in the nearly thirty years that I've been doing field research as an anthropologist. For most of the eight trips I've made to Anaktuvuk Pass, I was with Ed and Meryn, then just with Meryn, then with a student. This summer, 1999, I've come alone. Meryn, now sixteen, has insisted on staying home. With a new driver's license and a car, a boyfriend, and a summer job, what teenager would want to accompany her mother to a tiny, "boring" village in northern Alaska? Although I ensconce an adult in the house to supervise, Meryn is still wondrously free and no doubt relishing my absence more than I am hers. We are in touch—by e-mail and by phone when I can get to a village pay phone and am lucky enough to reach a live voice instead of my own on our answering machine.

The project that has brought me back is the nearly fifty-year-old village tradition of making caribou-skin masks for sale. The masks have been an economic mainstay of most village families at one time or another. Today not as many villagers make masks as once did; the nation's economy is strong here, too, with a plenitude of temporary capital improvement jobs paying high wages. In the three weeks that I'll be here, I'll interview villagers who make or have made masks and photograph them and their art. It's a straightforward project that has the endorsement of the city council and the North Slope Borough, which has helped fund my research.

I made arrangements for living in the village with unprecedented ease and efficiency; it took only one e-mail and one phone call. Two summers ago, after spending several nights in my new tent at the west edge of the village, I discovered that the school district rented unoccupied teacher housing to researchers engaged in broadly defined educational projects. In short order, I went from hauling water, cooking on a Coleman stove in the rain, and living in a tent that I couldn't stand up in to a small carpeted apartment with a La-Z-Boy lounger, cable TV, fully equipped kitchen, and a washer and dryer. I could hardly believe my good fortune, especially following several previous summers of securing at the last minute an unoccupied village house with no running water and no refrigerator.

My apartment, one half of an arctic-insulated duplex, is just steps across the road from the Nunamiut School, where I have been given access to a computer that gets me to the Web and my e-mail account back home. Two years ago I wasn't sure I wanted daily e-mail contact with family and friends from the field. This year, there's no question about it. I do.

My first morning in the village I dash up the arctic grating on the school stairs, walk down the hall to the science room, and turn on the computer. I spend almost an hour sending and answering e-mail. Two mornings later I am rewarded with an e-mail from Meryn; I save it till last to read. "Not much happening here," she begins and then tells me roughly what I expect to hear regarding her activities. What I don't anticipate is the last line: "By the way, I got my nose pierced. :)"

I remember a discussion we had in which I acknowledged that I found pierced noses less objectionable than pierced tongues, and I distinctly remember saying to Meryn that if she wanted to pierce anything other than her ears to please wait until she was eighteen and in college. My reply is immediate but measured: we will discuss the matter when I return home. Before I can hear from her again, the local server goes down, to remain out of commission until a replacement circuit board can be flown in from Anchorage. Sometimes the bush is still remote. Trying not to feel sorry for myself, I imagine Margaret Mead during her first field research in Samoa in the 1920s, thrilled to get mail once every six weeks when the boat came in.

I had carefully timed my arrival in Anaktuvuk Pass to be after the World Eskimo-Indian Olympics, an annual Fairbanks athletic and dance competition that draws Native villagers from all over Alaska. But I soon learned that nineteen members of one of Anaktuvuk's dance groups—people I needed to interview—were going to Whitehorse, Yukon, for a week. And one person I desperately wanted to interview had been in Fairbanks since before I came up. When I asked when she might be returning, I was told "before school starts." To make matters worse, just as I was arriving, one of the two museum curators was leaving for ten days. Most of the people I needed to talk with were headed out of town!

As a field anthropologist one can't have too much patience or flexibility. I'm a bit short on both, so I respond to the situation by doing what I do best: making lists. I make a list of whom I might reasonably interview before they leave for Whitehorse. I make a list of what I will do while they're gone (write an essay, take photos around the village, pick berries, hitch a tour of the village on the tourist van, spend time in the museum library, work on my courses for the fall, read the two novels, one nonfiction work, and two collections of essays I've brought). My lists work their magic: my week's schedule is full. I don't include watching CNN on my list, but I do a lot of that anyway.

My predicament is partly due to how anthropological research is conducted these days. The increasing ease of travel, the improvement of communications technology, the multiple demands on our time, and the growth of applied research have led to shorter and more frequent trips to the field. The yearlong or longer stays are still de rigueur for PhD dissertation research, but returning anthropologists, especially those who don't work halfway round the world from home, are doing more and more of what I call "hit and run" ethnography. I know I am. All of my work here has been like that— six weeks, a month, three weeks. And because I'm here so briefly I run the risk of missing some interviews altogether, not to mention events and even whole seasons. But doing a longer stint of fieldwork is no guarantee that the research will go smoothly or that everything will get accomplished. The washeteria or store or museum can still be closed when the sign says it should be open; the camping trip you were invited on can be put off for several days or maybe permanently because the Argo isn't working and the store has no parts; an interviewee can have something more pressing to do than the scheduled interview, and some people may never concede to an interview no matter how long you stay.

The first two days I walk around the village, taking in the changes, stopping to say hello to villagers on the streets, knocking on doors to visit people I know well. I manage to set up four interviews before the dance group's departure to Whitehorse.

This year I bought two lapel microphones, which provide better and clearer sound than the single stereo mike I was accustomed to using. The latter met its Waterloo at the washeteria when I tried to interview soft-spoken manager Doris Hugo over the jet propulsion sound of the water extractor and the innocent gurgle of her coffee maker. The lapel mikes are also good for interviewees like Doris whose voices trail off into nothingness at the end of a sentence or who occasionally look away from the microphone when talking. I spend several minutes testing the new mikes and set the record volume on the tape recorder appropriately. I toss this equipment into my backpack along with an extension cord, an extra tape, and my notebook of interview questions and set off for Justus and Ethel Mekiana's house.

"You interview him first," Ethel instructs, "He start it all." She gestures with a nod of her head, "He's across the road, you go get him." I find Justus, almost hidden from view in the willows and fading fireweed blooms, working on a sled that he's hoping the museum will buy. I hate to interrupt his work but he indicates that he's ready to be interviewed. It's an easy interview, and

Justus, as usual, is thoughtful and careful in what he has to say. All goes well until Justus gets up to fetch a cardboard template that he's telling me about. He's forgotten that he's tethered to my machine by the lapel mike. I hastily unplug it and put the machine on "pause." When he returns with the template, I plug his mike back in and we resume talking. Ten minutes later I look with horror to the idled tape in the recorder. I had forgotten to release the pause button! I confess my error to Justus, and with the tape rolling again, we try to reconstruct the lost ten minutes.

I interview Ethel after Justus. The mikes appear to work flawlessly. That night, as I'm turning in, I review the day's events and am suddenly stricken with the realization that I never plugged the tape recorder in to an outlet. For two hours it ran on battery power, on batteries that I last used two years ago when I played a demonstration tape to my research methods class. I know from having watched the gauge that the batteries were working during the interviews, but will Justus, Ethel, and I sound like ourselves or like Alvin and the Chipmunks? I can't believe that after having done hundreds of hours of interviews I'm still making dumb mistakes like this. Should I ease my mind and go listen to the tapes now, or wait till morning? If I've ruined the tapes, I won't sleep for sure. I leave them till morning.

Thankfully, the tapes of Justus and Ethel came out just fine, but by the time I head to the village washeteria the next morning, Doris Hugo has already heard from Justus about the problem I had with the mikes and the pause button. So, she helps me remember them each time she has to interrupt our recording session. Which is several times, as she goes to answer the pay phone on the wall across from us and turns to give customers change and soap for the washing machines.

The washeteria is a social place. People who come to do their laundry visit with Doris and each other, and small children trail after their mothers. This morning the only child in the washeteria is one unhappy little boy who lets us all know it in no uncertain terms. His anguish will be a real test of my new microphones. I remember this time to plug in the machine. We turn down the cb radio and begin the interview.

I had interviewed Doris a few years ago about mask making, but there is always more to be learned. I wish the Halloween mask with the caribou ears that she made for one of her kids was still around. "It really look like caribou," she laughed. Like some other homemade Halloween masks, it was purchased by one of the schoolteachers.

I am especially eager to interview Doris's husband Zacharias, who, in 1951, made the very first skin masks used at a holiday dance. Ed and I had tried to interview him for several years about his memories of walking to Anaktuvuk Pass to settle here in 1949. Zach's answer to our request was invariably the same: "If I'm around." He never seemed to be, and we never got the interview.

When I saw Zach the other evening and told him about my project, I couldn't help laughing when he responded with the expected, "If I'm around" to my request for an interview. At the washeteria, after our interview, Doris has advice for me. "He's coming back from Whitehorse before I do because he's got to go to work. He'll be bored. You go talk to him then."

After my interview with Doris I run into Ruth Rulland at the village store. She is available for an interview after lunch, so at 2 P.M. I go to her house. She clears a place at the kitchen table for my tape recorder, and I remember to ask her to turn down the CB. I've never interviewed Ruth before, but I like sitting at her kitchen table in a patch of sunshine, being the audience for the broad smile she wears as she talks about making masks. She tells me about a mask she made with a long, white caribou-hair beard that she placed on a Santa figure in her basket sled and put in front of the house. It won a Christmas decorating contest the village held a few years back. But, like the skin Halloween masks that Nunamiut mothers made for their children in the years before you could buy Halloween masks at the village store, Ruth's Santa mask has disappeared.

Ruth gathers up the wooden mask molds she uses for making her skin masks and tells me about each of them. As I am laying the molds out in the sunny doorway to photograph, a young grandson and his three friends jump over them on their way out the door with the two dollars Ruth has given them to buy Pepsis. Next I photograph Ruth standing and holding two of the molds, that same broad smile creasing her face. I wish her a good trip to Whitehorse as I leave.

The group going to Whitehorse is meeting tonight for last-minute instructions, but there's time before dinner to visit Lela and Noah Ahgook, whom I've seen only briefly in the store when I first arrived. Lela is in the back room that she uses for sewing. A box of partly completed masks sits on the floor, and she is hunkered over her new sewing machine, making a summer dance parka for a grandson. She's trying to finish it in time for tomorrow's departure for Whitehorse, but the machine isn't stitching properly. We visit while dismantling the machine and poring over the instruction booklet. Noah, as always, teases me. "No more Nunamiut Experience," he admonishes, referring to our camping trips by Argo. "You walk." And, "Your turn to take me to New York."

Lela decides to phone the shop in Fairbanks where she bought the sewing machine. "I'm gonna let you talk to him," she says, thrusting the phone at me. I have my doubts that the snaggled stitching can be resolved over the telephone, but sure enough, the problem is the upper thread tension, just like the shopkeeper says it is. Happily, Lela returns to her sewing, finishing the parka in just a few minutes. "I'll work with you, Margaret, when I get back," she promises, adding that she'll even teach me how to make masks.

My research here seems full of promise when I leave Lela and Noah's and return to my apartment to cook dinner.

On Wednesday I am at the airstrip when the second planeload of White-horse-goers departs. I wish them a good trip, but what really brings me here is an invitation to take the tourist excursion of the village. Although tourists still straggle here in small numbers (just under a thousand had signed up for tours in the summer of 1999), the tour has changed since I wrote about it in 1992. It's now run by a Fairbanks-based tour company. Subscribers start out in Fairbanks in the early morning and head north up the Dalton Highway, or "haul road," which leads to Prudhoe Bay. They cross the Yukon River and the Arctic Circle, visit a homestead, and from a pipeline station fly into Anaktuvuk Pass in the late afternoon. In Anaktuvuk the tourists are met by a van and resident tour guide. They spend about an hour and a half in the village before the return flight to Fairbanks. The guide for the last two summers, Sarah McConnell, is a former social worker from Fairbanks with a savvy sense of community outreach and a pied piper touch with the village kids, who crowd into the tourist van whenever they can hitch a ride. Today's twelve guests include three generations of an Indian family from Nairobi now living in Chattanooga; the others are from Argentina, Austria, and Australia. They listen attentively to Sarah's commentary as she drives around the village, and, like most Outsiders who venture here, they find this a scenic and friendly place. "This looks just like a movie set," exclaims one woman, looking first at the façade of the Nunamiut Corp store, then at the imposing mountains. "Imagine, to see the tundra," enthuses the Indian grandmother. "Even in my country we read about the tundra in geography, but to actually see it . . ."

Emily Hugo, whom I first met as a four-year-old, is now one of the several youth tour guides who assist Sarah, taking the "visitors"—never "tourists"— on walking tours of the village. The Native hosts are shy and speak quietly with downcast eyes, but they gradually warm to the visitors' inquiries about their village and their lives. Sarah looks forward to the day the tour will be completely in the hands of Anaktuvuk guides.

The museum, the cemetery, the store, the school, the community hall. They take it all in in less than two hours. Some days visitors might be lucky to catch one of the three Anaktuvuk Pass dance groups practicing in the community hall, or a mask maker might be persuaded to come and demonstrate mask making. Like everything else here, the tour is flexible.

Thursday. The day I locate and schedule interviews with the few mask makers who haven't gone to Whitehorse. At the top of my list is Bob Ahgook, who along with Zacharias Hugo made the first skin masks in 1951 that inspired the tourist art. I find him at coffee break, along with several others, in the community hall. I chat with everybody, about the weather, about how Ed is faring, about Meryn (I get a lot of mileage out of the nose piercing). "What brings you up here?" Bob gives me my opening. I tell him about the mask project, that I am interviewing mask makers and would like to talk to him as well. "If I have time," he chuckles, complaining, "How many more times do I have to talk about this?" "This is the last time," I promise, "I'll put it in a book so you won't have to tell it again." I ask if it's best to try him at home or here at the community hall. "This is the best place to catch him," the others gloat, "right here on the couch, drinking coffee." I try to pin Bob down as the others amble back to work after coffee break, and he allows as how home is better than the office. I tell him I'll stop by soon. "If I have time," he calls after me. Bob is as jovial, and as elusive, as Zach. Maybe the photo of the two of them holding that first mask taken at the village's recent fiftieth anniversary celebration is as close as I'll get to the story.

How different ethnographic interviewing was for some of the founders of anthropology. A. R. Radcliffe-Brown, a British social anthropologist working in the early twentieth century in the Andaman Islands of India, had a sure-fire technique for getting his informants when he wanted them. If they didn't show for a scheduled interview, he sent the police to round them up! I imagine that by the end of next week the old colonial anthropology will hold a certain appeal. Back at my apartment, I eat lunch to CNN's unrelenting coverage of a stock market day trader turned mass murderer in Atlanta. That evening I take a sauna at the washeteria and call home, but Meryn is not there.

Friday. The server is still down at the school and the defective parts on order, so it will be Monday at the earliest before I can check my e-mail. I go the museum and browse through their library for a while, but they are closing early today and I am left with time on my hands. I head down the hill to my apartment to write.

There is something else that has delayed my work. In the late hours of Thursday night, an elderly woman in the village died. She had not lived here for many years, but when her cancer was diagnosed as terminal she came home to die. A daughter has gone to Fairbanks to select a coffin, the family has chosen the gravesite, and village men are digging the grave. Her niece is one of the museum curators, and that is why the museum closed early today. Two of her siblings who did not go with the others to Whitehorse are mask makers I want to interview, but that will have to wait until after the funeral.

Late Friday afternoon. Trying to figure out what I can do to fight the in-evitable boredom that is settling in besides taking a shower at the washeteria or watching yet more CNN, I grab the soured milk from the fridge and head to the store for a refund. At the store, a young Native woman, whom I don't know, catches my attention. It isn't so much her bright orange hair that I notice but the big, shiny rhinestone stud in her left nostril. I wonder if Meryn's looks like that, and which nostril did she pierce anyway?

Saturday. I learn that the funeral will probably be Monday. I've already decided to spend the entire weekend writing, and I begin, with relish, after breakfast. I switch off CNN, put a musical tape in my interviewing tape recorder, and settle into the La-Z-Boy lounger with my laptop.

And I saw lightning in the sacred mountains, saw the dance of the turtledove when I was lying next to Katie on that old Navajo rug, Tom Russell sings in one of his cowboy stories, and I imagine myself in seclusion at a writers' retreat like Yaddo or MacDowell, looking out a dormered window onto manicured grounds, ancient trees, and formal gardens. My only obligation is to write.

Reality is a city bus that makes the rounds of this village of former nomads every 15 minutes from 7 A.M. to 10 P.M. five days a week. The bus brakes to a dusty stop before each of the three stop signs erected back in 1990. The Nunamiut expressed their sentiments about these signs of civilization by using them for target practice. Five years later the street signs appeared.

I have often wondered about the street names. I found them on a North Slope Borough map of the village from 1994, a year before the actual signs were put up. I don't know who bestowed these names. The Anaktuvuk Pass city council? The North Slope Borough? I only know what a shock it was to see the standard-issue green street signs with their anywhere names against a backdrop of tundra and mountains. Every town has its "Main Street," and Airport Way logically leads straight to the gravel airstrip at the east edge of the village. "Summer" Street is more problematic. It's an unusual name for a street in a place where it's mostly winter. Maybe the name is wishful thinking.

My personal favorite is the intersection of Maptegak and Illinois Streets. Old Morry Maptegak was the head of one of the large Nunamiut families, an outstanding hunter, and a runner reputed to be able to run with the wolves. It seems fitting, if you must have street names in this wilderness place, to call them after your own people. But why Illinois Street, I asked a resident the first summer the signs appeared. "Maybe because of the Chicago Bulls," she suggested. Everyone's a basketball fan in Anaktuvuk Pass, and during Michael Jordan's reign, the Nunamiut were all crazy for the Bulls. Another possibility suggests itself. If you follow Illinois Street west you come to Minnie Street. In Fairbanks, 250 air miles away, Minnie Street also runs right into Illinois Street. Beyond the memorable landmarks of two liquor stores and Sampson's hardware at the Fairbanks intersection, I'm not sure what inspired this borrowing of street names, especially since the Nunamiut never give a street reference in conversation, as in: "He's over on Maptegak Street." He isn't. "He's over by Pat and them." But street signs and names are a necessary part of being a legally designated "city." And, like the house numbers that were nailed up on house fronts at the same time, they belong on the mental maps of the non-Native police force.

The village is relatively quiet on the weekends. No honeybucket truck, water delivery truck, or village bus circles the village streets. The gravel trucks that deliver gravel to the several construction sites are stilled as well. Once when I glance up from my writing I see an Argo full of teenagers, each with a fishing rod, headed toward Iñupuq, or Giant, Creek and the John River for an evening of fishing. I work steadily until nearly 11 P.M., then put on my boots, grab a Ziploc bag, and hike up on the ridge below Oka Mountain to pick blueberries in the fiery pink of the setting sun.

Here on dry rocky ground where the arctic blueberries grow, I'm outside the village, looking at it from a distance. That's the anthropologist's gaze— looking in from the outside, all the while trying to understand from the inside. It is an odd kind of double vision. Most anthropologists not only have a great deal of regard for the cultures they study but many of my generation did their first fieldwork at a time when dissatisfaction with mainstream American culture and all it represented ran deep. Which may explain why more than one anthropologist has described themselves as marginal to their own culture.

While we may admire and respect the cultures we study, we can't belong to them and still maintain the kind of objectivity that anthropology demands. Not that we would necessarily be offered admittance in any case. We are left, at a certain remove, to learn and to wonder how the natives perceive us. Not always positively, we know from the widely circulated jokes natives tell about us ("The typical Navajo family comprises parents, children, a grandparent or two, and an anthropologist") or from the tongue-in-cheek description of the anthropologist immortalized thirty years ago in Vine Deloria's *Custer Died for Your Sins*:

> Go into any crowd of people. Pick out a tall gaunt white man wear-
> ing Bermuda shorts, a World War II Army Air Force flying jacket,
> an Australian bush hat, tennis shoes, and packing a large knapsack
> incorrectly strapped on his back. He will invariably have a thin sexy
> wife with stringy hair, an IQ of 191, and a vocabulary in which even the
> prepositions have eleven syllables. (78)

The uncertainty of marginality cuts both ways. Do people here see me as the hit-and-run ethnographer, visiting only with a mission ("What brings you here"?), leaving just when I've collected the data I want? On the other hand, am I a good enough anthropologist: Am I collecting enough information? Am I gregarious enough? Should I even be writing essays when I could be knocking on someone's door begging for an interview?

Fortunately, like some other areas of life, this anthropological soul-searching becomes less wrenching with time. I know that not every response I get from a villager, especially a reproach, is about me. The perceived slights and the disappointments roll off a bit easier now than they did when I wrote an anguished letter from the field to Ed (at that time, my dissertation adviser) nearly thirty years ago decrying the rebuffs I experienced, my intruder status, and being classed with all the nonanthropologists who came and, so quickly and erroneously, wrote about the people I had worked with all those months. In the long run, I suspect we anthropologists don't figure nearly as importantly in the lives of the people we work with as all the soul-searching we do might lead us to believe.

My blueberry picking hasn't kept pace with my racing thoughts. It's late, nearly 1 A.M., becoming twilight. I trudge down the hill with my small bag of berries to the village and bed.

Sunday. The beginning of the new week. The gnawing loneliness is gone. I am finally thriving in the absence of demands on my time and attention. I have no CB, no phone, and no e-mail contact. I come and go as I please, eat, sleep, and visit as I feel like it. I still haven't talked to Meryn, but I know she's OK. I've finished an essay, and it's too soon to worry about whether I'll complete my research by the time I have to leave. I like this freedom.

Monday. The funeral. My "freedom" doesn't last long. I did not look forward to this event and fret most of the morning over it. Funerals are emotionally wrenching anyway, especially with the body right there surrounded by weeping relatives, and they are socially awkward if you never knew the person. Nonetheless, the whole village attends, and attending is the proper thing to do. Moreover, rites of passage are the stuff of anthropology, so any fieldworker worth his or her salt goes. At 1:00 P.M., two young girls knock on the door to my apartment and ask if I am going to the funeral. They're going to look at the body they say, which is in the school gym. I follow them. At the door to the gym two teens are handing out a program of the service. I take a seat in the bleachers and begin reading the program. Villagers file into the gym, filling the bleachers.

The open coffin, a plain, light mauve metal casket with white satin liner, is prominently centered on the gym floor. Jane, the deceased, is dressed in a simple dark, mannish suit, her gray hair pulled straight back. Oddly, her mouth is open, as if she might have some last words to say. During my early fieldwork on the Queen Charlotte Islands in British Columbia, I attended several funerals and learned that the women of the church bathed and dressed the body. I don't know who does that here. Perhaps her sisters, who cared for her during her last days.

The coffin rests on a box stand that is covered with artificial grass. The Nunamiut gospel singers, an informal choir, take their seats in the four rows of chairs behind the coffin, and the white woman minister joins them. Off to the side, two guitarists strum gospel songs. Jane's large extended family fills the three of rows of chairs on the bleacher side of the coffin.

Villagers are filing past the coffin, and I join them. The funeral plays out in a lengthy series of speeches, Bible readings, and gospel songs, all of which largely follow the printed program. What strikes me, though, is how much a part of the event the kids are. Most of them, I'm sure, never knew Jane, but they all file by her coffin, some with tears in their eyes. The older kids hug members of the family. One little girl stands on tiptoe reaching up to put her hands on the satin padding of the coffin. She peers in at Jane for several moments. And a grandson—or great-grandson—of Jane's walks around and around the closed coffin during the service, patting its top, feeling the cold smoothness of the metal lid.

At the end of the very long service, the minister announces that, at the family's request, the coffin will be opened for a last viewing. She adds that she isn't comfortable with this but is honoring the family's request. It does seem unusual, according to church protocol, but after all, it is their family member. Why is the minister uncomfortable? Is God supposed to take over once the lid is closed?

Villagers collect outside the school to walk the half-mile to the village cemetery for the burial. On the school steps I greet Rosie, one of Jane's sisters. "How's Ed doing?" she asks. "Too bad he's not well, " she says, "or we could tease him like we used to." Behind her, in his old blue suit and clip-on tie, is her brother Johnny. He's smiling, like he always does. I reintroduce myself, but he draws a blank. "Ed Hall—" I jog his memory. His smile returns: "Oh, Ed Hall's used-to-be wife."

The caravan of walkers, Argos, trucks, and four-wheelers makes its way to the cemetery, following the coffin, which rests on the bed of a pickup truck. Villagers spread out among the graves. Young Kate Hugo takes a wind-mill she made in Bible school and announces that she is placing it on her father's—Willie Hugo's—grave. Little Aminilla Hugo scrutinizes the head and foot markers of her great-grandmother's—Jane's mother's—grave, and, lying down beside them, compares heights.

Two and a half hours go by as the coffin is lowered and the grave filled.

Jane rests beside her parents and not far from her teenaged son, who was buried here in 1991. Village men, joined by the women of the deceased's family, shovel the soggy earth into the grave. Villagers sit on nearby graves to watch the proceedings and they chat with one another. I end up sitting beside Ada, another of Jane's sisters. She can't help telling me a story about Ed. "People couldn't believe he was Ed Hall *Junior*. We only use 'junior' for little kids here. People saw Ed Hall walking around with a pack on his back and they said, 'He can't be junior, he's too big!' "

Some villagers hold fistfuls of plastic flowers, which they throw on top of the coffin before the last of the earth is shoveled in. Young men fetch buckets of fine gravel to spread on the grave. The kids stay throughout, helping to stomp the dirt and gravel onto the grave. Big blocks of sod are cut and placed. The kids help stomp that in place, too. The adults join in as well. Anna Hugo—mimicking the men's foot-stomping dance performances—dances a big clump of sod in place. As the grave is filled in and sodded over, villagers' moods lift.

Mine as well. Thinking ahead to the coming week of interviews, I suddenly remember Meryn at age two, when she was with her father and me as we worked on a project here in the village. We were interviewing subsistence hunters about all-terrain vehicle use, and she accompanied us on most of the interviews. As we zipped her into her parka one November morning, she exclaimed excitedly, "Oh boy, let's go anthropology!"

Fifty Years in One Place

Walking toward Giant Creek.

*In truth, the isolation and self-containment of Anaktuvuk Pass
are more illusion than reality. The settlement of the Alaska Native
Land Claims in 1971, and the establishment of a regional government in 1972, brought rapid changes to the village in the mountains. By the late 1970s, the village had arctic prefab housing, electricity, CB radios, satellite TV, and telephone service. What doesn't
belong to the Borough belongs to Nunamiut Corporation. It owns
the cable TV service, the fuel oil and propane distributorships, the
village store, and "camp," a jumble of mobile units at the south end
of the village.*

*By Alaskan standards, Anaktuvuk Pass is a "second-class city"
and, though it sits in the "middle of nowhere," it is one of eight
such "cities" in the North Slope Borough, the largest of Alaska's
twelve counties. The North Slope Borough is the least populated of
Alaska's regional governments, but it has as its tax base no less than
the developments at oil-rich Prudhoe Bay. Capital improvement
programs, police protection, water and sanitation services, housing
subsidies, a state-of-the-art school, a small museum—indeed, the
very quality of life in Anaktuvuk Pass—are directly traceable to the
Borough's presence. The North Slope Borough is also the principal
employer in the region, and, without it, it is difficult to imagine a
viable village here today.*

Anaktuvuk Pass is a village on the go. In 1997 the village had just begun
a 17.5-million-dollar water and sewer project that promised running water
and flush toilets to every village house by 2000. In the summer of 1999, you
can't escape the ear-rattling construction noise and the fog of dust that trails
the huge gravel trucks. To my astonishment, there's so much traffic that you
actually have to look before you cross the street.

I couldn't make the fiftieth anniversary celebration held in June, six weeks
before I arrived for my summer fieldwork. By all accounts it was marked
with great fanfare. Researchers and former schoolteachers who hadn't been
here in years came, along with pilots who used to fly here and ministers
who used to preach here. And a Fairbanks photographer came to document
it all. They donned anniversary T-shirts and showed slides from the past
fifty years. Greeting old Nunamiut friends at the community barbecue, they
shared memories of a valley dotted with sod houses and canvas tents.

The community the anniversary guests visited is very different from the
one most of them remembered. It's not just today's prefab houses, the street
signs, the big satellite dishes and the water tower, and the handsome Nunamiut School. It's the heavy equipment and the earth-ripping construction
projects; it's the fifty years of living in one place and a growing village pop-

ulation. It's belonging to the world outside the mountain pass as well as to the one inside it. It's living a modern lifestyle in a fragile arctic environment.

In front of the village corporation's rambling trailer-unit headquarters, there is a formidable yellow lineup of heavy equipment—dozers, front loaders, excavators, gravel trucks, pieces of equipment whose names and functions I don't even know. Every piece of it brought in on c-130 cargo planes. This summer they are digging the trenches and laying the pipe from the main line to the individual homes and buildings. The water and sewer project is welcome not only for the jobs it provides but for the improvement in waste disposal it will bring. Presently, the contents of every household's toilets wait in tightly knotted, ballooned garbage bags placed in buckets by the side of the streets for pickup. The logo for the project, a honeybucket with the universal "No" symbol across it, promises change. Ironically, the trench that will bring the village museum's water supply has been dug perilously close to the back wall of an old abandoned sod house.

While excavating for the water line, the construction crew discovered contaminated earth from a fuel oil spill in 1990—significant enough that you can still smell the diesel fuel when you walk by. They've posted a notice on the local cable TV channel and in public buildings.

Dear Parents of Anaktuvuk Pass

We have found soil contaminated with diesel between the school and the washeteria. Please make sure your children do not play in this area. This is a serious health risk and can cause serious medical problems.

Thank you. AKP Constructors.

I watch a group of small boys scrambling atop the pair of fuel tanks behind the washeteria. They take turns leaping from one to the other.

The water and sewer project is not the only construction in the village this summer. An FAA study of rural Alaskan airports revealed that the Anaktuvuk Pass runway was too close to the houses, especially given the big planes that come in with cargo and fuel oil. So the federal government is funding a 3.5-million-dollar airstrip realignment that will move the mile-long gravel runway seven degrees NE/SW and eight hundred feet away from the closest houses. Pilots aren't too happy with the realignment now that the airstrip no longer runs parallel to the mountains, but the runway project has created seventy-five more jobs with a local preference hire.

As part of this project, a wide swath of arctic willows along both sides of the airstrip has been cut to the ground. To non-Arctic folks this may appear no more serious than cutting back the weeds and bushes that edge up on the nation's freeways. But these scrubby willows are twenty-year-old "trees," once fuel and flooring and frame for Nunamiut homes. "All our good willows, cut down," exclaim dismayed villagers.

A hill just northeast of town is the latest source of gravel for the various construction projects. A rough gravel road has been built to it across the spongy tundra. Late into the twilit arctic summer night, the front loaders fill the gravel trucks that rumble across this road, down a short stretch of Main Street, over a new gravel causeway spanning the creek, and along the north end of the runway, where they dump their loads. All night long one hears first the accelerating trucks, followed by their backup beeps as they release their loads, then the front loaders scooping up piles of rocks. A shatter of large rocks hits the sides of the steel feed into which they are dumped, and the constant clackata-clackata of the conveyer belt moves the gravel to the growing pile by the runway. Loaders carry the gravel to its final location on the runway, and then the graders and rollers begin their work. All night long the cacophony of the machines fills the mountain air.

The availability of the heavy equipment and the newly mined rocks have spun off another summer project. The city council voted to fill in the small lake by the washeteria where kids frequently play. A villager explained, "So far Doris never let anybody drown. She holler at them. There's two kids that almost go in last year. Falltime, little bit ice in it, they try to go on it. It's been our concern for long time."

During the day, gears grind as the huge gravel trucks groan down the road to fill in the lake. Framed by the ancient mountains on the west side of the valley, the dark circle of a tiny arctic lake turns milky, and by the end of my stay half the lake has become a field of glacial cobbles. How many thousand years has this lake been here and how long will it be before the tundra takes hold and carpets its rocky fill? Kids could just as easily drown in the icy, fast-flowing waters of Contact Creek, where they fish for grayling. Or Summit Lake, just north of town, where they swim. But this lake has been identified as a "problem" that can be solved. Before the arrival of all this earthmoving equipment at the Pass it would never have occurred to anyone to fill in a lake.

Every morning I go for a run on the Anaktuvuk airstrip. On my way I pass the Nunamiut Corp's headquarters and "hotel," where I see soapy water gurgling from the drainpipe that pokes straight out from the bathroom wall, pooling in the gravel below. That's how it is with all the houses here. Gray water drains to the floor of the valley, a sanitation problem that will be corrected when the sewer lines are finally hooked up. Today, as I turn on to the runway, a grader is smoothing gravel along its shoulder. I hurry to get past the drone and clatter and its choking exhaust fumes, continuing to the south end of the runway and the headwaters of the John River. Kids still fish for arctic grayling here in the river's braided beginnings, but since the heavy equipment has been working, parents have cautioned their children not to drink its waters.

Just to the west lies the village landfill. Sometimes, on my final trip back up the runway, I return by the access road that runs from the dump to town. Here I pass through a graveyard of old Argos, school lockers, washing machines and dryers. Doorless refrigerators, snowmobiles, and bicycle frames crowd against the dump's fence. And in its center lies all the bagged garbage that has been retrieved from dumpsters. Aside from the Argos and snowmobiles, this dump appears no different from landfills elsewhere, save its smaller size. And smells no different either. Today they are burning it. Within the village one doesn't usually smell it because garbage is supposed to be burned in a north wind, which carries the smell away from town.

The village corporation has recently approved the site for a new landfill. Not only is the present one, which is nearing capacity, located too close to the village, but it is adjacent to the airstrip, and pilots are concerned about the ravens and gulls the dump attracts. It can't be moved any farther south, or it will end up in the pristine wilderness of the Gates of the Arctic National Park. Nunamiut garbage must stay on Nunamiut land. Quite the contrary to the lower forty-eight, where garbage from major cities is sent to western Indian reservation lands leased by waste management companies who avoid state environmental protection laws by dumping on federal lands.

The new landfill will be located a few miles to the north of the village, stopping short of Kanŋuumavik, a favorite spring camping place for villagers. A gravel road to this dump, already labeled the Anaktuvuk Pass Highway on the surveyor's map, will be built from where the road now ends at the cemetery. When the project is completed, one of the most scenic mountain passes in North America will be blighted by two landfills.

"Lots of people don't feel good about it, but where can we put it?" Rachel Riley asks me. I remember several years ago when the elders were worried about the fall migration of the caribou, about making sure that nothing would cause them to turn back and find their way south through some different pass. At one time the Nunamiut were concerned about the direction from which planes approached the runway, as the noise might affect the migrating caribou. Adults remember, as children, whispering in school when the caribou were passing through. Whether these actions had any impact on caribou behavior I don't know, but they express a deep concern for how human carelessness might jeopardize the Nunamiut's very livelihood. "If we put the landfill south, caribou, springtime, comes from south," Rachel reminds me. "So it's a problem either way—unless we put it on top of the mountain," she laughs.

When I ask village elder Bob Ahgook about the landfill, he doesn't think either the noise or the smell of a landfill would deter the caribou. "Caribou stay around sometimes close to the people, then sometimes they don't. Depends on where they pick for the winter." And, he suggests, caribou have become accustomed to the fingers of civilization—like the pipeline—extending into their vast territory. "Caribou used to be real sensitive to things like big noises and all that, get scared real easy. Not any more."

Back home the environmentalists and the liberals talk about "smart growth," about strictly limiting development and suburban "sprawl," while the conservatives and businessmen talk of every American's right to a piece of the American Dream. The Nunamiut settled in the John River valley at a time when they still had the freedom to live just about anywhere that the caribou were, before this part of Alaska became a patchwork of federal, state, and privately owned lands. As their population has grown, Anaktuvuk Pass has continued to be home for the Nunamiut. Even the teenagers, sometimes bored with the insularity and slow pace of village life, will likely choose to raise their families here. Now surveyors mark new sites for future homes at the north end of the village.

As for the landfill, where in the Arctic, 250 miles from "town," do you put your garbage? Your junked snowmobiles and ATVs? Your old mattresses and broken chairs? Fifty years ago, the Nunamiut had little furniture, few tin cans, no disposable diapers, and nothing plastic. They even reloaded rifle cartridges and shotgun shells. Fifty years ago, the Nunamiut could carry their possessions on their backs and sleds, caching what they weren't using that season for later. Today, like the rest of us, they have a lot more stuff. Today they need landfills.

I've talked with Bob Ahgook about these things. He concedes, "It's everybody's problem; its gonna hurt—someday." "Someday" may be sooner rather than later. Only a couple of years before Anaktuvuk people settled into village life, Levittown, a community of seventeen thousand identical, affordable suburban homes, was built in Hempstead, New York. A solution to the post–World War II housing shortage, it became a model for suburban living. It also became a harbinger of today's unchecked sprawl. Across the United States, each year new suburban developments gobble up farmland equal in size to the state of Delaware.

Today's suburbanites are nomads of a sort, commuting farther to their jobs than they did ten or twenty years ago, spending more of their day traveling to and from work. The traffic, the length of the commute, the occasional gridlock are offset by the big, comfortable homes with their "trophy" kitchens, their entertainment rooms and Jacuzzis, where, at the end of the day, the commuters can forget the long, frustrating ride home.

The Nunamiut dilemma revolves around "real" nomadism. A village (even one with a fifty-year history) looks different to people who once covered several hundred miles in their annual food quest. Anaktuvuk Pass—the village—is where your kids and grandkids go to school, where you buy things at the store, earn your money, and get your mail. When you are in the village, your mind travels out on the land—north to Narvaksrauraq, where the *akpiks* are plentiful, south to Qalutagiaq, where there are lots of blueberries, and farther south into the trees and the winter camp at Puvlatuuq—to everywhere that there are caribou.

Out on the land, beyond the village, is where you go every chance you get. And the new highway to the landfill will make getting there easier. "Never stay in one place long time," says Justus Mekiana, remembering Nunamiut life before the village. "Always moving. Stay little bit time here, then another place, another place, another place."

Now fifty years of living in one place have brought the environmental ills of life Outside. Sprawl, noise pollution, environmental degradation, waste, they're all here. If you go south, climbing the ATV trail that passes beside the filled-in lake, or if you walk west on the ridges up behind the museum, in just a few minutes you are out of sight of the valley floor. Gone is the landfill, the runway, the clear-cut willows. You can't see the houses or hear the construction noise. From these places, the pass and its serene mountains look as they must have to ancient caribou hunters hundreds, even thousands, of years ago. When I hike up above the village to pick berries, I can make it all disappear. But—a village teen told me—if you go a mile or so farther west and climb to the top of Oka Mountain, in the thin mountain air you can hear the backup beeps of the machines and the gravel marching along the conveyer belts.

In the wildness of the Brooks Range, these things seem all the more alarming.

Weekend Nomads

Coming home from camping.

Ironically, for all the talk of place, it is movement between places that defines the historic Nunamiut. "We never stay in one place. Always moving," Justus Mekiana is fond of saying. "Like the wolf we follow the caribou." In today's world of wage labor, such nomadism is a weekend and vacation luxury. Even more, it's a state of mind. The wandering wolf has become the school mascot and the pride of its sports teams.

Friday evening the parade would begin. I had watched it every summer we'd come here from the steps of our rental house. The parade of villagers—virtually everyone, it seemed, but Ed, Meryn, and me—leaving town. "Going camping," someone would shout, as they passed my reviewing stand. Doing, in the short space of a summer weekend, what the Nunamiut had always done—living and traveling on the land.

Until the 1970s they would have been on foot, setting up summer camps before breakup while they could still haul supplies by sled and dog team to summer campsites. When they moved over the land in the summer to new campsites or from kill sites back to camp, it was with dogs packing the gear and meat in caribou-skin packs strapped to their backs. Today villagers take to the land on eight-wheeled Argos. Heading out of town they resemble a convoy of miniature tanks in a toy army.

For an hour or more the loaded Argos would roar out of town, singly and in small caravans. Then they were out on the land, rising and dipping on the rocky ATV trails that run north and south through the Anaktuvuk Valley. It might be midnight or later by the time they reached their final camping place and set up the white canvas tent. There, away from the noise and the summer dust of the village, they would be real Nunamiut again. They'd roast caribou ribs over an open fire, visit other families camped nearby. Kids would roast hot dogs and marshmallows, wade in streams, play tag. No one would look at a watch. Sunday night, or perhaps in the early hours of Monday morning, the Argo loads of campers would roll back to the village, in time to begin the workday week.

Camping—being out on the land—is always on Nunamiut minds. People talk about where they're going on the upcoming weekend. And a lot of attention is devoted to the vehicle that gets them there. Summer evenings after work, men bend over the open hoods of their Argos. Heads disappear into the engine compartments; wrench-wielding hands dismantle ailing and broken parts. They hunker, checking tires and axles. In a pinch, a flat tire can be mended with a plug of caribou skin. They trade information, seek replacement parts, and solve Argo problems over the CB in conversations with other men. The intensity of their Argo activity increases as the end of the week approaches and they hurry to have their machines in good running order by the weekend.

By late Friday afternoon, piles of camping gear begin to accumulate in the gravel yards. What gear do you take camping? I asked Lela Ahgook and Becky Hugo, during one of our interviews in the summer of 1992. "Everything you need for camping," Lela grinned. I should have expected that answer, but I managed to get a list out of her anyway. The grub box, the Coleman stove, the white canvas tent and its three poles, sleeping bags, extra clothes, the rifle and ammunition box, binoculars and mosquito dope—these are the essentials. "Matches, that's the most important," Lela mused, adding, "I like to take sourdough, make sourdough pancakes out there."

Like all of us, the Nunamiut have accumulated more stuff as they have become more prosperous and more settled. And they take more stuff with them than they did in the years before ATVs. Becky had given the matter of camping gear more than a little thought because she and her husband, Willie, took all five of their children with them, and they invariably came back with game. Some people take only one fishing pole but Becky and Willie took four so everyone but the baby could fish. Becky economized in other ways: "No room for syrup. Because you would have to bring seven or six plates for the pancakes. We just carry two plates, and a big-sized bowl for the kids. We serve 'em plain." But she did take disposable diapers, baby wipes, towels, and shampoo.

True nomads travel longer and lighter. Justus Mekiana recalled a camping trip he took in 1950, in the days before Argos and wage labor and weekend family trips. He and three other village men walked in the Brooks Range hunting wolf pups, which they turned in for the fifty-dollar bounty that the Territory, and later the State, of Alaska offered for years. Each man brought his dogs to carry his camping supplies. Three of Justus's dogs carried his flour, coffee, tobacco, sugar, rolled oats, personal gear, and reloading equipment, and his other two dogs carried packs to hold the meat they would hunt and kill along the way. Their camping trip lasted for a month.

Today you have to be your own Argo repair person out on the land, miles from the village, so villagers travel with a tool kit to fix everything from flat tires to ailing brakes and axles. Kids add their dolls and Walkmans and electronic games to the growing pile of camping gear, and mothers pare it down. "They try to carry junk, you know. They come out, 'Mom, here is my bag.' But we don't have any room," Becky shook her head.

Somehow, everything that can't be lashed to the side of the vehicle is made to fit into the square depression behind the front and only real seat in the machine. The softest gear, the sleeping bags and extra clothing, goes on the very top, to provide cushioning for the back-seat passengers. A tarp and ropes secure the mounded gear. The kids hop onto the back, holding on to the ropes, and parents climb in front, Dad at the controls, baby snugged on mom's back inside her expansive parka. Someone holds the rope that is tethered at the other end to the family dog until they reach the village boundary, where freedom and the land begin.

"Qalutaq, Kuugukpak, Chandler. Cache Lake, Maggaqpak, Aŋmaġulik, Iġñivik, Tulugak, Masu, Ikiaqpak, and Anaqtiktuaq toward Ben Creek." Becky rattled off the list of camping places that they frequented. "Who decides where to go?" I asked. "The husband," both Becky and Lela answered emphatically. Exactly where they go depends on where the caribou are and whether the berries are ripe, but from the time the last spring snow melts until the snow flies again in the fall the Nunamiut repeat this weekend ritual. Even before the snow has melted, when the spring sun has moderated the temperature, the Nunamiut will go camping using snowmobiles pulling sleds. At these spring campsites they fish through the lake ice and hunt the season's first migrating ducks and geese.

By 9 P.M. or so, the parade was over, and I quit my reviewing stand. I would spend the weekend hiking, catching up on fieldnotes, pleasure reading, and wishing that I too were out on the land, far from the village, camping. My ethnographer's sense told me I should be doing just that. How else to understand Native life but to join in? The logistics of the three of us going camping with a Native family, however, were formidable. Families are big; they own one Argo, and there were none to rent. Finding room for one more small kid was not a problem, and Meryn got invited to go camping with the families of her village girlfriends. I was reduced to enjoying her experience vicariously as I sent her off each summer with Willie and Becky Hugo. It was, I told myself that first summer, an act of utmost faith. My seven-year-old daughter gone to some grizzly bear's territory, gone to wilderness I hadn't seen and could only imagine, gone too far away to track on our borrowed and not very powerful CB radio. Calming down, I reminded myself that her journey and destination are hardly terra icognita to her hosts. This was, after all, Nunamiut country.

Meryn returned to me three days later, smelling of woodsmoke and trailing a large Ziploc bag full of tiny arctic blueberries. Blueberry stains coursed the length of her sweatpants and sweatshirt, and blueberry leaves and toasted marshmallows were stuck fast to the French braid I had put in her hair three days before. She had seen the northern lights, she told me, a caribou being butchered, and mountain sheep in the high country. She'd been fishing as well as blueberry picking. She had done what the Nunamiut do in the summertime. In my envy, I vowed that not another summer would pass without seeing firsthand what Nunamiut camping is all about.

The Nunamiut Experience

"You're sure gonna be shocked when you hear how much your camping trip's gonna cost," Lela teases me. It's the summer of 1992. Ed, ailing from MS, has left the village to meet up with a colleague in Fairbanks, and I've persuaded Lela and her husband Noah to take Meryn and me camping, offering to help with the expenses. "Maybe we'll do old-style camping," Lela continues, "real Nunamiut Experience." We've been joking for days about the trip being a real Nunamiut Experience for us *tanniks*. "No matches, no Argo; we walk. Maybe I really take you on wilderness trip. Carry nothing," Noah laughs.

"You upside down yet, Margaret?" Noah comes into the house for lunch from his job driving the village garbage truck. "You gotta be upside down before I take you on Nunamiut Experience." I tell him I'm getting there, staying up later, sleeping in longer. "We're going to eat frozen meat and frozen fish, like in the video." Noah refers to Ansen Balikci's classic 1967 ethnographic video *The Netsilik Eskimo*, which Anaktuvuk people enjoy watching.

"If you don't like my cooking, you gotta carry your own food," Lela warns me, adding, "if you want something special, bring it." I tell her I'll bring my herb tea. "Herb tea!" she wrinkles her nose. In Anaktuvuk, "tea" means Lipton. She puts a steaming plate of sourdough hotcakes on the table and a big pot of caribou soup. "Everybody eat," she instructs. The hotcakes are delicious, even with Mrs. Butterworth's gooey syrup, and I tell Lela that above all else her sourdough pancakes have convinced me to go camping.

Three days later we have finished packing for the trip and are awaiting Lela and Noah, who are to pick us up after dinner. Meryn, ten years old and a self-proclaimed veteran of Nunamiut camping, fills my ears with nonstop advice:

"It's cold in the Argo, you'll want your sweatshirt, your winter jacket and that Gore-tex parka."

"And I hope you're not wearing your sandals."

"Your nose runs a lot in the Argo—you'll need Kleenex."

"You have to go to the bathroom a lot when you ride in the Argo, believe me."

"I hope you know, Mom, that we'll get our water from the river."

"And don't expect to go running when we go camping."

An Argo pulls up, braking with a spin of gravel, and they are here. We rush the gear outside, and I grab my video camera from its bag to photograph the beginning of our great adventure. Noah unties the rope that anchors the green tarp over the camping gear. "Anything breakable in there?" he yells as he punches our stuff sacks into position. "No," I answer, until he gets to my backpack with my four-hundred-dollar tape recorder I brought along to play some tapes of Eskimo songs that Lela was bringing. I look at Lela. "Maybe I should leave my tape recorder at home?" "Leave it!" she orders. I hand her my precious camcorder in its case to put in front, where it becomes an armrest for Noah. Her own purse is tied to the handhold on the passenger side of the Argo. Among other things, it contains the mosquito dope and numerous Ziploc bags, which would prove to be the most practical item brought on the trip.

The load secured, Meryn and I hop on the back, and finally we are headed out of town, into a light north wind and rain. I sit backward on the Argo, holding on to the bar that runs across the top of the front seat. Going through the smooth streets of town is easy, but I gasp once Noah hits the Argo trail, grabbing the rail even tighter. A mistake, Meryn is quick to tell me. "Don't hold on tight, Mom, your hands will get tired; hold on to the ropes instead." I am a human accordion, teeth clacking, vertebrae thwacking, joints pounding each time the Argo noses into a swale. My shoulders are wrenched from holding onto the bar, and I find it slightly disorienting to ride facing backward. I want to turn and sit in some more comfortable position, but I fear if I let go I'll bounce off. Finally I am able to swing around to sit sideways, one hand on the ropes, one on the bar, my feet dangling over the side. Meryn, with her back to me, sits similarly on the other side, her admonitions continuing over the next couple of miles: "Don't sit on your feet." "Don't hang your feet over the back end or they'll get wet."

Despite its chiropractic side effects, the amphibious Argo is a marvelous machine. It rolls smoothly over glaciers in the Anaktuvuk River and easily spans narrow crevices in the ice. It climbs and descends nearly vertical slopes, and its tires squish flat (no one seems to measure how much pressure they put in, they just "fill 'em up") as it plows over big boulders. It is watertight and will float (though it is liable to drift in very deep water). It runs up or down shallow, fast-flowing streams, takes on tussocks, and cuts a path through five-foot-tall willow thickets. In the village it rolls effortlessly over gravel streets, transporting groceries, laundry, and people. In Anaktuvuk Pass, Argos are more common than automobiles; virtually every family has one.

Not everyone in the north views the Argo as favorably as the Nunamiut. In the wilderness set aside as the Gates of the Arctic National Park, which borders the village on three sides, the Argo is seen not so much as the modern means to summer subsistence hunting and gathering but as the cause of the muddy scars that course the green summer tundra. Argo wheels flatten the delicate vegetation, and other Argos following the same path eventually churn up the earth. For a time the Park Service tried to limit, even ban, Argos within the 8.5-million-acre park, but park lands stand between the village and other Nunamiut-owned lands that villagers could not access short of going through the park. And subsistence hunting within the boundaries of the park by Nunamiut and other rural residents is perfectly legal. In 1991

Nunamiut protested the park ban on Argos, speaking out at meetings, signing petitions, even marketing bumper stickers that gloated, "No Park, No Problem." The following year the matter was resolved to the satisfaction of most. Argos are allowed in the park but only on certain already-established ATV trails.

The land holds many memories, and Lela shares a few of them with me as she identifies landmarks along our route: the place where the bear bothered Bob and Justus last summer, keeping them up all night trying to get their meat; the spot where Elijah killed his big bear; Arctic John's fishing hole. She names the creeks, valleys, and mountains for me. She points out the caribou trails, thin, branching tracings across green mountain slopes that come together toward the bottom of the slope, marking the very recent passage of large numbers of animals on the move. After a couple of hours we stop at a flat place at the mouth of Aŋmaġulik Creek to stretch our legs, relieve our full bladders, and spray our heads with mosquito dope.

A small caravan of Argos and their passengers has assembled. People typically travel in groups to camping places, meeting up at customary stops along the way. Aŋmaġulik Creek is a favorite, judging by the rock rings of old campfires and the litter of more-recent cigarette butts. Traveling together the Nunamiut are able to help one another in case someone has Argo problems. Not everyone camps in the same place, but they keep in touch on the CB throughout the weekend, and some or all of them will meet up here again on the way home.

We follow Aŋmaġulik Creek upstream, slowly climbing. Lela and I carry on an intermittent conversation over the loud hum of the Argo, and every now and then Noah looks back, laughs and exclaims, "Nunamiut Experience!" We watch the sun begin its momentary descent behind the mountain ridges, which ring us on all sides, and then we descend toward Narvaksrauraq Lake, a mile-long shimmer in the distance. Just above the lake, Minnie and Pat Mekiana have pitched their tent. We stop to have tea with them. Rachel Riley, Molly Ahgook, and her daughter Elfreda, traveling with us in two other Argos, have stopped as well. Minnie is frying caribou meat. We crowd into the tent; teacups are washed out and fresh tea poured for all the visitors. Their food supply—fried caribou meat, lunchmeat and bread, cookies—is offered to all. There is seasoned salt for the meat, and catsup. I am surprised both by how hungry I am and how good the fried meat tastes. Most of the conversation is in Iñupiaq, and Molly, widowed for many years, jokes about when she was young and used to go with Zach and Noah. "And now I got no one," she laughs.

I had thought we were going to camp right beside Pat and Minnie on the lakeshore, but we continue on, a bit north from the lake, Rachel and Molly following. We stop on some dry, stony ground, and everybody hops out of the Argos to walk around this probable campsite. Noah asks whether we should stay here or continue to Sukkak, about an hour to the west. Lela is noncommittal. We stay, while Rachel and Molly motor on toward Sukkak.

As Noah unwraps and unloads the gear from the Argo, I grab my camcorder to continue my record of the Nunamiut Experience. I train the camcorder on Lela and Noah as they secure the tent's guy ropes with large rocks. They gather more rocks to put inside to hold taut the tent corners. Their tent, like most others in the village, is an Alaska Tent and Tarp white canvas model, eight by ten feet. This particular one is riddled with holes eaten by arctic voles, and Lela has patched some of the holes with scraps of fabric or pieces of sock, or just simply stitched them together. Lela says their son John is going to buy them a new tent. Meantime, Noah hands me pieces of paper toweling to stuff in the unpatched large holes. Fortunately Noah has brought along a plastic tarp, which he puts over the tent. Good thing, because it rains much of the night and at least half of the next day. The tent plugs and tarp work and we remain nice and dry all weekend. A tarp is spread across the ground inside the tent before the Coleman stove; air mattresses and sleeping bags are brought in. The wooden grub box is left outside with Noah's rifle leaning against it. As soon as the Coleman stove is in place by the front wall of the tent, Lela lights it to heat water for tea. As I settle back to drink my cup of Lipton, I wonder what time it is. I have purposely left my watch at home, but Lela is wearing hers. It is nearly 1 A.M..

The sleeping bags are laid out across the back of the tent—Noah, Lela, their daughter Valerie, Meryn, and me. As soon as we are snuggled in, like so many anchovies in a tin, Valerie begs for a story: "Mom, tell me a story about your life." I can't help retorting, "She's afraid I'll tape record it!" Lela laughs: "Someday I'll tell you my life story, Margaret." Lela resists the life story that Valerie continues to beg from her, but she relents to tell a scary—and true—bear story.

Lela talks softly to Noah in Iñupiaq, noting to me first, "Don't worry, Margaret, we're not talking about you." Frankly, I don't care if they are. My back aching from the Argo ride, I sink into my soft air mattress and am almost instantly asleep.

I awaken to the rhythmic pumping of the fuel tank of the Coleman stove and the whoosh of the flame as it is lit. Noah puts the coffeepot of cold water on the burner, and Lela, seated by the stove with a Tupperware bowl in her hand, stirs furiously, adding flour, water, and baking soda to her sourdough pancake mixture. The bright light that filters through the tent walls doesn't hint at what time it is. It is summer, and it is always light.

We fill ourselves with Lela's sourdough cakes soaked in Mrs. Butterworth's syrup and warm our hands on steaming mugs of coffee. We linger over our coffee. "You want more coffee?" Lela asks. "Nope, I've already had two cups," I answer. "Tanniks," she exclaims, shaking her head. "Tanniks always set limits. Too much cholesterol, too much this, too much that."

It is raining when we finish breakfast, so we break out the cards and play snerts. I am too slow. "Snerts!" Lela exclaims triumphantly, playing her last card and leaving me with a fistful.

When the rain slows to drizzle, we venture outside to pick berries while Noah scans the ridges for caribou, his rifle at the ready. Voices from scattered campsites play on the CB, the airwaves like threads connecting the far-flung Nunamiut campers. Justus, over at Sukkak, has killed a caribou. Raymond Paneak and Gilbert Lincoln, a mile or so across the valley and just visible through the binoculars, are going for one now. Noah listens as they report their progress over the CB. They get a caribou in the late afternoon, and later that night we head out in the Argo to their campsite for fresh meat.

The two families' tents are pitched close together on a wide, flat rocky area that looks north to Nanmautik and Miluk Mountains, both named for their shapes, "dogpack" and "breast," respectively. The campers are gathered round the blazing willow fire. A side of ribs on a strong willow branch roasts in the fire, and on some flat rocks nearby are a pot of hot tea, the cooked caribou liver, and the uncooked long bones, which are cracked for *patiq*, fresh marrow. The fresh skin lies stretched on the ground, hair side down, and the remainder of the meat, which is substantial, is neatly piled on a bed of leafy willow branches.

"Eat meat," Ada Lincoln instructs, and Lela, taking an *ulu*, deftly cuts a rib from the cooked rack, scoring it in several places to make the meat pull easily from the rib. I eat three or four ribs, washing them down with hot tea. Meryn and Ada's little granddaughters heat willow branches in the fire, making firebrands. They raise the burning ends to their mouths and blow on them to make them glow. Sated with fresh-cooked meat and the story of its capture, we leave the warmth of their fire in the late evening, bumping over the tundra in the Argo to our campsite and bed.

There's no story tonight, just one comment by Noah from his sleeping bag. "You never get lonely when you go out camping, Margaret." Suddenly, I feel at home, in the company of old friends.

For the Nunamiut as for anyone else who lives by the work week, a weekend of camping passes all too quickly. So soon, it is Sunday evening and time to head home. The round rocks that held our tent walls and poles in place and the charred remains of our campfire mark one more campsite on the ancient landscape of Nunamiut habitation in the Brooks Range. I don't know if this one tenting place will be named, but campsites are sometimes named for events that occurred there. Like the place we camped two years later, in the summer of 1994, several miles to the southwest of Anaktuvuk Pass. On that trip Lela gave me the task of making the morning's sourdough pancakes.

Zach Hugo, camped nearby, showed up one morning just as I was piling the silver-dollar-sized hotcakes on a plate. "New York hotcakes," he laughed at me and at my tiny pancakes. "We'll call this place 'New York Hotcake Country.'"

The gear repacked into the Argo, we are on the move homeward, in a rain driven on a strong south wind. I sit sideways in the back, my legs wrapped around Meryn so we can benefit from each other's body heat. We travel in a caravan of returning Argos—Doris and Zach, Molly and Elfreda, and Rachel, Justus, and Ethel. We stop twice en route, first at Aŋmaġulik, where we stopped on the way north, and then at a place called Kawasaki Creek, named for the abandoned snowmobile that died on its banks. Molly, well behind the rest of us who have already reached the rest stop, begins singing on her cb as she approaches Kawasaki Creek. The other women decide to dance for her. They spread across the Argo trail in their colorful summer parkas, raising their arms, turning and swaying to her Eskimo singing. "See how happy we are," Doris says to me. "Yes," I answer, noting as I watch the dogs, still free from their village ropes, exploring the vicinity, "and the dogs, too."

The remainder of the journey goes quickly, despite the cold and the wind. We pass Kanŋuumavik, the spring camping place just north of the village with its bare tent platforms, and we see in the distance the white tent at Poker Hill. In minutes we are at the cemetery and finally on the streets of town. It is nearly 10 P.M. when we arrive and Noah unloads our gear.

At one point during our Nunamiut Experience, Lela had confessed to me that she had been afraid to take me camping. "Why?" I wondered. "Because you might be too tannik," she explained. "Was I too white?" I wondered. "No, you were ok," she said.

By the late 1990s Nunamiut camping patterns had begun to change. Construction jobs in the village, which would bring running water and flush toilets to all households, and the realignment of the mile-long airstrip provided employment opportunities for just about every able-bodied adult. Many of these jobs kept people working six and seven days a week, leaving little time for camping. Fewer people were going camping, and those who did were not venturing as far from the village as they did a few years before.

I once asked Justus Mekiana what he missed most about the old days, about life before the forty-hour workweek. "I miss only camping," he replied. "I never miss much about the dog packing, I never miss much about the dog team. I like to be camping around, you know. Everybody likes it."

In the summer of 1999, I was preparing to leave Anaktuvuk Pass after a brief field season. I walked around town saying my good-byes, and when I came to the Ahgooks, Noah and his son Richard were packing the Argo for camping. "Nunamiut Experience, Margaret," Noah called to me, "You wanna come?" "Going home," I smiled wistfully. "Next year."

The Things We Carry

Returning from caribou hunting, 1959. Photo by Edwin S. Hall Jr.

We never stay in one place. We're moving all the time to where there is a lot of caribou. If there was caribou at Nigu, we stay there. Next year no caribou there, so some hunters check up this way. There is some caribou coming this way again. So stay in here, maybe two months or one month or three months, stay in here. The caribou move on somewhere else and we move again. We never stay in one place all the time. Move around. Travel.

Justus Mekiana

January days of darkness. This would be my first winter in the North, the one place I never wanted to spend winter. But I'd happily agreed to the honor of being a scholar-teacher in residence for the spring semester at the University of Alaska during my sabbatical year. I could have opted for the fall semester, but if I was going to go for a semester I wanted to arrive in the darkness so that I might emerge into the light as the days lengthened into spring. Now I was about to become a modern nomad, leaving behind my western New York home to camp out in Fairbanks for a few months.

In the late 1960s Simon Paneak made a series of drawings for University of New Mexico archaeologist Jack Campbell that told a story of Nunamiut life before snowmobiles and Argos. The simple pencil drawings are minimalist yet rich in detail. In one, a caravan of three sleds moves along the frozen river. Their winter possessions and food are covered with caribou skins and lashed to the sled. Three dogs pull each sled, and linked to the front of each dog line walks a woman in snowshoes, breaking trail for the dogs. As if that weren't enough work, she also carries a baby on her back. But the men work hard too, walking beside the sled, helping to pull while steadying the unwieldy load so the sleds won't capsize. The little Nunamiut group trudges across the wintry page of Simon's sketch, perhaps en route to a destination where they will build a sod house and remain for a few months.[1] Today's older Argo—and snowmobile—nomads still remember that life.

To listen to Doris Hugo describe it, leaving a sod house at the end of winter for a summer of camping seemed very matter-of-fact. "They would empty the sod house, save it for next year. Take the floor out, windows out, clean it real good and they can use it again." The dog harnesses for the sled and valuable household goods too bulky to carry—like the phonograph Doris's father, Homer Mekiana, owned in the 1940s—were placed on a cache built five or six feet off the ground. The winter sled was secured nearby. Pieces of cloth that would flutter in the wind, or tin cans that would rattle, were tied to the cache to scare away the bears.

Travel in the summertime was harder than in the wintertime, for all the household goods that had to be transported, including the tent, poles, cooking pot, and stove, were carried by the dogs. "We had lots, lots," Doris remembered. "Maybe nine, ten dogs. Lots of family, lots of dogs." Mothers carried babies; fathers carried rifles and packed on their backs small children too tired to walk.

"How much longer? That question, all the time," Doris recalled. "Our dad used to get mad, I guess. We were right behind him, 'How much longer?' You just can't wait to camp. Can't wait to relax, instead of walking. I think my dad used to get tired of us like that. Same question . . ." Her voice trailed off.

Leaving home in the winter for several months seemed much more complicated than heading for Alaska for a month in the summer. It was, after all, winter in the snowbelt, and I would be gone from snow-plowing season well into lawn-mowing season. On the plus side, I was now shed of all pets. One by one our five cats had died and were all buried in the back yard of my former home. Following my divorce, Meryn and I had moved into a new old house, less than half a mile away. I had thrown myself into remodeling, planting and tending its gardens, and shepherding Meryn through high school. She was now a freshman in college, and the only remaining pet, a goldfish named Moby, had, at my insistence, accompanied her to school, sloshing in a styrofoam cooler the four hundred miles to the Rhode Island School of Design.

Before leaving for Alaska I tried unsuccessfully to rent my house, but I decided to leave it empty when kind friends offered to check it regularly. All of them were more than happy to start my new PT Cruiser once a week and back it up and down the driveway. The driveway would be plowed as usual; lights were on timers; and a lamp would go on in the kitchen window, alerting the next-door neighbor should the temperature inside dip below forty degrees. Five pages of miscellaneous instructions left on the kitchen table spelled out how to fill the humidifiers, water the plants, and search for mice. They included a list of phone numbers for every conceivable household emergency. On top of all that surveillance, the local police would check the property daily. So, one January morning, two hours before dawn, I turned the key in the back door for the last time, leaving behind the Navajo rugs, the teenage love letters from my first boyfriend, most of my clothes and books, and my antique Shaker rocking chair. More than half a lifetime of stuff.

My thoughts were on Alaska as I struggled into the bathroom cubicle at the airport with my carry-on luggage. In one hand I gripped a weekend-sized suitcase bulging with important papers, favorite pieces of jewelry, and my laptop computer. In the other, a portable cervical traction device for the ruptured disk in my neck. I nudged open the door of the stall with my left foot, set the bags down inside, and then realized I would have to stack them in order to close the door. I was already sweating in my heavy winter parka that I wore on top of the wool blazer that was too bulky to fit into either of the two suitcases I had checked through to Fairbanks. I peeled off the parka and piled it on top of the suitcases, balanced on top of that the plastic grocery bag containing my water bottle, a banana, a newspaper, and my airline ticket. I shoved the whole pile perilously close to the toilet in order to free the door. Finally, it closed.

I long ago learned to use the U.S. mail to get the overflow of my belongings to my destination. This time, I'd mailed just four wine boxes of belongings to Fairbanks. The rest was crammed into one capacious, expanding duffel bag and one rolling suitcase. It was a reasonable amount of gear for four and a half months in a furnished apartment, but at that moment of reckoning, trapped behind my mound of carry-on bags in an airport toilet stall, I felt hopelessly overburdened with stuff. I would make a lousy nomad.

I straggled out of the restroom with my embarrassment of luggage just as my plane was announced. As guilty as I felt for what I was carrying, I couldn't help noticing how much baggage every passenger had. Air travelers seem to carry more every year: rolling suitcases that, without even being packed, must exceed the weight limit for overhead baggage; overnight bags that hold two weeks of clothing. Didn't these folks check anything through? Or were they, like me, going away for several months?

Nobody ever measures their carry-on bags in the containers the airlines provide for just that purpose. That's because they wouldn't fit. I know the overhead compartments have gotten bigger too. I've often flown an old Boeing 727–200 that still makes the run from Fairbanks to Barrow. None of the suitcases that were rolling onto my flight behind their owners would fit in its shallow overhead compartments. I boarded the plane and found my aisle seat, stuffing my own largesse of luggage and my bulky parka into the overhead compartment. As I buckled myself in, I gave passing thought to the possibility of the overhead compartment giving way in a glut of overweight luggage. All of which would land on the heads of the passengers in the aisle seats. My own computer could do me in.

Were it not for the computer I would have had even more luggage. My small laptop contained the course I'd be teaching at the university along with every other anthropology course I'd taught in the last fifteen years. Years of field journals, research notes, and interviews—virtually all of my academic life. And not just that, but the Christmas card list, the most recent love letters, and the digital photos of my home, gardens, and the Erie Canal that I had added at the last moment. The only things I seemed to be missing were a cell phone and palm pilot, which the majority of other passengers appeared to have and were using in the last moments before departure. It is odd how we've all "gone smaller," embracing tiny portable technology at the same time that we're schlepping around more and bigger luggage. Dave Barry got it just right when he portrayed a suburban soccer mom driving an suv equal in mass to a school bus while talking on a cell phone the size of a Chiclet.

The second leg of my journey, from Chicago to Fairbanks, took us above the snow-covered, rectangular fields of the Great Plains. I thought of Meryn, who, like so many other kids, once believed these fence lines were state boundaries that surely were as visible on the ground as they were on a map. This vast geography of lines and mountains and ribbons of rivers separates my small family. My brother and his family are in Ohio, Meryn in Rhode Island, my mother in California, my stepson and his family in Michigan. Such vast distances to connect with e-mails and phone calls. We seldom think about that distance until its sheer expanse unfolds before us. The Nunamiut once covered two hundred, maybe three hundred miles of territory in their annual cycle, every bit of it on foot. Families who had been together for part of the year would split up when resources were scarce or when other hunting options drew them apart. There were times when, as a youth, Justus Mekiana remembered that his family was all alone. Still, the Nunamiut people always gathered at Christmastime for Eskimo dancing. "No matter how far they are—other families," Justus said, "they come to the one place."

What meaningful things—aside from the gear and supplies needed to survive—did these nomads carry as they moved from camp to camp? A woman never went anywhere without her knife, her skin- and meat-cutting curved-bladed *ulu*. A man, too, always carried a knife, along with a rifle and ammunition. But meaningful as these things were, they were also essential to survival. In 1942 Simon Paneak bought a Zenith radio powered by a twelve-volt battery. He carried his precious radio and its battery, wrapped in a caribou-skin bag, from camp to camp. And he always had the journal in which he recorded northern bird life, and his worn English dictionary.

My mind wandered to an exercise I have students do in the life history class I teach. To make the point that we talk about our lives with things as well as words, I ask students to bring to class four or five possessions that tell their stories. What's really interesting are the items shown by students who forgot the assignment. They stand before the class, pulling key chains out of pockets, pointing out the mementos that dangle from them. They dig for pictures in wallets and talk meaningfully about a necklace or a ring they are wearing. When *don't* we carry things of significance? Only in the common dream, where we find ourselves suddenly, excruciatingly, naked in a public place. We're horribly embarrassed, of course, but there's something else. There is nothing that defines us, only the absence of the things that do.

It was just after dawn when a flight attendant announced our descent into Fairbanks. At 10:30 the wan northern sun was barely above the southern horizon, spinning a pale ribbon of pink below a bowl of ice-blue sky. The frozen coils of the Chena River shimmered in the early-morning light. Black spikes of spruce rose from an expanse of snow that extended to the very edges of the earth. I had come North. In winter.

My good friend and colleague, Molly Lee, greeted me at the airport, wearing only a heavy sweater and jeans. The January temperature that morning was a welcoming twenty-four above zero; I was lucky. I had walked into one of the warmest winters in modern Fairbanks history. I moved into a one-bedroom third-floor furnished apartment just a couple of miles from campus and conveniently located next to a shopping center. My tiny quarters had everything I needed for my stay, including pots, pans, and dishes, even sheets and towels. The only things missing were a corkscrew and a garlic press, which I quickly purchased. My accommodations proved so quiet that I hardly saw or heard my neighbors the entire time I was there. And I never came to know any of them.

Two colleagues loaned me their away-at-college son's 1984 Subaru, which got me handily from my apartment to the university and the shopping center. Within a week of my arrival I had begun to wear the rituals of home like favorite clothing. In the predawn hours I headed to the university gym for my morning workout, then returned home to eat breakfast with the morning paper accompanied by the local NPR radio station. I tuned in to NPR on the car radio as I drove to campus. I ate lunch at the student union with anthropology colleagues, drank an afternoon coffee on the way back to my office. In the late-afternoon darkness I headed home for a glass of wine and the *Jim Lehrer News Hour* with dinner. Weekends brought a matinee at the movies, a gathering with university friends, the Sunday *New York Times*.

From my classroom I watched the returning light. In January it was already dark when my afternoon class began, but by early February the sun was sitting on the lip of the horizon as we gathered in the classroom. By the end of February, daylight lingered through my hour-and-a-half seminar. The late-afternoon sun, still barely ten degrees above the horizon, sent gossamer strands of pink through the dark spruce. The light beckoned; I drank it in. I smiled as I watched the ravens outside my classroom. Those fat, black trickster birds that had hung around all winter swaggering in the snow and squawking from their dumpster perches now spun and whirled in mating dances.

My house-tending friends teased me by e-mail from home: "Everything's fine, though I have seen pieces of your art showing up on walls in the neighborhood. And the other day your front door was wide open. Your new car won't start, but everything's still standing." I didn't care. There was no art on my walls in Fairbanks either. The car I drove wasn't new but it started and it got me to my destination. I had few obligations. I was living a pared-down life.

Town

Going to town.

To its residents, Anaktuvuk Pass is the antithesis of "town," that is, Fairbanks: Anaktuvuk is quieter, safer, and unfailingly friendly. No cold stares greet strangers walking the village streets. There are no bars; possession and sale of alcohol are against the law, even though from time to time villagers bring it in. Residents smile, wave, and say hello to each other and to visitors, no matter how many times their paths may cross in a day.

Not by any measure is Fairbanks a big city. No tall buildings announce the treeless commercial downtown, barely a half-mile square in size. The old residential part of downtown is a jumble of bungalows, log cabins, and the occasional trailer. The town's water treatment facility, which ought to be out of sight somewhere, is planted squarely in the heart of downtown on the Chena River just blocks from the new tourist hotels. The route from downtown to the airport is lined on both sides by a continuous sprawl of strip malls. Fairbanks is a zoning nightmare. Its frontier town ugliness is softened by the spruce- and birch-forested hills that ring the city and the several sleek white buildings of the University of Alaska up on College Hill.

Notwithstanding its looks, Fairbanks is a lively, friendly place. Its hearty residents don't complain about the bitter winters; most of them would rather be here than anywhere else. Fairbanks draws people too from the surrounding bush communities that it serves. Anaktuvuk Pass is one of them.

I was looking forward to seeing Anaktuvuk people in town during my semester in Fairbanks. Summers when I would pass through Fairbanks at the end of the field season I would occasionally run into a villager at the Tanana Valley Fair, or in the Fred Myers store, or at the airport waiting to go home with a load of clothing and toys purchased in town. And I'd usually traveled from the village in the company of people going to town. But now I was the Alaska urbanite, and I could invite village friends to my place.

My friend Lela came to town the first of February for some doctors' appointments and stayed at the Klondike Inn less than half a mile from my apartment. The Klondike is an unremarkable one-story strip of a motel with a huge parking lot perpendicular to busy Airport Way. The Nunamiut and other Native Alaskans like staying at the Klondike because its rooms have kitchenettes and it's within walking distance of Safeway, Fred Myers, Sears, a liquor store, and Value Village, a secondhand store.

"All right!" Lela responded to my dinner invitation when I phoned her. "I'm cooking tannik stew," I warned. I had thought for some time about the menu and decided meat should be a substantial component, but I also wanted it to be different from standard Nunamiut fare. I cobbled together a Greek beef stew, seasoned with cinnamon, feta cheese, and walnuts and served purposely over a mixture of wild and basmati rices, not the white Uncle Ben's they buy in huge bags in Anaktuvuk. A salad (for my tastes), bread, and a Marie Callander's blackberry cobbler completed the menu.

"Oh, I like that hug," Lela said, when I greeted her at the Klondike. Her daughter Valerie had come with her to see the dentist, and though she'd been invited for dinner, she had opted not to come since she was just getting up from a nap.

Lela and I started laughing the minute we got in the car, and we continued throughout the evening. "Remember when you kicked over the sourdough starter when we were camping at Qalutagiaq?" Lela asked with a grin. I couldn't forget that; I'd felt terrible at the time and had been endlessly teased about it while we were camping. "But," I countered, "remember the New York hotcakes I express-mailed you from Brockport that fall to make up for it?" That had really fixed them for the teasing I took for making small hotcakes on the camp stove. Over dinner I learned two things about those hotcakes: they actually ate them after Lela heated them in the microwave, and Noah told the entire town about them over the CB.

I stabbed at a piece of stew meat. "Were there lots of caribou this year?" They hadn't come through the pass this fall, she explained, but there had been plenty around all winter. "Lots of young people are not hunting today when they easily could," she lamented. Lela's son Richard hunts for several people. "I tell him to feed the old people," she added.

And how do people feel about opening up ANWR for drilling? I wondered. With the new Bush administration looking for additional sources of energy, the possible opening of the Arctic National Wildlife Refuge was all over the local and national news. The Anaktuvuk people depend on the western arctic caribou herd, not the Porcupine caribou herd that calves in the Refuge, but the future of ANWR is a North Slope issue, and both oil revenues and caribou are of concern to Anaktuvuk people. Villagers are divided; Lela's against opening the refuge. But the Iñupiat people in the coastal villages of Kaktovik and Nuiqsut are all for it. "Caribou are not as important to them," she explained. "Just whales?" I teased. "Just whales," she echoed. Lela noted that when Anaktuvuk people haven't had enough caribou, other North Slope villages have helped out and sent caribou meat. "But it doesn't taste the same," she noted. "I can hardly eat it. Ocean caribou tastes funny."

"Well," Lela said at 8:30, "You ready to take me back?" I nodded and loaded up the rice, stew, bread and the rest of the cobbler for her to take to Valerie. "Valerie asked if we were going to drive around," she offered. I recognized the oblique hint. When villagers come to town, there are places they want to go, and getting there by taxi is expensive. "Sure," I said, "Where do you want to go tomorrow?" "I need to get a new cover for my snow machine," she said.

Lela threw me a big smile through the window when I pulled up to their motel room the next afternoon. "No gloves?" I teased her, "boy, you're tough." "It's warm," she retorted, snickering good-naturedly at my down vest and down jacket and particularly at my gloved hands and the pair of outer gloves she spied on the car seat. It was minus six, and a dusting of new snow glittered in the bright afternoon sun.

We headed for the snowmobile dealership, Lela laughing at my constant shifting of the gears. "Too busy shifting to drive," she snorted. "That's why I never learned to drive a car like this."

Northern Power Sports proved easy enough to find. On the way, Lela explained her mission. Her son Richard ran into a rock with their 1998 Arctic Cat Ventura, damaging the chassis. "I need a new body for my machine," she said. Lela had shopped here before, she knew Karen in the back office with the three overweight Chinese pugs, and her most recent purchase was easily located in their computer. They bought the machine two years ago and haven't driven it since last spring, when Richard had the accident with it. "Don't you have much snow there?" wondered Steve, the sales agent, trying to figure out why Richard had hit a rock. "We live in the mountains," explained Lela. No extra snowmobile "bodies" were to be had, but Steve was happy to show her a new Ventura for fifty-one hundred dollars. Lela asked me what I thought. I told her I knew nothing about snowmobiles. Steve told her she ought to be able to sell the engine of the old one for at least seven hundred dollars, and he sent her off with a brochure on the new model to take home to Noah.

"Can we go by Wright Air so I can get my money?" Lela asked as we settled into the car. "Sure," I responded, and we headed for the east ramp of the airport, where the bush air services are located. Someone from the village, she explained, promised to send her money on today's flight. I guessed she was calling in her debts. "People always want to borrow money; it's hard not to loan it," she confessed. Unfortunately there was no money for Lela at Wright's, and the next plane was not due in until 5:30. I could read the disappointment in her face. I hoped she had enough money for the two remaining days she would be in town.

"What time is it?" I asked her as we turned around at Wright's and headed back into town. She looked down at her watch. "Three o'clock. Only three!" She was surprised. "Time sure goes slowly in town." "Not at home," she added. "Nothing to do here." I smiled, seeing the situation quite the reverse. "If Noah were here I wouldn't be as bored." Once Lela had taken care of her doctors' appointments and done some shopping, she had exhausted her thirst for town. "Ready to go home?" I asked. "*Ready to go home*," she asserted.

We made one more stop on our afternoon jaunt. Lela wanted to buy some lambskin for lining mukluks and a parka hood, and I asked if she was familiar with a nearby fur store. She wasn't, so off we went. This was, Fairbanks colleagues told me, a wonderful place to take Eskimo friends who come to town. What subsistence hunter and skin-sewer wouldn't appreciate the racks of prime wolverine, wolf, fox, lynx, and beaver furs? The store smelled invitingly like smoked moosehide. My eyes went immediately to a beautiful hooded, fur-lined wolverine jacket on display. All I could think of was my vegan daughter's reaction if I came home with a fur jacket from my Alaska travels. There were no lambskins, but Lela admired the furs, stroking the folded caribou hides. She held out a beaver fur—too red, she noted. "We use 'em for cuffs on parkas. They should be real dark."

We climbed in the car and headed back toward the Klondike. She asked what I was doing on the weekend. "Going to a writers' workshop all day Saturday," I answered. She looked at me incredulously: "Haven't you learned how to write yet?"

"Say hi to Noah, and e-mail me," I called after her as she got out of the car. "And call me whenever you come back to town." "I will," she agreed. She turned at the door to her motel room and gave me a last wave.

Less than one month after my visit with Lela, on February 27, 2001, in the middle of the afternoon in the parking lot of the Klondike Inn, a forty-six-year-old man from Anaktuvuk Pass shot his forty-two-year-old estranged wife in front of two of their children and then turned the gun on himself. I was shocked, not only because such violent deaths had occurred just around the corner from me, and not just because the victims were from Anaktuvuk, but because it was so incomprehensible. These were two outstanding people from the community. Both had been former mayors of Anaktuvuk; he was named trapper of the year on the North Slope in 1995 and was completing a college degree in business administration. She was a talented guitar player and gospel singer with a warm, outgoing personality. She worked as a youth group leader and served as a member of the local search and rescue team. Two summers before, the couple had taken a trip across the continental United States on their Harley-Davidson. They had also traveled to Sweden and hosted a Swedish student in Anaktuvuk.

If there was a clue that trouble lay ahead, it was his job. He'd been the head of utilities services in the village, managing the electric, garbage, and water services to village homes and public buildings. He'd managed them so well that he accepted a promotion to head utilities services for the entire North Slope Borough. That meant being based in Barrow and commuting home to Anaktuvuk. It also meant a more stressful job. People say he started drinking to relieve the stress.

Not long before the murder-suicide, his wife had come to Fairbanks with the two young children for something that Anaktuvuk Pass doesn't offer—a woman's shelter. She had asked her husband for a divorce, and something in him snapped. He had come to town intent on his mission, packing a sawed-off rifle in his duffel bag, or so villagers speculated. She had stopped at the Klondike to deliver separation papers for him to sign but left when she saw he was drunk. She returned later that afternoon with the papers and the kids; he was even drunker. That's when it happened.

The Festival of Native Arts, held at the beginning of each March at the University of Alaska, draws a large crowd of Native dance groups and sellers of Native arts and crafts from all over the state. The largest contingent was coming from Anaktuvuk Pass. No one came. The village was in mourning. A moment of silence was observed at the festival, and four days later a double funeral was held in Anaktuvuk Pass. A trust fund was set up for the children. The couple was laid to rest side by side in a shared grave in the little village cemetery.

"The tragic issue here is alcohol and its effects," wrote an in-law of the family in a letter to the editor of the *Fairbanks Daily News-Miner*. Anaktuvuk people know the effects of alcohol and its impacts so well that, like many other Native villages in Alaska, the village has an ordinance banning alcohol. In Anaktuvuk, not only can you neither *buy* nor sell alcohol, you can't legally *possess* it. That doesn't stop some people from occasionally bringing it in their luggage from Fairbanks, and neither would you have to look too hard to find a bootlegger in the village. But, unlike my East Coast college town, which braces for the Thursday, Friday, and Saturday night ruckus of drunks heading home from the bars, public drinking in Anaktuvuk is more an occasional annoyance than a serious problem. The ordinance has been in effect for many years, and though it is periodically questioned, each time it appears on the ballot, the people re-endorse the ban. The city council has even written the Bureau of Alcohol, Tobacco, and Firearms seeking permission to search peoples' baggage when they come into the village, because, as it stands, public safety officers can search baggage only when they have probable cause. The vigilance at the local level reduces drinking in the village but it makes the bars on 2nd Avenue in Fairbanks attractive.

Alcohol is a relatively recent problem in the community of Anaktuvuk Pass. Nick Gubser, a Yale University anthropology undergraduate who lived with Simon Paneak's family for fourteen months in 1960–61, wrote in his 1962 Yale bachelor's thesis, "Alcohol has not yet been introduced. . . . Time and the White man will probably change that." And, of course, he was right. Today Anaktuvuk is still a relatively quiet, peaceful place, and it is considered the best village assignment by the North Slope Borough's public safety officers. Even so, seventy-five percent of the incidents requiring the intervention of public safety are alcohol-related. The signs are impossible to miss. Posters on the walls of the health clinic list the symptoms of fetal alcohol syndrome and fetal alcohol effect, warning of the dangers of drinking during pregnancy. Vanilla extract, mouthwash, and Nyquil, which all contain alcohol, have been removed from the store's shelves. You have to ask for them at the counter. A sign in a village home taped on the inside of the front door reads: "No alcohol in this house. No drinking in this house. E. M."

I didn't know the couple well who died in that February tragedy, but in a village of three hundred people you "know" everyone after several field seasons. Their deaths hovered over me for weeks. That May when I visited Anaktuvuk, I talked to the brother-in-law of the man who committed the murder-suicide. The dead woman was his sister. He pointed to his daughter's wedding picture on the bookshelf, taken the preceding summer in Fairbanks. He hadn't been able to get a seat on the plane from Anaktuvuk to Fairbanks to get to the wedding because the plane was full of tourists, so his brother-in-law, who was already there, gave his daughter in marriage. And less than a year later he killed the man's sister. "I don't know why he did that," he said simply. Neither could I possibly know.

Every community has its underbelly of jealousy, mistrust, unhappiness, domestic violence, and failed marriages. Anaktuvuk Pass is no exception. But those were never the things that captured my attention. So much more compelling were the friendliness of the people, their joking and laughter, their knowledge of the land and its resources, their stoicism and making do. I smile when I recall old Johnny Rulland one summer in the early 1990s driving backward through the village on his four-wheeler, eyes fixed on the rearview mirror. Reverse was the only gear that worked, and it got him where he wanted to go.

Here's how I think of the Nunamiut: out on the land, embraced in the long light of summer, remembering what it's like to be nomads again. And as the days get shorter, focused on the fall caribou migration, their excitement growing as the snow starts to fall. And always reminding the young, "You have to learn to hunt." I see the Nunamiut in their mountains, not on 2nd Avenue in Fairbanks.

But I'm startled out of my reverie—often. A villager is denied permission to board a flight from Fairbanks to the village because she's drunk. One of the members of a village dance group doesn't appear for the group's scheduled performance at the World Eskimo-Indian Olympics—too drunk. A village teen is arrested in the city for underage drinking.

Back home the elders sigh, "Too much Fairbanks."

May—North of North

Anaktuvuk Valley, May.

From an airplane, the village of Anaktuvuk Pass is a patchwork of houses and buildings stitched onto a vast blanket of tundra and mountains. "The land," Barry Lopez writes in Arctic Dreams, *"is like a kind of knowledge traveling in time through them. Land does for them what architecture does for us. It provides a sense of place, of scale, of history; and a conviction that what they most dread— annihilation, eclipse—will not occur."*

In this country of the mind, as Lopez calls it, the landscape of the Anaktuvuk Valley is dotted with stories and camping places and crisscrossed with the journeys of generations of Nunamiut people. The journey begins with Ayaġumaġałqha, the giant culture hero who, in time beyond recall, taught the Nunamiut how to live in their country and left behind as a reminder of his lessons his giant mittened hand, which forms the Arrigech peaks of the Brooks Range.

Spring comes slowly to Anaktuvuk Pass, where the wilderness is still frozen white. The rushing waters of Contact Creek and the John and Anaktuvuk Rivers are locked tightly in ice. The mountains of the Brooks Range are a confectioner's creation that might have been made by Ayaġumaġałqha with a giant sifter of powdered sugar. The northern sun, confident now, is already high above Napaaqtualuit Mountain at seven in the morning, and by midafternoon it is squintingly bright, its warmth felt through a winter parka. Not till midnight does the sun slide behind the near mountains, and even then its light lingers.

In Fairbanks—where I've come from, 250 miles to the south—winter's brown grass is greening; Hot Licks Ice Cream stand opens to a brisk business. Canoeists take to the open waters of the Chena River, and the mighty Tanana has officially broken up. Dozens of species of birds have already passed through on their way to nesting grounds farther north. Mother's Day brings the season's first tourists.

In Anaktuvuk, snowmobiles course the streets of town and the trails beyond, taking people out on the land for spring camping. Sunburned villagers return from a weekend at Chandler Lake, where they drill holes through the thick ice with power augurs to fish for lake trout and arctic char. On a sunny Sunday, teenagers head up to the Anaqtiktuaq Valley for a late-evening picnic in the snow. Men race snowmobiles north to hunt the season's first ducks and geese. Duck soup, complete with heads and feet, simmers in big pots on stoves.

The afternoon sun melts a set of snowy tire tracks in the road. Small kids don rubber boots, splashing and hauling toy trucks through the ribbon of slush. Older kids try their bikes, skidding across the snow.

Inside, the Nunamiut School gym is festooned in blue and white balloons. The strains of "Pomp and Circumstance" announce the five members of the class of 2001. One by one, in blue and gold robes, they take halting, unfamiliar steps down the balloon-lined walkway, pausing in front of the bleachers to smile shyly at their proud parents, grandparents, aunts, and uncles, who cheer them exuberantly. In their senior speeches, they thank teachers and coaches for helping them and their parents for waking them up on dark winter mornings to make them go to school. And they don't fail to offer thanks that they are finished with high school. The lone villager with a university degree (earned in 1997) encourages them to further their education, acknowledging how hard it is without Native foods, your village family. But it's worth it, she says, adding, "I'm here for you." Three of the five graduates are making plans to go to college.

The room darkens and everyone watches the senior slide show. Pictures of the graduates as babies and toddlers, as high-school athletes, and in formal graduation garb flash on the screen. The little kids, huddled in front on the gym floor, hold their arms high and waggle fingers, making shadows on the screen, till adults make them quit. At the end of the show, villagers share the blue and gold graduation cake and thin slices of *maktak*, whale blubber, brought by a guest from Barrow. In a splash of blue and white balloons, the graduates leave the school, their jubilant voices rising into the sunny, frosty May evening.

Ed's Place

Anaktuvuk Pass, 1959. (Ed Hall, standing, in the middle.) Photo by Stephen C. Porter.

Anaktuvuk has many moods. On the Fourth of July, 2002, it is serene and beautiful. The sky is achingly blue, the gray mountains dusted with a surprise of summer snow, the tundra Ireland green. A day you would want to be nowhere else. And then, right before midnight, cold fog, blown on a strong north wind, blots out the blue. And just three days before that, on the first of July, biting snow funnels down the Pass at fifty miles per hour, whiting out everything in its path. Embracing, freezing, unpredictable. The Arctic is like that, even in summer.

How was Anaktuvuk, Ed asked first thing when I saw him a week after my return in August 2002. His caretaker had brought him over to Meryn's and my house for dinner on the patio. He was wearing the Anaktuvuk T-shirt I had sent him from the field. I grilled steaks, and while we sipped our wine I told him about the Fourth of July celebration and how similar it was in outline to the one he attended in 1959.

Anthropologists are territorial animals. "My village, my people," they used say matter-of-factly, describing the sites of their field research. As graduate students in the late sixties we used to mock that blatant proprietariness. We would never speak those words. But we knew we couldn't wander into another anthropologist's territory without permission, without appropriate homage to those who pioneered there. Should we wish to work there, in addition to the ritual payment of acknowledgment, the research project had to be different than anything done by those who had staked the territory. And, though we didn't see ourselves as possessive, we wanted to find our places too.

Anaktuvuk Pass was Ed's territory, not in that possessive sense of the anthropologist who has built his or her career and reputation on one place, but in the sense that he was there first, twenty-one years before me. He knew Anaktuvuk as a nineteen-year-old, before snowmobiles and electricity, before the school and airstrip. He knew it when . . .

At one time, I was Ed's student. As a fledgling anthropologist I went off to do my dissertation field research on the Northwest Coast of British Columbia and Southeastern Alaska and, as my dissertation adviser, he sent me letters of encouragement, reassurance, and advice during that year. It was only many years later, after we married, and were both full professors at the same college, that I came to the Arctic to work with Ed, first in Barrow and then in Anaktuvuk Pass. Meryn, almost two years old, came with us to Anaktuvuk in the winter of 1984, and villagers laughed as Ed packed her around the village in the back of his roomy parka like Eskimo mothers.

After that we both wanted to continue our studies in this friendly, welcoming village. There was much oral history to be recorded, especially Anaktuvuk people's accounts of the dramatic changes they experienced as they moved from a nomadic life to settling in one place. Ed also wanted to write the biography of Simon Paneak, whom he had first met in 1959. Our skills and knowledge complemented one another. Ed knew the Arctic, the people, and the geography; having published two life histories of two Native American women, I knew oral history research and biography. We would work as a team.

As for professional territory, Anaktuvuk was now squarely the domain of Grant Spearman, since he had been living and working in Anaktuvuk Pass since 1978. But we wouldn't be treading on Grant's toes, as his anthropological interests ran backward in time to the era when the Nunamiut were still nomadic, before the modern world embraced them and they it.

Was there room in a small village for three anthropologists at one time? The Nunamiut have a long history of welcoming outsiders bearing questions, beginning with biologist Laurence Irving in 1948, followed by the first census taker in 1950, then Army research scientists studying the effects of cold on metabolism, and then geologists, archaeologists, and more. Ed and I would not be in the village for long periods of time. We could interview Justus Mekiana in late July, while Grant had eleven other months of the year to sit and talk with him. Besides, the information from our research would all eventually go to the Simon Paneak Museum anyway.

We had two Anaktuvuk summers and quite a few interviews under our belts before things began to unravel, before territory began to matter, before Ed's illness starting taking over his life—and mine.

July 21, 1990
Then there is the matter of my/our project. I want to do a book on the village, a personal portrait that explores several themes. Ed thinks the project too ambitious and me too inexperienced with this place to bring it off. The end result, he says, would be a "cream skimmer" book which would detract from the book on Anaktuvuk he has in mind to write. I elaborated on one of my ideas for the book, but we ended up in a nasty argument. I would, I think, do well not to bounce half formed ideas off Ed, particularly when they bounce into his "territory." Besides, his response to incomplete ideas is not to build upon them but to challenge their logic and completeness.

Our problems had a history longer than Ed's MS. In fact, they began not a year after our marriage in 1977. "You were so unhappy," Ed said, and no doubt there was some truth in his statement. I shared our small town with his ex-wife, who was understandably both furious and sad that Ed had left her for his former student. I could hardly expect her to be welcoming. Neither was I fully prepared to become stepmother to a five year old with sizeable needs and a set of parents whose ideas about discipline and child rearing conflicted with each other's and with mine. Moreover, I hated the weather in Brockport; the grayness and the constant wind made me homesick for Delaware, where I had lived for the past four years. The spring of that first year I had looked forward to a visit from a close friend, but shortly after she arrived I spiked a fever, got pneumonia, broke a rib coughing, and took to my bed. I later learned that my "friend," escaping marital problems of her own, took to Ed's. That might not have been so bad had they not fallen in love and had I not learned about it several months later, when I discovered a box of her letters in the front hall closet.

"I chose you," Ed said, after he burned her letters, assured me he'd broken off the relationship, and followed me, at my insistence, to a marriage counselor. I mended, but the visceral memory of betrayal lingered. In the end it made me tough, so much so that people called attention to my hard edge by noting that motherhood had softened it.

Several years later there was another exchange of letters and phone calls between Ed and my former friend. I started looking for a divorce lawyer. A wise friend, noting how rich our intertwined professional lives were and how close Ed and I both were to our young daughter, suggested we give counseling another try first, so off we went, with Ed muttering, "I'd rather have a root canal than talk to a counselor."

We returned to Anaktuvuk in the summer of 1991. Ed's slurred speech and stumbling had improved, but the disease found other routes of attack. He was taking steroids to accelerate his recovery from a recent flare-up, and the drug made him irritable and edgy. The disease was exacting its toll on me as well.

That field season I began to suspect that MS was affecting Ed's mind. What was the first clue? Maybe it was the instructions he wrote for the research assistant back home that were out of character with his usual incisive logic and practicality. Maybe it was the jokes he told with the punchlines that had lost their punch. Ed was a consummate joke teller, delighting in long stories, puns, and fast delivery. Maybe it was all the things he had forgotten to bring and maddeningly called home to have mailed to us, or maybe it was the files he started to lose on the computer. Whatever it was, I wrote it off to the stress of our makeshift living conditions, the steroids, and the exhaustion he suffered from walking everywhere with a cane. But I knew these weren't the real reasons.

In 1992 we spent another summer in the same tiny village house. A few light moments interrupted a tense field season. At the washeteria one day we ran into Rachel Riley, whom Ed had first met in the summer of 1959, when she was eighteen and he nineteen. Rachel had been a beautiful young woman, and Ed had taken several photos of her that summer. In one she poses, dreamily, arms entwined around the eave support of the log cabin the geological survey crew occupied. She wears her colorful summer parka, and her lipsticked red lips break in a half smile. She appears, too, in Ed's journal. One day, he recorded, Rachel had hiked into the mountains to help her father bring home three mountain sheep that he had killed, a round trip of eighteen miles. Undaunted after her all-day errand, she went dancing that evening. Ed was admittedly smitten, but too shy to do much except take photos and write. Thirty-three years and considerable girth later, they stood together in the laundromat, reminiscing about that long-ago summer: Ed, smiling and leaning precariously on his cane toward Rachel, a still-handsome woman with a husky laugh; Rachel, teasing, "I follow you guys and flirt, flirt, flirt!"

Ed's journey north as a field anthropologist ended in 1992, in Anaktuvuk Pass, just as it had begun there thirty-three years earlier, After that summer Ed was too incapacitated with MS to make the trip again. Other doors were closing for him as well. In the fall of 1991 he was forced to take a medical leave from teaching, and by the beginning of the following fall semester he was on permanent disability leave. I oversaw the remodeling of our eighty-year-old house to make the first floor accessible for Ed, who fell frequently as he struggled up to the second floor or to our attic study on the third floor. Ed was resistant to the project and feigned indifference because it was such an obvious reminder of his accelerating physical limitations. I tried to reason with him, stressing the safety benefits of being on one floor, reflecting on how fabulous the final results would be. "You always have to have your own way," he barked. I soon resented that the remodeling project was eating up my sabbatical and that Ed was unrelentingly hostile toward my efforts in pursuit of his well-being. What little writing time I had, I devoted to spilling my guts in a journal devoted to ugly thoughts about MS and Ed, which I fantasized turning into a tell-all memoir that would become a best-seller.

February 4, 1993
I have separated myself from him, for a variety of reasons not the least of which is not to feel "there but for the Grace of God go I." He is the "other," an emissary from a strange culture who bears little physical or intellectual relationship to the man I once loved, the scholar I once admired, or the father Meryn had as a little girl. I don't know the Ed who resides in the private recesses of his mind, though I know he struggles to be who he has always been. Nonetheless, I am xenophobic, quick to judge his behavior exotic and inappropriate, to exercise my impatience at his mental shortcomings. I find myself physically repelled by him, so much

*so that when we go anywhere together I walk ahead of him. I keep my
distance under the guise of facilitating his way, but my body language
says, "I am not part of you, I am not under the influence of this horrific
disease; I am healthy and whole, while you have crossed the border into
the hinterland of the infirm and disabled."*

*I chronicle his dementia, approvingly almost, as if its gathering force
is justification for my disgust and disdain, yet I feel guilty that I cannot
love him at a time when he so needs love. We cannot legislate love, you
know; it comes, unbidden, from the heart. This loss—my loss, our loss—
is especially agonizing, for there is no finality to it. Ed is here, in the flesh,
with moments of clarity even, especially when he talks to me late at night
in bed. But most of the time I am an unwilling witness, perhaps even an
accessory, to his long slow decline towards death, which he is surely aware
of too. The reality of it is just too awful.*

When did I decide to leave? There was no decisive moment. It happened
by stages. I waffled: I would keep my family intact by maintaining the surface
appearance of being the caring and devoted partner. No, I would leave; that
was the only way to have a life.

October 26, 1993
*I am not prepared for the stress of a divorce. I have only recently gotten
our finances in working order, gotten the household running smoothly,
and settled into my attic garret free from the incessant sounds of Ed's TV
downstairs. I love my house, my space, and I am not prepared to lose
them right now.*

March 19, 1994
*I came to a place after Christmas where I convinced myself that I had to
live with the situation—as a kind of death one can't run from—but now
I'm not so sure.*

April 9, 1994
*I teeter once again on the brink of calling it quits. . . . I cannot stand to go
on about the day's routine with feigned grace and good cheer . . . I have
taken over his checkbook, his credit cards, his driver's license, his life. He
calls me "the Warden." I am sick of being "the Warden."*

But it was another year before I told Ed in no uncertain terms that I
wanted a divorce, before I told our families, and before I consulted a lawyer.
Then I stayed on for months after doing so. Moving out was complicated; Ed
needed full-time care and a legal guardian, both of which he fought. Meryn

and I needed a place to live. In the spring of 1996 I watched our magnolia birth its glory of pink blossoms from my attic study for the last time. The tree, a fragile sapling with all of two or three blossoms on its spindly branches when we bought the house, now stretched its full crown toward my third-floor window. I carried out my nineteen years of possessions and memories through the crowds of red and yellow tulips that lined our driveway. I hunkered down into the new old house that Meryn and I now owned. I wanted to go nowhere; I just wanted to make this place my own.

Anaktuvuk Pass eventually drew me back, as I knew it would.

July 13, 1997
I am going because I think I need to, because I have stayed home for too long and have a tendency to entrench myself in the comfort of familiar Brockport places and faces. I am going so I can write more about Anaktuvuk Pass. I am going because I need to go to the field to feel like an anthropologist again. But I don't really want to go.

In all my past trips, it was not so much Ed who paved our way into the village, but Meryn. It was she who dived into village life, who brought the village children to our little house, who was called on the CB radio. And now it is Meryn who has refused to return, opting to spend the time at her paternal grandmother's instead. And I am no longer with Ed, my original connection to Anaktuvuk Pass.

I have been reminded by my soon to be ex-mother-in-law that I do not belong in Anaktuvuk Pass, nor even in Alaska: "I hope Ed will not be too depressed that you are in his beloved country and he is not."

That summer I was so uncertain in my new status as singular anthropologist and Ed Hall's former wife that it was difficult to confidently introduce what fieldwork is about to the student I had invited to accompany me. Everywhere I was reminded that Ed would not be returning. At the store, the store manager, who knew only that things had changed, asked me, "Are you and Ed still together?" "No," I answered, and with the swipe of her pen she crossed his name off the account. At the city council meeting where I explained the essays that I had been writing about the village, a council member asked my student, "Are you taking Ed Hall's place?" "Oh, no," she exclaimed, "I couldn't do that." I briefly explained Ed's physical situation. "Oh," they said, and one by one added, "Well, tell Ed Hall a big hello from Anaktuvuk Pass."

In the summer of 1999 I was again in Anaktuvuk Pass, with a purpose and research project that was beginning to gel. I had a personal mission too. 1999 was Ed's sixtieth birthday. In my spare time I went around the village with a sheet of white paper and pen, collecting signatures and birthday wishes from villagers to have framed for him. "A big hello from Anaktuvuk Pass," wrote one. "Ed, we're praying for you," wrote another. They shared their memories with me as they signed their names. "I remember Ed Hall in that red hat." "Ed Hall was just like a big brother to us."

Now, in 2002, I have been to Anaktuvuk Pass almost as many times without Ed as with him. The project I began in 1999 has come to fruition, and I have a generous National Science Foundation grant to do a two-year project, documenting the history of the Anaktuvuk Pass caribou-skin mask. My grant is ample enough to allow a research assistant and a professional photographer to document the process of mask making. It's a collaborative project with the museum as well, so Grant Spearman is part of it, too. This field season I've apprenticed myself to a mask maker in order to make a mask while I am in the village. "If I'm going to write about it," I told myself, "I have to learn to do it."

Ed doesn't talk about returning to Alaska any more, but Anaktuvuk is in his bones, as it surely is now in Meryn's and mine. Our shared library of Alaska materials—notes, slides, tape recordings, art—spread now over two households, spans four decades of our separate and joint lives. On Ed's shelves there is a row of handwritten field journals, one for every field season. In each, on the first page, he has carefully penned the words of the Spanish explorer Casteñada (1542): "Granted that they did not find the riches of which they had been told, they found a place in which to search for them."

There's a photo on my bookshelf I took when Meryn was seven. She and her father are crouched on hands and knees on the tundra beneath Suaqpak Mountain in Anaktuvuk Pass. They're picking blueberries and smiling at each other. Ed's teasing her: "I can pick blueberries faster than you." Meryn, confident, giggles, "No you can't. I'm the fastest." The camera snapped just as she seized the bounty from one tiny bush. She doesn't remember him then, before he got sick. Sometimes now I don't either.

I find him in my journals and photo albums. In one photo Ed and seven-year-old Justin pause from their hike in the meadow at Summerland in Mount Rainier National Park to look up at the mountain that Ed once climbed. Justin, the father of two young daughters, is now defining his own fatherhood. He remembers Ed only too well before he became ill. Now Ed calls Justin "the Warden" because he's Ed's legal guardian. When Justin and I talk he teasingly calls me his ex-stepmother, and I reciprocate by introducing him as my daughter-in-law's husband. We laugh at this clever dance of kinship, but it hurts.

After dinner that night I showed Ed the mask I had made during my stay in Anaktuvuk and a couple of others I had purchased. I passed on the "big hello's to Ed Hall" from his Anaktuvuk friends. We didn't get to look at the photos I took because Ed got tired and wanted to go home. "When will I see the pictures?" he asked, as he and his caretaker were leaving. "Next week," I assured him. "Thanks for dinner," he said. "It was good." The lift hoisted him in his wheelchair and he disappeared into the van.

Happy July Fourth

Anaktuvuk women on the Fourth of July, 1959. Left to right: Jane Rulland, Rose Ann Rulland, Rachel Mekiana (Riley), Doris Hugo (holding son Roy), Margaret Hugo (Gordon), and Lela Ahgook with son Chuck. Photo by Stephen C. Porter.

New snow on the 4th. Nothing much happened in the morning except that Homer Mekiana raised a 49-star flag before Jack [Campbell] which made him rather mad. We spent the morning taking pictures of the women and kids all dressed up in honor of the day in new parkas and boots. Around 5:00 all of the Eskimos went to the church and had a short service followed by a 4th of July feast. After this the shooting match was held. It cost a quarter to enter and many of the Eskimos and most of the white men in camp shot. The Shell Oil crew from down the valley was up for the fun. The target was impossibly small and shooting Ken's unsighted 30/30, I doubt if I came anywhere near it. Gene the 'copter pilot won and was tossed in the air by the other men.

The rest of the evening until about 11:00 was just more or less of a social gathering on the tundra outside of the church. The men competed by jumping and running while the others watched. There are many more men in camp now than when we first arrived because the Wolf hunters have come in. They were not too successful this year—mainly because the airplane shooters have killed so many Wolves. Since the bounty is one of the main sources of income for these people it is a shame plane shooting is allowed. Also the reason for setting the bounty was to protect the caribou herd—now getting far too large for the grazing area.

Around 11:00 we went across Contact Creek and played Lop-game—almost everyone playing. [1] *I lasted until 4:00 and then to bed.*

Ed Hall, fieldnotes, 1959

The maintenance crew at the school had hung a flag from a classroom window the night before. By noon when the first upside-down villagers were rising, a flag sprouted from a rooftop across from the school. Soon, down the street, there appeared another, and then another.

Up the hill by the Presbyterian church a small group had gathered for the shooting contest. They had set up a target 175 yards away on the tundra, and by the church they had placed a board on the ground for the prone shooter along with an upright board to prop the rifle on. The list of men and women participants ran to two pages. Each had paid a twenty-five-dollar registration fee. A scatter of bicycles, Argos, pickups, and a van ringed the activity. Villagers stood on the steps of the church watching the shooters, ducking inside now and then to replenish their styrofoam cups with coffee. Rhoda and Bob Ahgook gave us a wave from inside the van, where they sat sipping coffee; kids climbed off and on the bed of a pickup truck and rode their bikes up and down the steep hill leading to the church. Shooters prepared for their turns by sighting their rifles through the space between the back and seat of an old chair. Bets were taken on the side.

Even before Alaska became a state, even before 1949, when they came together at the pass to form a village, the Anaktuvuk people had, in their own way, wholeheartedly celebrated the most American holiday. To them, this Fourth of July, 2002, was no different than any other in recent memory. To us, Anaktuvuk was refreshingly far away from the heat and heavy security of Washington DC on our nation's first birthday following the horror of September 11. It wasn't that September 11 had little impact here. To the contrary. "We heard about it on the CB," Rachel Riley told me. In the early-morning hours of September 11, some villagers had picked up the news from TV, and they spread the word to the rest of the village through the CB radio. At the Nunamiut School, where Rachel teaches the Iñupiaq language and culture classes, the classroom TVs were on all that day so students and their teachers could follow the aftermath of the terrorist attacks. "The little kids were scared and we had to calm them down. 'Are they going to bomb us here?' they asked." And what about the high school kids, I wondered. "'Where's our future, where's our future,' they kept saying." I was not really surprised that these teens, who will probably spend most of their adult lives in Anaktuvuk and raise their kids here, see their futures so tied to the financial and cultural capital of the United States. We'd all come to that realization. Yet, on this brilliant July Fourth, in the cradle of the Brooks Range, how could one not feel secure?

"Happy July Fourth," people greeted each other and us, shaking hands or giving a hug. When we arrived they had just finished the shooting without scope and begun the shooting with scope. Rachel Riley was getting ready to shoot. I knew she would be in the competition; she's an avid hunter. I stood on the church stairs talking to Effie Lincoln—now Mekiana, she corrected me, reminding me of her marriage to Kenny Mekiana a few years back. Effie's a former teacher's aide in the school, a fine beadworker and the proud mother of a three-year-old daughter. "Three years now, I haven't had a drink," she announced, "and I don't even miss it." She rolled two rifle cartridges in her hand as she talked. "I'm shooting today, and my sisters too." One of her sisters had given Effie the cartridges and was letting her borrow her rifle. "Sure would be funny if I beat her with her own rifle," she mused. Effie turned to demonstrate the shooting posture of the one sister— in Fairbanks—who was not shooting today. She leaned forward, sighting her imaginary rifle, balancing herself on her left leg and crooking her right leg backward. "Ping," she announced in a high voice, emphasizing the kick of the rifle with a little jerk of her crooked leg. The real shots were startlingly loud. The little kids covered their ears.

Three hours and several pots of coffee later it was all over. Rifles were put back in cases, and the procession of shooters and their gallery moved down the hill to the community hall, where the targets were laid on a table to determine the winners of the prize, three hundred dollars. The shooters huddled around the targets, inspecting and measuring. Nearby, at another table four young men cut watermelons into big bite-sized chunks. Effie joined in to prepare a huge mound of grapes and big California strawberries. Plastic tubs of potato salad, piles of hamburger and hot dog buns, and a neat row of catsup and mustard jars on another table, all provided by the city council, foreshadowed the evening's feast.

A group of kids on bikes had gathered in front of the community hall and were wrapping crepe paper and sparkly strands of blue, red, and gold stars around their bikes. Some taped little American flags to the handlebars and tied red and blue balloons and cans to the backs of their bikes. Beside the hall three men were firing up a big grill for hamburgers and hot dogs. I recognized the fuel—those charcoal briquettes had come up on the plane with us two days before. Dinner at six, announced one of the men stoking the grill. The hall cleared out, and people went home for awhile. We followed suit. Suddenly there were sirens, and the village fire truck and ambulance pulled up to the community hall to lead the procession of children on flag-decorated bikes. The sirens whined and the kids pedaled, racing the trucks. Balloons and crepe paper fluttered from handlebars as the little parade threaded the dusty streets of town.

People were already eating when we returned to the community hall. They sat on folding chairs that ringed the perimeter of the hall, balancing paper plates and bowls on laps. Kids carried their dinners outside into the Fourth of July sunshine. Some older people sat on the floor, Eskimo style, legs stretched straight in front of them. Big pots of caribou soup on the long tables reminded everyone that this was not just the Fourth, but the Nunamiut Fourth. "Eat soup, get a bowl Margaret and Judy," the women instructed. We filled our plates and soup bowls, joining Lela and Noah, who were sitting along the side. Lela nuzzled her newest grandson, four-month-old Austin, outfitted for the holiday in a new red, white, and blue shortalls, T-shirt, and cap. Across the room, Gilbert Lincoln, a veteran, was also dressed for the occasion. He had donned his Alaska vfw cap for the evening's gathering.

By 7 p.m., the hall had emptied again. The city clerk and a few other young people were pushing big brooms across the community hall floor and folding up the long tables in anticipation of the Eskimo dancing that would begin in a couple of hours.

By 9:30 people had begun to gather again. The work crew had lined up three rows of chairs along the back of the hall in addition to those ringing the perimeter, leaving a large open area for dancing. A few small clusters of villagers occupied the chairs. A crew of usgs geologists doing survey work in the area arrived wearing red jackets and carrying digital cameras. Small boys chased each other in and out of the hall; smokers talked over cigarettes in the entry. At the back of the hall the drummers had placed their drums and flat-sided hickory drumsticks on the first row of chairs. A North Alaskan Eskimo drum resembles a big quilting hoop with a short handle. The drumheads used to be made of whale, walrus, or seal bladder, or, here in the interior, a caribou skin, but nowadays, REI ripstop nylon works just about as well and stays taut despite changes in the humidity and temperature.

The drummers took their seats in the folding chairs. Years ago, three or four drummers might sit straight-legged on the floor in a cramped sod house or skin tent. The ten men drummers tonight included some young recruits, and as the evening wore on their number swelled to thirteen. They took their seats, holding the drums in their left hands. Click, click, click, the thin flexible drumsticks tapped the undersides of the rims as the men sang. The full-moon faces of their drums rose and fell to the rhythm of the song. Drumsticks connected with taut drumheads. After a few songs, some young girls walked in a group to the center of the floor to "motion dance." They stood feet together, knees bent, swaying to the music, their arms undulating and torsos turning to the rhythm of the drums. The women's dance movements are all in the knees, shoulders, arms, and hands. They remind me of flowers, firmly rooted in the ground, bending with the wind.

Throughout the evening, dancers flowed off and on the dance floor. If the vitality of a culture could be measured in peoples' enthusiasm for dancing, drumming, and singing, Nunamiut culture would surely rank as one of the most vital. There are three dance groups in this small village, and just about everybody belongs to one of them. Many of the songs they sing are old ones, but old and young men alike compose new songs.

Tommy Rulland, an agile, wiry little man and a showman of a dancer, stood up, set his drum down, and strode to the middle of the dance floor. I love to watch the men dance. With knees bent, arms outstretched, feet and fingers spread, necks craned and heads thrust forward, they are bold and powerful performers. They move suddenly and dramatically, stomping first on one foot, then on the other, hopping forward then back. When the men dance, the community hall floor shakes as if an earthquake had rattled this peaceful mountain valley.

Tommy owned the floor. He hopped, punctuating his hops with guttural animal sounds. He lunged at the audience; he teased and clowned. Suddenly, Vera, Effie's sister, jumped onto the dance floor behind her strutting uncle, following him closely, mimicking his every move. The crowd laughed as she made good-natured fun of the preening man.

And then there was the solo performance of little Courtney Mekiana, a wisp of a two-year-old with a tiny bow of a mouth and the bowlegged walk of a diaper wearer. Courtney may have had other intentions as she wandered onto the empty dance floor, bottle in hand. Perhaps she was headed for some person sitting on the other side of the room. But midway, she was overtaken by the singing and drumming. She stopped, bent her knees, and bobbled her head and swung her arms to the boom of the drums, all the while keeping a tight grip on her bottle. People on the sidelines urged her on with applause, but it was Gilbert Lincoln in his veteran's cap who caught her attention. He gave her a big smile, moving his arms as if he were dancing, while Courtney faced him, swinging her arms just like his. They made an interesting pair, the old war veteran and the tiny girl he was teaching to dance like a woman.

Anaktuvuk people's love of small children is especially obvious in public gatherings. Everyone holds babies, passes them around, and talks to and plays with small kids. Earlier in the evening, Courtney was swept up by a teenaged boy who carried her outside. A younger boy later stopped to tie one of her shoes. The young mother of a nine-month-old boy hiked up Courtney's pants when they started to slip, and later I spied her in a stroller pushed by a teenage girl. Following her dance performance, she got a hug from elder Rhoda Ahgook, and then she made her way down the line of women singers sitting behind the drummers. Who is her mother, her grandmother, her father, her siblings? It was impossible to tell. Everyone knows Courtney, and she them. She was perfectly comfortable in this noisy, multigenerational crowd of people and perfectly free to wander throughout the community hall. Were she to venture into anything that might harm her, someone would pluck her to safety. On this July Fourth I celebrated the exquisite freedom of a small child in a safe place.

The drums would pound for two more hours after we left at 11:30. The next evening there would be foot and bike races in the shadow of Suaqpak Mountain, and the evening after that, card games and traditional Eskimo games in the community hall. Over the long holiday weekend villagers would continue to greet each other with "Happy July Fourth."

We stepped outside the community hall into the street. Amidst a tangle of flag-decorated bikes splayed across the ground, kids twirled and ran with sparklers. The boom of the drums followed us down the street, past Mark Morry's house, where the American flag was flying in the north wind.

Faces of the Nunamiut

Wooden molds for masks.

We take off to the north. The day is bright and clear, still sum-
mer. I watch the plane's shadow speed over the rooftops, across
the ribbon of Contact Creek, across the cemetery. We turn sharply
to the southeast, climbing, climbing, up toward the headwaters of
Giant Creek. I look back at the village slowly being swallowed by
the valley. We level off just above the mountaintops. I glance to
the west, and there on a ridge are three mountain sheep, tiny and
white against the gray-brown peaks.

Flying back to Fairbanks my mind floats somewhere between
the mountains and Brockport, between my time in the village and
my impending immersion in my other life. The small, scratched
plastic window of the plane reminds me of the focused view I have
of Anaktuvuk Pass. There are a few villagers I count as friends who
have let me into their lives during the brief periods of time that I
am here, but there is so much I don't know. It's like the view from
the arctic windows in village houses, thrown open on a warm day
to let in the breeze and sun of the brief arctic summer, then sealed
tight as the cold and dark of winter descend.

Fieldnotes, 2002

"It was a cold, bitter winter, and food was so scarce the Nunamiut had to eat their masks!" Jim Barker, the photographer who's come with me on my latest project, announces in a deadpan newscaster's voice as he makes a sandwich during our break for lunch. In the two weeks we've been here we've had our fill of Anaktuvuk Pass caribou-skin masks—thinking about them, talking with mask makers about them, photographing them, measuring them, and for me, even making them. We laugh at this little bit of imagined irony.

This has been a nearly perfect field trip. Short so that we had to work intensely, which was fine. No long lapses without doing something that seems like fieldwork. Not even time to languish in the sauna at the washeteria. And this time I not only have the luxury of hiring a professional photographer, but my research assistant is my dearest friend from graduate school. Judy Gussler and I met in the fall of 1966 as first-year anthropology graduate students at Ohio State. We shared an office that year, and we were students in the first class that a new twenty-six-year-old professor named Ed Hall taught. Over the years I attended the weddings of her children, and she attended Justin's wedding. We saw each other through divorce and new relationships. But perhaps most meaningfully, I had accompanied Judy on her first fieldwork in 1972 to St. Kitts, sent there by her husband to lend a hand, cheer her up, and take photographs for her. Now, exactly thirty years later, I am able to return the favor.

This is the field season I have always longed for. Having colleagues along to help has made it less lonely, and we work well as a team. Jim doesn't wait for me to tell him what to photograph; he knows what this project can be visually. Judy sees the village and people with the eye of an anthropologist who has worked in a different part of the world. Together they offer ideas and suggestions about the research: why not take close-ups of the details of mask construction, and how about shots of masks simply as they appear about the village sitting on a shelf by the TV, or in a box with other partially finished masks? Judy and Jim accompany me on interviews and take pictures, leaving me free to focus on talking with people. No short tempers here; everyone is simpatico. Even better, we have similar political views. Sitting on the couch each evening, dinner plates balanced on knees, we talk back to CNN *Headline News*, offering our resolutions to the world's problems.

I feel good about this project for other reasons. With luck and hard work it may culminate in a museum exhibit "Outside," and we hope to collaborate with the school and local museum to do an online exhibit. We present the project to the city council at their July meeting, explaining what the research involves, what the final product (book and exhibit) will be, and how the village will benefit. Villagers ask the questions I never considered when I put together the handout on the project. Why aren't you paying the mask makers more? Why is all the money from the book going to the Simon Paneak museum and not to the individual artists? What about all the pictures you're taking, what happens to the ones that aren't in the book? I explain that the mask makers are being paid the North Slope Borough's standard wage, twenty-five dollars an hour, for Iñupiat cultural resource experts and that the book won't be a best-seller like Hillary Clinton's memoir with its eight-million-dollar contract, so why not give the modest royalties to a community institution? The council members smile and nod. And the photos—we won't use them without people's permission. In the end the council gives its stamp of approval.

"I'm retired now; I'm ready for interview. You can interview me anytime," Lela tells me the first night I visit her. I can hardly believe what I am hearing. "You bet, I still haven't interviewed you about masks," I say. "And," I add, "I want to make a mask. Will you teach me?" She grins. "You wanna make masks? First you gotta get a caribou." As enticing as that challenge sounds, fortunately her son Richard has already gotten the caribou and the skin has been stretched and dried. "You can scrape my skin for me." I roll up my sleeves, taking the long-handled scraper (a straight dowel fitted to a short segment of sharpened two-inch pipe) from Lela. Noah fetches the skin from the back room and Lela unrolls it on the living room floor. I sit on the skin and, beginning at one edge, start taking off the remaining bits of flesh and dried blood with long strokes of the scraper. It is hard work, but satisfyingly physical and rhythmic. We talk while I scrape.

"Aren't you married yet?" I laugh and tell her that two marriages and twenty-seven years was enough. "Tell me your story," she demands, so I tell her about the biking trip I've just completed across northern Spain on the Camino de Santiago along the medieval pilgrimage route to that city. I show her photos of my mother's ninetieth birthday celebration just a week before I flew north and describe the food and culture course I taught last spring in which I showed the video of her cutting up caribou. I have a new grandchild, too, I add, and I haven't even seen her yet. "And how's Meryn," Lela asks. "She's housesitting for me, painting houses this summer and getting ready to go to Italy to study for a year."

For several days, between visits to Lela's, I trudge over to Doris Hugo's, as she had agreed to let Jim photograph her making masks from start to finish. Far better that the official photo record of mask making be of the Nunamiut mask maker than the anthropologist apprentice. Even more fitting that Doris sits outside on a piece of plywood board, her legs stretched straight out in front of her, her mask-making supplies to her side. The gray mountains nicely frame her in her faded blue- and rose-flowered summer parka, and the outdoor location makes it seem all the more "authentic." She might have worked inside, especially to avoid the ever-present mosquitoes, but her husband doesn't want any photos taken inside the house. I set my tape recorder on Doris's plywood work board and point the mike at her. There's no need to conduct a "formal" interview. Doris effortlessly talks about what she's doing at each step. Jim moves silently in and out of my visual field, the click of his camera the only audible record of his presence.

Back and forth. Doris sits outside in the quiet afternoon, occasionally slapping at mosquitoes. Inside I sit on the couch beside Lela so she can monitor my sewing and correct my mistakes. *Great Balls of Fire*, Jerry Lee Lewis's biography, plays on the big-screen TV across the room, and I occasionally look up from my work to watch the movie. My tape recorder, stationed on the coffee table, indiscriminately records the cacophony of the TV, our conversation, the gurgles and cries of Lela's baby grandson Austin, and the coming and goings of the Ahgook household members. Sewing on an eyebrow, I prick my finger trying to poke the skin sewing needle through the thick caribou skin of the mask. Blood splatters over the forehead of my mask and drips onto my sneaker. Lela laughs and hands me a band-aid. Doris, on the other hand, hardly pauses in the stitches she makes, her needle piercing the tough caribou skin like it was the finest Egyptian cotton.

It takes me two hours to sew on a pair of eyelashes and one eyebrow (then, exhausted, I quit for the day); Doris has sewn hers on in minutes. In just a couple of short afternoon sessions Doris finishes several masks to take with her to the World Eskimo-Indian Olympics in Fairbanks the following week. Hours and hours—the exact number noted somewhere in my fieldnotes— I spend at Lela's just completing a single mask. One day when I am up at the museum, Darryl, Doris's grandson, brings some tourists to me with a question about mask making. I can't help taking a bit of pleasure in this spontaneous deferral to my "expertise." Their question is the one that I had once been fond of asking: How long does it take to make a mask? Suddenly I understand the Native frustration with these "how long and how many" questions that seem on the surface so uncomplicated. "Forever," I truthfully answer.

Being an anthropologist in Anaktuvuk means walking a lot, even though distances are not far. Back and forth to the store, the museum, the washeteria, over the bridge spanning Contact Creek to visit people "across." A morning walk for exercise, a stroll after dinner. This time I show the points of interest to my companions. Judy wants to stop at the health clinic—she's a nutritional anthropologist—to learn about health care issues. We visit the cemetery, where I show her the graves of Susie Paneak and Willie Hugo. And the new graves, from last year: Willie's mother, Grandma Ellen Hugo, and the single grave of the couple who died so tragically in Fairbanks. Jim too walks to the cemetery, to take photos in the early-morning light.

For me our daily walking tours are a stock-taking of what has changed and what has not since my last visit. I see Steve Wells's battered pickup with four flat tires and broken windshield parked in the willows by his house just where he left it the last time he drove it. Steve died, nearly a year ago, well before his time, from complications of diabetes; I didn't expect to see his truck. Neither did I expect the Nunamiut Corp restaurant—"camp"—to be located in another building. At least the menu seems the same as last year. Why does change surprise me, even though I look for it? Perhaps it's the romantic ethnographer in me that wants Anaktuvuk Pass to be the isolated, self-contained, unchanging village that it never was. If there's one constant about culture, it's change. I can't help but see some change as loss—the loss of knowledge as the elderly die, the loss of culture as villagers begin to resemble, in their embracing of American popular culture and their consumerism, the rest of us from Outside. It bothers me that each weekday morning a villager in her new SUV drives three hundred yards around the corner, stops in front of her cousin's house, and repeatedly honks the horn with the impatience of a Manhattan taxi driver until the passenger emerges from the house and hops in for the five-hundred-yard ride to their workplace. The horn echoes off the mountains and rings in my ears like a slap to the face. But sometimes I forget how much my own life has turned upside down over the fourteen years I've been coming here.

Vehicles are on my mind this summer. The new tourism has its own vehicle, a comfortable middle-aged van belonging to the Northern Alaska Tour Company. It's a familiar sight on the streets of the village during the summer months, driven by the company's community coordinator, Sarah McConnell, who's completing her fifth summer here. It spends the frigid arctic winter parked in front of a villager's home, for a large storage fee. Tourism is down this summer, all over Alaska, though Sarah still seems to fill the van several days a week. The village tour guide program is going so well that a couple of former guides, like Darryl, have branched out on their own. Darryl specializes in Argo tours, taking people about town and out on the tundra. One day he came rolling down Airport Way with two tourists in the back of his Argo sporting those brimmed camouflage hats with mosquito netting veils. The little vehicle and its cargo looked like they should have been crossing the Serengeti instead.

There's a new crop of Native youth tour guides this summer, and to train them Sarah has devised a clever exercise that involved village residents. The story is hers, but I can't resist telling it. So that villagers could see for themselves what visitors are shown and told, and so that they might offer guidance on what to say and how to say it, she offered villagers a tour on the van. The youth guides would try their new guiding skills on village members, who would pretend to be tourists. To entice folks to take part, the tour company offered door prizes, which are always popular in Anaktuvuk Pass. The big prize was a free trip to Fairbanks on the tour plane when space was available, but the eight hours of babysitting proved to the be the most popular door prize. On the appointed day the tour van picked up the "visitors" at their homes. As each climbed aboard, the youth guides asked where he or she was from. "I'm from South Carolina," drawled Doris Hugo. "California," Rachel Riley answered. Rachel wrapped her arms around herself and affected a shiver, exclaiming, "It's so cold here. It's so cold here!" "Texas." Ruth Rulland offered her wide Nunamiut smile. Rhoda Ahgook drew a momentary blank, then blurted out, "Chicago-miut," followed by her infectious giggle. The role playing held up well until the little group arrived at the museum and the "visitors" fell out of their tourist roles and became elders again, telling the youth guides about the artifacts of their culture as they toured the collection. The "real" oral history began, Sarah relates, when the little group paused at the photo wall in one corner of the museum. Here the elders met themselves as youngsters and young mothers and here they shared their stories with the young guides-in-training.

My early-morning walk takes me north beyond the village, but not scrambling over the uneven tundra. The road no longer ends at the cemetery but continues north toward the camping ground of Kanṇuumavik, "gathering place." This is the Anaktuvuk Pass Highway, dashed in as a proposed road on maps just three years ago. It's the road that leads to the new dump located down the valley. No sooner did I walk into the silence of the broad Anaktuvuk Valley, far enough away from the village that I could no longer hear the hum of the generator, than I could see in the distance, in the center of the valley, the large square outline of a wire fence. Will the trash destined for this space soon be visible too? The village flexes its fingers into the wilderness.

I finish my mask in the nick of time and place it carefully in the box that holds the ones I have purchased in the village. The masks are coming home with me on the plane, not being mailed with my sleeping bag and extra clothing. I don't know where I will hang my mask when I return. Does it belong with the "real" Anaktuvuk masks on the walls of my home, or should I take it to the office so my students might see an artifact of ethnographic fieldwork?

"Choose your mold," Lela had said, spilling the contents of a box of a few dozen molds. Two of her young granddaughters, Judy and Josie, dived into the pile of wooden faces, each coming up with a wooden mold. Like kids everywhere who are handed a mask, they held them up in front of their faces. "Who made this mold?" I asked Lela, holding up my choice. "My uncle, Amos Morry," Lela replied. I already knew about Amos as a carver. Rachel Riley, who also has some of his molds, told me. "Amos had a big nose, so he always made his molds with big noses." Amos Morry died before I came to Anaktuvuk Pass, but villagers are still making masks from his big-nosed wooden molds.

Given all I put into making this little Nunamiut woman and the hours of instruction Lela had offered, she isn't just a piece of tourist art. I begin to think of her as my alter ego, my Anaktuvuk self. She needs a name, so I decide to call her Kamikpak. That's the name Lela's son Chuck jokingly confers on me as I sew the mask. "You got an Eskimo name yet?" he asks. "No," I answer. "All right then, I'll give you one. I'm going to call you Kamikpak. Kamik [boots] because you always walk around a lot. Kamikpak [big boots] because you're from New York, the Big Apple. Big Boots from the Big Apple." I remind him that though I am from New York, I'm not from the city. That doesn't matter. "You're from New York; New York's the Big Apple."

Not bad, my artist daughter says when I unpack my treasures from the summer and show her my mask. As I am unpacking, she is packing, preparing to spend her junior college year abroad in Rome. She thinks now about how she wants to live in another culture. "I don't know how you can pry into other peoples' lives," she exclaims during one of our discussions over dinner. "To tape-record people, interview them. It seems so intrusive. I would rather go as a visitor." Sometimes I would too. Then I wouldn't have to appear before the city council, badger people for interviews, or answer for what I write. But would I follow up on my curiosity, would I understand Anaktuvuk and myself in the same way? Is it the anthropologist who made that mask, who plucked those geese on the tundra the year before? And, I ask Meryn, as the child of just "visitors" could you have gone camping with a Nunamiut family when you were little? Would the people and the place have settled in your visitor's bones?

She thinks for a moment, but it's a moot point. "You know," she says, "I really would like to go back to Anaktuvuk Pass sometime." "I'd like you to come with me," I tell her, adding, hopefully: "Maybe next summer—after Rome."

Unattributed epigraphs to essays come from my essay "99721, The Place of Many Caribou Droppings," *Folklore Forum* 33(1–2): 35–44 (2002).

Anaktuvuk Pass, You Copy?

1. Argo is the brand name of an all-terrain amphibious vehicle manufactured by Ontario Drive and Gear that comes in six- and eight-wheeled versions. Most Argos in Anaktuvuk Pass are the eight-wheeled variety with a four-cycle, twenty-horsepower engine and a load capacity of one thousand pounds. The vehicles are shown on their website, *www.argoatv. com.*

2. Several articles document the growth of CB radios in the 1970s, among them Dannefer and Poushinsky's "The CB Phenomenon: A Sociological Approach," *Journal of Popular Culture* 12(4): 611–19 (1979); Kerbo, Marshall, and Holley's "Re-establishing Gemeinschaft? An Examination of the CB Radio Fad," *Urban Life* 7(3): 337–58 (1978); and Marvin and Schultze's "CB in Perspective: The First Thirty Years," *Journal of Communication* 27(3): 104–17 (1977).

Fieldnotes

1. The quoted material on fieldnotes and the survey mentioned come from Jean Jackson's "'I Am a Fieldnote': Fieldnotes as a Symbol of Professional Identity," in *Fieldnotes: The Making of Anthropology*, edited by Roger Sanjek (Ithaca: Cornell University Press, 1990), pp. 3–33.

Writing History from the Pass

1. Homer Mekiana's journal is located in the Naval Arctic Research Laboratory's collection at the Polar Regions Archives, Elmer Rasmuson Library, at the University of Alaska, Fairbanks. Simon Paneak's journals and correspondence with Laurence Irving are located in the same archives in the Laurence Irving Collection. Simon's correspondence with Ethel Ross Oliver is in the Ethel Ross Oliver Collection, also at the Polar Regions Archives at the University of Alaska, Fairbanks.

The "New" Eskimo

1. The term "Eskimo" is still used regularly in Alaska to refer to the Inuit people. "Nunamiut" means "people of the land" and distinguishes the interior north Alaskan Eskimo from their coastal relatives. It is the most commonly used self-designation by the people of Anaktuvuk Pass. "Nagsragmiut," "people of the summit," is more geographically specific, referring to those who settled at the headwaters of the John and Anaktuvuk Rivers,

that is, the people of Anaktuvuk Pass. "Iñupiat" (Iñupiaq, sing.), "real [or genuine] people" refers to the Eskimo people from northwestern and northern Alaska, thus both the coastal and interior Eskimo. "Inuit," or "people," has several different references, most notably "Canadian Eskimo," but most broadly it refers collectively to all the Eskimo-speaking peoples from Siberia to Greenland.

Of Meat and Hunger and Everlasting Gob Stoppers

1. Carl Henkelman's comment on Nunamiut dentition comes from Laurence Irving's *Birds of Anaktuvuk Pass, Kobuk, and Old Crow*, Smithsonian Institution Bulletin 217 (Washington, D.C.: Government Printing Office, 1960). Henkelman accompanied Irving's expedition to Anaktuvuk Pass in 1948.
2. Discussion of the marketing of Canadian Inuit foods comes from "Picture it on the Menu: Arctic Hare Ragout," *The New York Times*, March 8, 1995.

Masks

1. The Anaktuvuk Pass mask was first brought to public attention by Sarkis Atamian in a 1966 article entitled "The Anaktuvuk Mask and Cultural Innovation," *Science* 151(3716): 1337–45. A recent treatment of this artform can be found in my 1997 article "In Their Own Images: The Anaktuvuk Pass Skin Mask," *American Indian Art Magazine* 22(4): 58–67.

The Only Road That Goes There Is the Information Superhighway

1. Ethel Ross Oliver's account of her census work comes from a 1989 tape-recorded interview at the Simon Paneak Memorial Museum.
2. Dicussion of the Internet in the Canadian Arctic comes from Sheldon Teitelbaum's "The Call of the Wired," *Wired* (November 1997): 234–43, 278–84.

The Exhibition

1. The story of Minik is told in Kenn Harper's *Give Me My Father's Body: The Life of Minik, The New York Eskimo* (Iqaluit, NWT: Blacklead Books, 1986; New York: Washington Square Press, 2001.).

The Things We Carry

1. Simon's 1967 drawing of winter travel is Plate 51 in John M. Campbell's *North Alaska Chronicle: Notes from the End of Time, The Simon Paneak Drawings* (Santa Fe: University of New Mexico Museums Press, 1998).

Happy July Fourth

1. "Lopgame," mentioned in the epigraph to the essay, is also known as "one-base baseball" or "Lapp game." It originated with Sami (Lapp) reindeer herders, who introduced reindeer herding to Alaskan natives in the 1890s, and it is still played in village Alaska.